C000069962

COINCIDENTAL
DESTINY

COINCIDENTAL
DESTINY

Living with Cancer and Refusing to Die From It

BILL ARIENTI

 KHARIS PUBLISHING

Copyright © 2019 by Bill Arienti

All rights reserved. This book or parts thereof may not be
reproduced in any form, stored in a retrieval system, or
transmitted in any form by any means – electronic, mechanical,
photocopy, recording, or otherwise – without prior written
permission of the publisher, except as provided by United States
of America copyright law.

Published by Kharis Publishing, imprint of
Kharis Media LLC.

ISBN-13: 978-1-946277-37-4
ISBN-10: 1-946277-37-1

Cover design by Emma Elzinga and Shelby Taplin
Interior design by Kristina Starr

All KHARIS PUBLISHING products are available at special
quantity discounts for bulk purchase for sales promotions,
premiums, fund-raising, and educational needs. For details,   contact:

Sales Department
Kharis Media LLC
Tel: 1-479-5998657
support@kharispublishing.com
www.kharispublishing.com

*I dedicate this book to my wife Nancy.
Without her love, care and devotion, I
would not be a fraction of the man that I
have become.*

VICTORY

*The battle is finally over. Although I emerge
victorious, I am far from unscathed, and my
wounds, serious. I leave the battlefield slowly,
measuring each step, and lay down in a field of
clover. I lie here not to die, but rather to rest.*

*I shall tend to my wounds, close the tears in
my skin, splint the breaks in my bones, and
grow strong once more. Tomorrow I shall
once again face the challenges which I may
encounter, and confront them with the
determination, resolution and might that only I
can amass.*

Bill Arienti

WHAT OTHERS ARE SAYING ABOUT COINCIDENTAL DESTINY

'Coincidental Destiny' is an inspirational true story of how to deal with whatever life 'throws your way'. The author, Bill Arienti, introduces you to his family and his caregivers in a way that makes you want to be there with them. Everyone should read this book. With warmth and humor, Bill educates the reader on what the patient and his family and friends go through. Seeing things through Bill's optimism in himself and how he sees the good in all of us will encourage you to do the same in your daily life.

— Dr. Steven Brustin

For each of us, life is a personal odyssey. Who am I? Why am I here? Where did I come from? What is life all about? This is a survivor's story, the odyssey of one man who has fought the fearsome trials life throws at each and every one of us, and has overcome anxiety, anger, and despair to find within himself the courage to live his life to the fullest, and embrace with humanity, love and joy the precious gift that is life itself. We all share and can learn much from his experiences.

— Louise Sironi
Pembroke, Massachusetts

TABLE OF CONTENTS

FOREWORD
By: Jerry Thornton

I would love to begin this with some variation of "We all know someone like Bill Arienti." But that is objectively not true, and I want our relationship to be built on a foundation of trust.

The fact is, not all of us know even one person like Bill Arienti. And knowing more than one is rare. Having several in your life is a longshot along the lines of hitting a Powerball jackpot. Because, the sad truth is the world suffers from far too many substandard people and a deplorable lack of Bills.

I'm not a good enough student of history to know what they called guys like Bill Arienti during the actual Renaissance, but my guess is it wasn't "Renaissance Man," because nobody today calls anyone "a true 2000s Man" unless they're trying to insult them.

A generation ago they used the expression "a hail fellow, well met" to describe a hearty, congenial man with a quick wit and a lust for life. Hundreds of years before that, an ocean away, they used the term "Warrior Poet." Like in the final scene of *Braveheart*, a movie that not only is required to view if you want to be my friend, but also perfectly sums up my friend Bill Arienti. Except he has never turned that warrior spirit against rival clans and kings, but against threats to the health and well-being of his neighbors.

Bill is one of those rare souls who is as comfortable running into a burning building as he is at a keyboard. As much in his element resuscitating a stranger back from the brink of death as he is preparing a top-quality meal for dinner guests. As perfectly fitting into his own skin telling filthy-but-hilarious jokes as he is writing a book of uplifting Christmas stories.

I'll try to sum Bill up for you with some of my favorite personal stories. And just out of an excess of caution, let me warn you I talk in a LOT of sports metaphors. And have enjoyed the pleasure of coaching youth sports with Bill. My first story involves a game where we were both assistants coaching a football team of 10-year-olds who had just had their heads metaphorically handed to them by a bigger, stronger, faster, more athletic team. One voice among the postgame speeches was raised to lift the kids up. To remind them that they made every effort. And while it's OK to be disappointed they lost, the takeaway should be that they fought hard to the end and should be proud they refused to quit. Although it was hard to make out the voice over the sound of our fellow coaches rolling their eyes so hard they were in danger of rupturing their ocular nerves, rendering themselves blind, it was no shock that message meant to build kids up came from Coach Arienti.

But my favorite story is from the time I was an assistant on the baseball team of 11-year-olds he managed. We were the Pirates. A ragtag collection of fun-loving misfits so clichéd that Disney executives would have looked at a description of them and said "Oh come on, this is embarrassing! Who's gonna buy into a movie about these kids winning anything? Get out of my office with this crap! NEXT!!!"

Bill operated off this crazy idea that maybe – just maybe – youth sports was about kids enjoying themselves. That perhaps if you gave them a chance and built up their confidence instead of tearing them down by reminding them of what you think they CAN'T do, they'll succeed. So, the fat kid got his chance to play middle infield. The small kid had a turn at first. If you lacked confidence but had never pitched before? Here's the ball. There's the mound. Do your best. Like I said, crazy. But, just crazy enough to work.

I have a vivid memory of the Pirates trailing 9-0 early in a game while this collection of middle school class clowns, goof offs, and wise guys horsed around on the bench. Out of a thousand managers, 999 would have lit them up and told them to act like winners. Bill was that one exception. And a relaxed group of preteens who weren't made to feel like they were committing a hate crime against the sacred sport of baseball came back and won the damned game. Cause. Effect.

That team ended up squeaking its way into the playoffs. And winning. And winning again. Eventually making it into the town championship. According to town legend another manager whose team got eliminated – the kind who believes children are born into this world to shine a spotlight onto his coaching genius – screamed with a purple-faced rage in front of a bunch of families, "I can't believe the fucking Pirates are in the finals!!!" And in the finals, we were.

And won it all. As a matter of fact, we won it in extra innings, with the go-ahead run scored by a kid we all loved and I respectfully thought of as the Neville Longbottom to my son's Harry Potter. Not only that, he had walked, advanced on wild pitches and scored the championship-winner off of the pluperfect stereotype of the athletically gifted mean kid who had tried to make Neville's life miserable. Again, Disney's script doctors would never have purchased the rights to a story this hokey. But it happened. I saw it. It was real. And one of the single most gratifying things I've ever seen.

I warned you I talk in sports metaphors. So, what does this mean? What does the long-forgotten story of a bunch of 11-year-olds playing a game have to do with anything? Nothing. And yet, everything. Bill Arienti deserved most of the credit. But in typical fashion, accepted none of it. As with everything else he does, he was just merely trying to be a force for good. To make others feel better instead of tearing them down. To heal rather than harm. It shouldn't be a novel concept, but it is. Human beings like him shouldn't be rare, and yet they are. Which is what makes this book so worthwhile.

When Bill hasn't been fighting back against fires, medical emergencies, psycho parents' approach to their kids or the corrupt vulgarians governing our country, he's been fighting his own health problems. Not to mention the problems of his fellow first responders and his own loved ones. With the same joy of battle and appreciation for what's truly important in this one short trip around this little spinning blue marble we all get.

Like I said, I hope you have your own Bill Arienti. If you're not so fortunate as we who know him are, the book you have in your hands should help you appreciate that people like him are among us. Enjoy.

— **Jerry Thornton**
Author of From Darkness to Dynasty

BILL ARIENTi

INTRODUCTION

I s life based on fate or coincidence? This is a question which underlies everything from the big bang theory to something as commonplace as finding a parking space today at the mall. If the gases that traveled throughout the Milky Way had not combined into an explosive compound great enough to create this world, you would not be reading this, for I never would have written it. Was it all just coincidence or were we forever meant to be?

Personally, I consider myself to be a fatalist, but not in the traditional sense of the term. I am not downtrodden or pessimistic, but rather optimistic and hopeful. I see life for the goodness it holds and the pleasure which one derives from it. The fatalist part comes into play when I look to the future. I am a firm believer that everything in this world happens for a reason. Although I am not a religious man, I am truly and deeply spiritual. I appreciate the beauty of the grain in a slab of wood that no artist can truly capture. The colors of sunset were not created by the Crayola Company, but inspired by nature for the Crayola Company to mimic. Nature is a gift given to us by whoever or whatever one wants to believe. Everything and everyone is here for a purpose; what that purpose is we may never know, even after we fulfill it.

Coincidence, contrarily, is random. It is an event or series of seemingly unrelated events that happen to correlate to a specific happenstance. Coincidence is also known as a twist of fate; from a belief that fate is inevitable. My belief didn't just happen to appear one day, it is based on a number of series of unrelated events that had they not occurred in a specific order would not have produced a greater event. Even the most devastating experience could very well be an integral link of a much greater happening.

The day before my nineteenth birthday, my father, a Quincy Firefighter, died from fire related-injuries. Four years later, I was appointed to the Quincy Fire Department. As a firefighter, I saw a surprisingly large number of firefighters being diagnosed with cancer. These firefighters were in relatively good physical condition, only a few smoked cigarettes or had an otherwise hazardous occupation. Although their cancers were varied, many shared one specific thing in common, among other organs affected, their kidneys showed signs of cancer or pre-cancerous lesions.

As part of my job, I studied to become a hazardous materials technician. In my studies became aware of the effects that different chemicals have on the human body. One of the chemicals was benzene, a direct derivative of diesel fumes. With that knowledge, I was able to begin to put the pieces together and found the single thread that connected many of these firefighters. In the professional firefighting service, firefighters work, live, eat and sleep in the same building that diesel powered fire engines are garaged. Each time a fire engine is started in the station, diesel fumes fill not only the garage area, but infiltrate the living quarters of the fire station as well. In addition, the fumes also permeate the protective gear that hangs right next to the fire engines. It became both evident and ironic that the gear we use as protection from fire was in actuality slowly and silently poisoning us.

Being president of the Firefighters Union, I began a crusade to eliminate carcinogens, like benzene, from inside the fire stations, but removing it from their protective equipment as well. After months of research, trial and error and negotiations, the City of Quincy installed equipment to completely eliminate diesel fumes from the fire stations. It was not long after that we began to see the number of Quincy Firefighters suffering from kidney cancer drastically drop. Using these facts, I then filed legislation with the Massachusetts House of Representative to mandate diesel fume eliminators in all Massachusetts fire stations when any renovations of the stations were performed. No one can ever know how many Massachusetts Firefighters are alive today because of this advancement; but the chain of events, how tragically it began, resulted in firefighters living longer lives.

This is just one of the many chains that I have experienced. The idea of serendipity is a pleasant thought, but ultimately, we are here on purpose for a purpose. Fate is not necessarily a bad thing, especially if it drives us to make a better world.

—⟋⟍—

I have always been an admirer of the works of John Steinbeck, the great American author. I find his grasp of the human struggle to be quite insightful and resonates with my experiences so that reading his work is almost like becoming a character within the story.

Everyone knows his works like East of Eden, the Grapes of Wrath, and Of Mice and Men, but two of his lesser known works are my favorites. Cannery Row tells the stories of a group of people left behind in the port city of Monterey after the collapse of the fishing industry. The characters were created with such detail and complexity that each one could carry a novel on their own.

In "Sweet Thursday," once again Steinbeck reprises the cast of characters that he created in "Cannery Row". He deepens even more the players' intricacies, and the relationships established during these difficult times. Both books are so moving that they caused me to take a vacation to Monterey, California, just to, in a small way, experience the atmosphere from which this author gathered his inspiration.

To honor this great author and his works, I have adopted the style he used in a few of his works. Each odd numbered chapter tells a part of the true story of how destiny saved my life. The even numbered chapters offer you, the reader, the ability to understand me, my beliefs and the changes I experienced throughout a life changing ordeal. I hope you enjoy it.

—ᴧ—CHAPTER 1 —ᴧ—

E veryone who truly knows Paul would not consider him their friend. The reason for this is not what you would expect; but something much more inspiring. You see, Paul, an immigrant from Lebanon, offers more love to everyone than most people offer to their families. This makes Paul not just a friend, but a family member; at least, to all the people I know who know him. There is no better friend, father, husband rolled into one good person as there is in Paul.

One major passion in life that Paul and I have in common is food. Both Lebanese and Italian families consider preparing food as a form of love. To enjoy food made by another is the greatest compliment one can pay people whose ancestries hail from the Mediterranean ring. Whether the meal is a twist on traditional American fare or unusual delicacies passed down by generations, tasting the new food is a sign of respect; enjoying the food is a sign of love.

Paul prepared food nightly for his family. Although he only has his wife and one daughter living at home, he cooked a special treat for them for dinner; and each dinner was truly appreciated by his family. When he began to lose weight, he went to his doctor and was diagnosed with cancer in various parts of his body. There are times in life where the cure seems worse than the ailment; for someone who honors the pleasures of food, the cure for cancer is one of them.

Cancer causes a body and a metabolism to work at an accelerated rate to fight the internal infection. As the body works harder, it eats calories at a much higher rate to fuel its efforts. What makes this even more difficult is the fact that chemotherapy and radiation, two of the most widely used therapies to fight cancer often destroy and eliminate both appetite as well as the pleasure of eating. This just adds to the danger the cancer patient faces, as insufficient nutrition reduces the ability of the body to fuel its immune system.

Paul quickly became weak and his appetite diminished just as fast. Knowing how Paul is, and knowing what he would do for me if I were in a similar situation, I began to prepare meals for him and his family. Three or four times a week I would shop and create two meals; one for my family, and one for his. I would make enough food to allow for sufficient leftovers for the next day in case I could not prepare next nights meal. Each time I would deliver the meal to Paul's family, I would receive copious thanks and hugs, along with compliments on my culinary abilities. This practice was in no way work to me, as I enjoyed every morsel of food I created for them.

The anticipation of a scheduled trip to Italy was growing greater and greater inside me as the date of departure continued to draw near. Although my wife and I had already been to Europe, this was our first time visiting Italy, with all its history, splendor and excitement. This would be the culmination of many aspects of our lives. It would be a celebration on our reaching our retirement; a reward for doing without some comforts to assure family responsibilities be fulfilled, and a gift to each other for being the most important person in each other's life for thirty years. It was a trip that we had been planning for a number of years now, and we paid meticulous care to address even the smallest of details.

One of the details most important to me was memorializing the trip with visual media. Although I had a very nice camera, I wanted to use it more than as a point and click toy. I wanted to take pictures that not only captured the moment in posterity, but also captured the heart, the soul and the imagination of everyone who sees it. To accomplish this feat, I knew that I would have to learn a lot more about my camera other than setting it on automatic mode. I contacted the photography store down the street from me and signed up for lessons beginning April 6, from six to eight PM.

After coming home from delivering the dinner to Paul, I sat down and began to relax. The television was on and I was waiting for my wife Nancy to return home from work before serving dinner.

Nancy finally got home around five-thirty. As she walked into the house, she looked surprised to see me in the clothes that I had been cooking in. "What are you doing here?" Asked Nancy. "I thought you were going to the photography class tonight." With all the duties of my hectic day, I had completely forgotten about the class. "I think I'm going to skip it and go next month instead." Nancy shook her head; this course was one of her Christmas gifts to me, and I had already put it off for two months due to work obligations. Postponing it another month for any reason would have made it seem that I was not interested in her present. "You have time, it's only around the corner. Go get changed and go."

I rushed up to our bedroom, found a shirt, washed my face and changed. By the time I left it was five-forty-five, and if the traffic lights were kind to me, I would be at the camera store in five minutes. With no traffic, I was able to get there on time, albeit I was the last student to arrive.

The course was interesting as well as informative, and the instructors were able to explain the different topics with both a professional, yet down to earth style. At the end of the class we were given a homework assignment that I looked forward to completing; this class was going to be fun.

Earlier in the day before the class started, I had prepared a ham dinner not only for my family, but for Paul's as well. Although it always seems to cause indigestion in me, I like the taste of ham, and since it was on sale, this was a no brainer. I made ham dinners, they tasted good, but I knew that I would have to pay for it later.

When the class ended, I left the building with my camera, notebook and homework assignment and walked back to my car, about eighty feet away. About half the way there I realized that I had left my leather jacket in the classroom. I walked back, donned my jacket and again began the walk to my car. After a few steps, I began to feel a pressure in my chest, not too painful, but enough to know it was there. "That goddamn ham; I knew this was going to happen," I thought to myself. I tried to take in a deep breath but was for some reason unable to fill my lungs with air. My car, which originally looked only eighty feet away, now looked over a football field away. All I wanted to do was sit in my car and get a deep breath.

This particular event was the first in a series of seemingly unrelated happenings that, of themselves, would have been nothing but coincidence. However; when the providence of one coincidence is compounded by a number of subsequent events, coincidence must give way to fate, destiny or maybe even divine intervention. Whatever you call it, me forgetting my jacket at that opportune moment is one of the circumstances that allowed me to write this book.

It was at that moment I experienced the first of what would be too many times, my life, for all intents and purposes, clinically ended. Many people relate different experiences when they have a near death event. I have heard people say they see old family members who have already passed, white lights, music, a beautiful woman or a saintly figure. They are quite adamant about their recounts, and I do not deny anything they state. I can however say that maybe I didn't get close enough to death, or maybe I don't deserve the traditional welcome into the afterlife; whatever the reason, there was no light, no people, no music. It was a few days later before I truly understood the situation and circumstances surrounding this life changing event.

A few moments, or hours later; I still had no idea how much time had passed; my eyes opened up to see a number of people gathering around me. I was not afraid, but rather confused. I recognized no one, yet felt that I was in the hands of people who cared. "Don't move, don't move" repeated the voices around me. I tried to speak, to ask what was going on, but my mouth did not work for some reason.

My face was wet. The more I moved, the wetter it became. It was then that I tasted a familiar flavor in my mouth; it was blood. The puddle in which I laid was composed of my own blood; it was then that the feeling of fear began to grow in the pit of my stomach. Again, I tried to speak, but my tongue was not able to reach the roof of my mouth to form words. It was at this time that I didn't know if injuries were caused by a fall, a stroke or something else. The more I tried to talk, the more I came to the realization that my teeth were not in the normal vertical position, but rather were positioned horizontally into my mouth from just under my nose. I realized at that point that I had broken the maxilla portion of my upper jaw. The uncertainty of me having a stroke was now less of a concern; but I still had no idea what had befallen me.

I gave my phone to one of the people who surrounded me and asked them to call my wife. With the understanding that my injury was the cause of me being non-verbal, I then adjusted my tongue to fit what little room was left in my mouth to speak. The attempt to reach my wife was fruitless; however, a few moments later my phone rang, and my wife's picture appeared on the screen. I informed her that I did not know what had happened, but I was in trouble. She asked where I was and she rushed to be at my side. It was then that I realized how fortunate I was to have forgotten my coat in the store. If I had not returned for that garment, I would have been in my truck driving at that critical moment. Would I have driven off the road and into a tree? Would I have crossed the yellow line and driven into a head on collision with an innocent victim? I, through all the goodness of the world, will never know.

A few minutes later, the Hanover Fire Department Ambulance arrived. The three paramedics who arrived were all friends of mine, and the expressions on these hardened medical professionals gave me the indication that I was in more trouble than I had thought. In accordance with protocol, the medics put a cervical collar on me, got me onto a stretcher and rushed me into the ambulance. As the medics worked feverishly inserting intravenous, giving me an EKG and driving with what seemed reckless abandon to the hospital. I was tired. As we drove my eyes kept closing, and I felt myself falling asleep. Butch, a close friend who was tending to my injuries in the back of the ambulance kept shouting at me "stay with me buddy, come on Billy," and "stay with me". As hard as I tried to keep awake, the desire to sleep was a great challenge to overcome. I began to will myself to stay awake; knowing that if my eyes closed, they would never open again. The ambulance finally arrived at the hospital, and I drew in a deep breath; I had made it.

As the stretcher to which I was strapped was pulled from the back door of the ambulance, I felt the jolt of the wheels falling to the ground and locking in place. The medics wheeled me into the emergency room through the double glass doors and were directed to take me straight into a room known as Trauma One. I laid there, unable to move, my eyes staring directly into a bright circular light above me. A number of nurses congregated around me, removing my jacket, my clothes and inserting additional needles filled with a myriad of pain killers and antibiotics into my arms. My vital signs were taken over and over again; my wife and son now in the room watching. A number of the nurses whom I worked with in the hospital were working furiously to insure my safety and wellbeing. Noticing just how serious the nature of my injuries were, I wanted to break the tension, so I began to make light of the situation. "If this is what dying is like, to be honest with you, it's not that bad," I joked; not knowing how prophetic my words actually were.

Since I still did not know the cause of my syncopal episode, I had a sneaking suspicion that the level of stress that I had been recently under caused by the vindictive personnel director of the City of Quincy had more than just a slight impact. This woman had made it her crusade to destroy my reputation, my career and my retirement on the basis of nothing more than a few lies told to her by a disgruntled deputy chief. Even though the Chief of the department told her the claims against me had no basis, her blind rage prevented her from dismissing the libelous statements. The hostility among all the players reached a crescendo at a five-day grievance hearing, where the director and city attorney twisted and manufactured a number of events that they claimed happened over my thirty year career. Fortunately, both the Chief of the department as well as a number of witnesses who were present for every event cited by the city of which I was accused, were rebutted to an impartial arbitrator. The arbitrator later found the whole case against me unsubstantiated, and ruled wholly in my favor.

This constant stressful pressure, even though baseless, had now taken its toll. Even knowing my troubles were nothing more than a smear campaign, hearing untruths about something I held as sacred as my career was none the less devastating. Insomnia, nightmares, depression and irritability now were an unwanted part of my life, cast upon me by a city employee that had been moved from department to department without any formal training in any.

Not a day since the first accusation against me was made was I able to separate myself from this ordeal. This whole chapter of my life had now in some way taken up residence in my mind and tormented me every moment of idle time. Since there was nothing else I could think of to have caused my situation, I assumed this was one of the most significant contributors.

Chris, one of the paramedics who transported me, is an old friend. My house in Hanover was diagonally behind his parent's house and we have maintained a very close friendship for many years. He is a hardworking firefighter dedicated not only to the citizens of Hanover, but to his fellow firefighters as well. Once in Trauma One, Chris never left my wife's side, reassuring her and offering her support in this difficult time. I called Chris closer to me and asked him for a favor, to which his answer was "Anything Bill, name it."

"Chris, could you please take a picture of my face?" I asked; a strange request to say the least by most people, but with me, nothing is out of the ordinary. "You really want a picture?" asked Chris. "I want the bastards who caused this to see that their actions have consequences." Chris smiled, shook his head, snapped a picture and messaged it to my phone.

After ordering an X-ray and a CAT scan, the doctor in charge made the decision to send me into Massachusetts General Hospital, where an orthodontic surgeon was on duty. To ensure that the broken jaw did not interfere with my breathing, the doctor required an advanced life support ambulance take me into Boston. Once settled in the ambulance, I reached into my pocket and retrieved my cell phone. I then found the picture that Chris had taken minutes earlier, and for the first time, I then understood the concern, fear and panic on the faces of all those involved. I took a deep breath, exhaled and closed my eyes. Although worried about the injuries I saw in the picture, this ride, after being seen by a doctor, seemed to trigger much less anxiety. On the way into Boston, I fell asleep.

CHAPTER 2

In everyone's life there are certain natural occurrences or locations that have the power to rejuvenate us. The most exasperating day can be neutralized by just listening, watching or smelling the world around us. One of my most favorite places to unwind is at the beach. I enjoy the experience long before I get there; not by the anticipation of relaxation, but by the feeling of the humidity of the air slowly increasing, and with it comes a faint fragrance of salt, sand, drying seaweed, and the marsh grass of the ocean. The closer to the shore I get, the greater the humidity and the beach essence grows. Even though I have yet to arrive, two of my senses are already well on their way of decompressing. My sense of touch and smell are stimulated in a positive direction, lifting the yoke of stress from my already overloaded shoulders.

Soon my first view of the ocean is visible through a space between the tall apartment buildings that line the side opposite the beach. The dark green and blue hues of water and sky are highlighted by the white crest adorning each wave as it makes its way to the shore. Once the wave finally reached the shore, the sounds of fury, strength and power join the vision of unrelenting might as a roar of incomparable power accompanies each wave as it crashes onto the hard sand of the beach.

The cycle of each beach wave begins with the sight and sound of the undertow. As the wave grows off shore, the ocean begins to churn and pull whatever may be situated on shore back into the surf, as if the ocean is reclaiming what it recently gave up. The sound of gravel grinding against itself is the first sound as the sand on which it sits flows without resistance down the slight incline of the beach, with all the water from the last wave being reanimated as it is sucked into the superseding wave. Once rejoined with the ocean, the wave is again forced upon the shore, rushing up onto the shore, leveling anything and everything in its path except the immovable boulders.

It is at this time that I realize that I am not the wave, not the stone, not the gravel, but nothing more than an insignificant grain of sand in an ocean of tumult. My problems, in the workings of the world as a whole, mean virtually nothing. People who live in war torn countries, or who are caring for children with life threatening diseases; people who have no place to keep warm on a cold night, people who haven't eaten for a day, and know not if they will have food to feed their family that night; these are the problems that matter, these are the rocks, these are the gravel, and the ocean, life's waves of relentlessly pounding difficulties and challenges in their way.

These are the problems which I have never known or experienced. My life, although never rich or without worry, has been a sequence of events of good fortune; starting with my parents and family's love, care and generosity, to never having to worry about food or shelter. From my health and the health of my family to the unconditional love of my precious wife; my life has been a river of peace flowing through a forest of happiness. Even my death, although it may make some sad at my passing, wouldn't create a ripple on the ocean which is life.

CHAPTER 3

U pon reaching Mass General Hospital, a stream of nurses, doctors and aids began to administer to my wounds. I was immediately given additional pain killers through the intervenors, the cervical collar that held my head and neck motionless was removed, and the extent of my facial injuries could be better evaluated. The oral surgeon came into the room, it was now about 2:30 AM. The surgeon was a young, blonde man; tall and thin. He introduced himself as the oral surgeon. I did my best to form a smile on my face, then in garbled words, I asked the doctor to smile for me. Although he looked perplexed, he honored my request and smiled a smile befitting a movie star. I then said "OK, I make it a practice to always use a dentist with better teeth than me." What little laughter that he could muster at 3 AM, was discharged by the surgeon, as well as my wife and nurse, who were both standing beside my gurney.

The surgeon began his work by applying a topical pain reliever to the mangled mess that was once my mouth. A few moments later he began to inject Novocaine into my upper jaw gum line. I lost count after ten injections. "I'm just going to let that sit for a while," said the surgeon as he walked away from the gurney to look at the X-rays of my face. I was beginning to think how bad my mouth was going to feel after the Novocaine wore off; the pins and needles feeling from one shot of Novocaine is torturous, having over a dozen will surely be pure horror.

The doctor returned, changed his blue latex gloves, and began to touch my upper lip and gums. "Can you feel this?" asked the surgeon. I shook my head in a negative fashion, and the reconstruction commenced. An assortment of wires of different gauges was set on a metal table beside my head. The surgeon took each individual wire and placed it between my teeth, anchored it to another and twisted the wire. The doctor then reached into my mouth and pulled my front four teeth forward, bringing my upper jaw back into place. He then quickly worked to insert and twist more and more wires until my mouth was stationary (a condition my mouth seldom stays in for very long). Upon finishing his craft, he asked the nurse to hold a couple of clamps in place while he took pictures of his handiwork. A combination of stress, medications and sheer exhaustion allowed me to fall asleep, as my wife stood vigil beside me. Although I remember being transported to another room, I was in a different world as the transfer took place.

I was brought to a medical ward where I was transferred off the emergency room gurney onto a regular hospital bed. Even though I would say any other time how uncomfortable the bed was, compared to the gurney it felt like a Serta Perfect Sleeper. Once in the bed and covered, I fell fast asleep. At 7:30 AM I was awakened by a young nurse who apologized for waking me, but she had to take my vital signs. My wife Nancy still beside me, I told her to go home; "Take a cab to the T station and go home" I told her. "Someone will pick you up at the T station in Braintree and drive you home." The nurse overheard our conversation, and informed us that the Red Line of the MBTA had a stop in walking distance. That happy circumstance allowed Nancy to visit me daily, without having to drive or find a parking space in the hospital parking garage.

Having been awake the whole night, Nancy was understandably exhausted. She kissed me goodbye and began her first, of what would be many trips home. I closed my eyes, still quite sedated by the effects of pain killers and fell asleep. What seemed a moment later, a hospital transport person entered my room and asked if I was William Arienti? I said yes, and he told me that he was there to take me to an ultrasound test. The young man helped me to my feet and into another hospital gurney, even less comfortable than the first. I laid back on the stretcher, rested my head on the plastic pillow and even with the discomfort of the gurney, I quickly fell asleep for the ride.

I again was awakened by a woman's voice. "Mr. Arienti?" she said with a question in her voice. My eyes opened to unfamiliar surroundings; the silhouetted figure of a woman stood between me and a blinding light behind her. "Mr. Arienti, could you please tell me your whole name and date of birth?" I answered her directly and she brought my gurney into a room and pulled the curtain securely behind me. The room was much darker than the area in which I had been waiting and sleeping. There were a number of machines around the perimeter of the room, as well as a chair and a television monitor immediately adjacent to the gurney on which I was positioned.

The woman requested that I lower the head of the bed and lay supine, as she pulled a sheet over me, up to my waist. She then pulled the hospital johnnie I was wearing off my body and began to ready me for the gel medium they use to perform the procedure. I braced myself for a cold thickened liquid, but was pleasantly surprised when the application of a warmed viscus cream was applied to the middle of my chest.

The sounds within the small room reminded me of a time twenty years earlier when I heard my son's heartbeat for the first time while he was still within my wife's womb. The squishing noise with a rhythmic beat let us know that he was healthy. This time the noise coming from my chest let me know just the opposite. Unlike my son's regular beat, mine had a slight yet unmistakable echo after every second beat.

Upon the completion of the procedure, I was returned to my room. I transferred from the gurney back into my hospital bed, and once again attempted in vain to sleep. My eyes had not closed for more than a few seconds when a man in a well fitted suit accompanied by two other men and one woman wearing lab coats adorned with stethoscopes entered my room.

"Mr. Arienti," began the suited man. He introduced himself as well as the other doctors, and then started to explain my medical condition to me. The fatigue which I was experiencing, combined with the number of medications that I was taking, limited my understanding of the extent of my condition. The only detail that I was able to understand and retain was the cause of my unconscious event; the atrial portion of my heart, the artery leading to it were involved, and the valve controlling the flow of blood to the rest of my body had somehow become stuck in the open position. The malfunction of this valve prevented my heart from blood to the rest of my body.

As luck would have it, it was then that Nancy and my sister Marie returned to the hospital. The doctors introduced themselves to my family and continued to explain the situation. It was a relief having them there, because I knew that I was only hearing half of what the doctors were saying, and understanding only half of that.

The doctors had ordered a few tests and procedures be done to make certain that their theory were correct. My broken jaw also complicated matters by adding the danger of infection. It would be in my best interest to wait to perform any invasive surgery, especially heart surgery. Since the chances of infection resulting from mouth wounds are much more aggressive than injuries to other part of the body, the doctor's wanted to wait until my mouth healed, then perform the heart surgery. Taking this direction would allow me to go home, recoup from the broken jaw and nose, and insure a more sterile atmosphere for a serious surgical procedure. The doctors all took a turn listening to my heart and lungs, they then thanked me for my time and left the room.

Nancy, accompanied by my sister Marie had just arrived for a visit. It was then that good fortune again shined down upon me. Nancy, Marie and I began to discuss the situation which I was facing. Although the Mass General

Hospital is ranked as one of the top cardiac hospitals in the world, getting the right doctor for the procedure is paramount. Marie called my brother Charlie, who recently retired as a director of South Shore Hospital, and asked if he knew the name of a good cardiac thoracic surgeon. Charlie asked what was wrong, and was fully briefed by Marie. He then told her that he would call her back in an hour. Charlie was true to his word, as about fifty minutes later my sister's phone rang. My sister answered the call and heard Charlie's voice say, "I've talked to a few doctors, and they are unanimous in their opinion, try to get Dr. MacGillivray."

Having lost my mother thirteen months earlier, the closeness of my family was never greater. My sister, who had been my mother's primary caregiver, was still grieving our mother's death. With the serious medical issues I was facing, I did not know how she would be affected emotionally. It didn't take long to reassure me as there are no greater players under pressure than my family. We began to discuss my options when yet another doctor entered the room. This doctor, a very well-spoken and distinguished looking man of Indian descent introduced himself as the cardiac groups' surgical liaison. He, like every other doctor, began by asking me what happened to bring me there. I explained, in detail, the series of fortunate events that caused my admittance into the hospital. The physician then said that he would be following me and my case throughout the entire procedure. This was a very friendly, yet extremely professional doctor. He explained to me that I required an atrial valve replacement, and educated us about the differences of mechanical valve versus tissue valve replacement. The one issue that caught both my attention as well as my sister's was the fact that I would be required to take blood thinners for the rest of my life once I had a mechanical valve. Since my late mother was on blood thinners, we both knew the drawbacks of taking such medication. Although the mechanical valve would most likely last me the rest of my life, the fact was that I would have to be monitored bi-weekly for the rest of my life. Knowing myself better than anyone else knows me, I realized that I am not sufficiently disciplined to follow such a strict regimen. I asked him if it would be possible to have Dr. MacGillivray as my surgeon. The doctor nodded his head, told me that he would see what he could do. He wished me well, said goodbye to my family and me, and then left the room.

"Your face doesn't look bad at all", said Marie in a voice she tried to disguise as surprised. Having seen the picture of my face earlier in the day, as well as the inflexion of her voice, I knew I looked pretty bad.

I took a deep breath in through my nose and blew it out of my mouth, which is my first act of accepting a difficult situation. "I think I am going to go with the tissue valve, I don't want to be on blood thinners for the rest of my life," I stated to Nancy and Marie.

"Blood thinners are a pain, but the mechanical valve never has to be replaced" countered Marie. "He said the tissue valve lasts ten to fifteen years.

In medical technology, ten years is a lifetime. By that time, they may very well have a better option for me." I answered.

In the few minutes that passed as we conversed about the prior evening's events. I could see how tired Nancy. She had been awake the entire night and only got a few hours of sleep that morning. I asked the two women to leave so that I could get some rest, but my concerns were solely on Nancy's condition. They agreed, kissed me good bye, and left me to my own devices.

Even if I wanted to sleep I wouldn't have gotten the chance. Just moments after they left the room a young man pushed a stretcher to my doorway. "Mr. Arienti?" he asked, butchering the hell out of my last name. "Close enough," I laughed and slowly got out of bed. "You have to go to the cardiac cath lab for a test." I walked to the stretcher, climbed on, and was covered by a sheet. The young man pushed me down corridors and through doors. On the ride I began to feel like Quasimodo in the Hunchback of Notre Dame. The looks my battered face received from everyone I passed ranged from shocked to horrified.

When we finally reached the cardiac cath lab, the lab techs slid me over to a very thin table and strapped me in tightly. They inserted a bag of I.V. fluid to my already positioned intravenous, and began talking with me while we waited for the arrival of the doctor who was to perform the procedure. The techs explained the procedure to me and what to expect. From what little I could comprehend, the doctor was about to put a needle in my thigh, push it up through my femoral artery and feed it directly into my heart. I knew this test; it was called an angiogram and was a very common procedure. I did not worry about it, as I was in the best hospital in the world with the best doctors.

I suddenly felt a whoosh of air on the top of my head, as the doctor entered the room. He positioned himself at my side and asked me what had happened. As I spoke, I felt a warm sensation in my arm from the fluid passing into me from the I.V. The tech had added an additional smaller bag of fluid to the first. As I tried to tell the doctor about the night before, I felt woozy but conscious. When he heard the details, the next words out of his mouth still ring in my ears. "You're lucky, I've heard of this happening. Your valve stayed in the open position, not allowing your heart to pump blood to your body; basically, you were dead before you even hit the ground."

Dead? I was dead? I thought I just passed out. "What do you mean by dead?" I asked. "Your heart was not able to pump blood to your body, therefore there was no perfusion of blood to your organs. If you were lying down when that happened, you probably wouldn't be here right now, but the force of the blunt trauma on your chest when you fell may very well have caused the valve to close and the heart to start pumping again."

Although in a drug induced stupor, I began to run through the links of the chain of events along with the consequences of each link that led me to this point. Going back to get my coat after I was so close to my truck; if I hadn't done that, I would have driven away and when my valve stuck I probably would have driven into traffic or driven into a tree, either way the results would have been disastrous.

The next lucky link, my face planting on asphalt. Had slid down the side of a car, or landed in snow or a field of grass, the impact would not have been severe enough to cause the valve to close, which would have left me dead on the scene.

Breaking my jaw necessitated my emergency ambulance trip into the Mass General hospital because South Shore Hospital did not have an oral surgeon available or on call. Because of the advanced medical practices at the Mass General, the doctors were able to precisely diagnose my condition, my ailment and what course of action was necessary. As I stated earlier, I was never one to believe in coincidence, and this series of fortunate yet seemingly unrelated events were not random, but more like the universe taking the steps necessary to keep me here for some reason or another. My fate was not to die in a dimly lit parking lot that night, but rather fate had something very different in store for me: what that is? I have no idea.

On Sunday morning Nancy called around 10 o'clock. "I'm coming in a little later; Mark wants to come in and see you, so does Laura and Tom," Nancy informed me. "I'm trying to get Mark to go in with Laura because he has never been to Mass General, but he wants to come by himself." Shaking my head, I could understand both sides of the argument. Being a parent, I did not want my son to get lost driving into Boston, but being a man, I understood that doing something like this would be a coming of age event for Mark. After measuring both sides, I told Nancy to let him drive in. "He has a GPS in his car, he should be alright." Nancy reluctantly agreed, and as she had foretold, my cousin's Laura and Tom came in a few hours later for a visit. Soon after they left, Nancy arrived.

"Mark said he is coming here right after work." Nancy said with a little worry in her voice. "He gets out at 3, so he should be here no later than 4." I nodded. We sat and had a light conversation punctuated with the occasional "I hope he's alright" by Nancy. At 4 PM Mark had not yet arrived, and so the countdown began. At 4:15 Nancy asked if we should call Mark to see where he was. I told her not to, "Give him some time." I recommended, assuring her that he was alright.

At 4:30 Nancy's apprehension began to creep into my mind as well. "Should we call him?" Nancy asked with a little more urgency. I said, "Don't call him," this time with a little less certainty.

At 4:45 Nancy stated unequivocally "I'm going to call him." This time I agreed, and Nancy called Mark. The phone rang twice, was picked up and immediately hung up. Again, Nancy tried to call, the results were the same. With such responses, Nancy and I both began to worry. This is just what I needed, already stressed to the max, now I have to worry about where the hell my son was.

Our fears were short lived, as a few moments later Mark walked into the room. His tall frame loomed over my bed as he bent down to hug and kiss me. "Where have you been?" asked an agitated Nancy. "I was on my way in following the GPS on my phone when it rang and disconnected the GPS." Mark explained. "Then, once I reset the GPS, the phone rang again, and I missed the exit." I looked at Nancy and laughed, "Well, you're here, that's all that matters." I laughed. We sat, had a nice visit and then they hugged me, kissed me and said they loved me. It was a very warm and comforting feeling for me to savor as they left the room to return home.

CHAPTER 4

There are certain smells in life that can transport us to a different time and place. The scent of pine may evoke the memory of Christmas's from years gone by. The smell of the salty ocean may conjure up thoughts and memories of summers on Cape Cod. Whether it be a natural scent, a manufactured perfume or something cooking, the sense of smell is the most powerful of all senses.

The power to recognize familiar scents allow us, if only for a minute, to leave the situation we are in along with all its stressors and return to a time of comfort and happiness. Even the thought of those smells, without the manifestation of the scent itself can reduce tension without even changing your position. Just for laughs, ask a friend near you to close their eyes and try to remember the smell of cinnamon buns cooking, the watch closely for their reaction; more times than not, a small smile will appear on their face.

People go through life unconsciously gathering a collection of aromas. The more prominent scents are recognized immediately once they again present themselves. From skunk to cinnamon, from warm bread to a baby's dirty diaper; whatever, recognizing the scent is just a subconscious reaction by our brain.

I enjoy trying to gather smells whenever I go to new place. Years ago, it seemed that each neighborhood often had their own special aromas. Depending on the ethnic makeup, age and businesses in the neighborhood that created its character. Those characteristics had their own aromas. Irish neighborhoods often smelled of freshly cut grass in the summer time, as they kept their yards pristine. In summer as you walked down the street in an

Italian neighborhood you could smell basil and tomato plants, as there usually was a good-sized garden in every other yard. Indian neighborhoods had the distinct smell of curried foods. If there was a bakery, a restaurant, a gas station or any other business these entities created their own atmospheres. To this day just the thought of warm bread brings me back to Sumner Bakery, and the smile I spoke of earlier readily appears on my face.

Think of some aromas that bring you back to a happy memory; a new puppy, a new car, cooking chocolate chip cookies, or meat on a charcoal grill…anything. It is truly a gift when your subconscious brings you to a better place without you even having to move.

CHAPTER 5

The soles of his shoes made a distinctive sound as they met the floor; they were not your ordinary, run of the mill Buster Browns, these were quality shoes this guy was wearing. As he got closer to my room the sound was distinguishable from any other shoe that I heard. He entered the room without a word. He was tall, over six foot and quite fit. His white lab coat was unbuttoned making visible his wrinkleless shirt with a necktie hung precisely to the proper length. His appearance was nothing less than impeccable, but it was his deep commanding voice that impressed me the most. It's funny how just a voice can offer a level of confidence, even if you have no idea how good someone is at their craft. He sounded like the actor Robin Thick, but with a higher level of decorum.

"I take it that you are Mr. Arienti" boomed the voice, not with volume, but with a resounding tone. "I'm Doctor MacGillivray." I sat up in my bed and reached out my hand to greet him. "Hi Doctor, I've heard a lot about you" I replied as I shook his hand. "This is my wife Nancy," I continued. The doctor greeted her with a respectful hello, and then took a chair next to my bed.

This was the man; the guy who is going to cut me open and dig into my chest. He sat back, crossed his legs and clasped his hands around his knee. "So, tell me, what happened?" He asked. I took a deep breath, and with as much detail that I could recall, I related the events of that evening to him. As I spoke, he was silent, no question, no comments, not even a nod of the head. He was stoic. When I finally finished my accounts of the event he pursed his lips and nodded his head. "Well, after reading your file, that is absolutely consistent with the results of all your tests." He then told me what course of action was necessary, and explained in much greater depth the benefits and the drawbacks of the procedure and my choice of valve.

Although he told me my decision on the valve was not needed immediately, I told him that because of the dedication needed to maintain the Coumadin regiment, I decided to go with the tissue valve. Dr. MacGillivray nodded, "That is a very logical explanation and choice you've made" he nodded. "Actually, either choice for a person your age would have been the correct choice." He then explained that the tissue valve was created from the stem cells from a cow, as their valves are exactly like ours.

"What do you do for work?" asked the doctor. "I'm a firefighter" I responded. "I've been a firefighter for thirty one years, but I guess I reached the end of the line now, at least after this." The doctor stood up from his chair, put his hand on my knee and looked into my eyes. "I have the utmost respect for you guys and the job you do. If I can do anything at all to help you I will, you can be assured of that. I won't know until I get in there, but you may be able to go back to the job. Do you have light duty?" I bit my bottom lip and said "no" realizing that my career was most likely over one year earlier than I had planned. "Well, let's cross that bridge when we come to it" he replied. "The first thing we are going to do is get you up on the cardiac care floor."

He then told me that I had a few more tests to take, and he would check up on me daily. We again shook hands goodbye, then he said goodbye to Nancy, and left the room with the distinguishable sound of those shoes.

It did not take long for his words to ring true, as just a few minutes after he left, a nurse and a young man came into my room. "You're going up to the tenth floor" the nurse informed me. Nancy stood up, collected what few items I had and put them into a green plastic bag that was given to her by the nurse. The nurse and the young man worked together to unlock the brake on my bed and begin to push it out of the room and down the hall on our way to the tenth floor.

The journey to the tenth floor stopped at the last room down a long corridor. As the bed stopped at the door, I could see that there were already two beds in the room, and a tall nurse with definitive Irish features was folding the hospital corners on the bed closest to the door. The young man walked into the room and spoke quietly to the nurse. "Can you walk?" asked the nurse? "Sure," I answered as I began to make my way out of the bed. "Hold on, let me put the rails down" laughed the transporter. As the rail went down I hopped out of the bed and walked into the room rolling my I.V. pole beside me. "Your face isn't as bad as they said it was," said the nurse. I wanted to respond with neither is yours, but not knowing this woman from Eve, I decided, discretion was the better part of valor. And knowing this woman was in charge of managing any pain or discomfort I had with medication, I kept my mouth shut.

"Oh, by the way, I'm Cathy." The tall nurse had a very welcoming voice, and her manor was sincere. I realized that her first comments were actually compliments to make me feel better about my situation. "Hi Cathy, I'm Bill, it's a pleasure to meet you," I replied with the best smile I could muster with a spool of silver wire stabilizing my upper jaw.

As I surveyed my new room, I was stunned by the expansive view I had of the Charles River and the Boston University Bridge. It was a view that any Yuppie with a seven-figure income would die for. Even though my bed was next to the door rather than the window, this window stretched across the whole room, and gave me a panoramic view of the city of Boston second to none.

Settling into my new room, Cathy explained to me what was going to happen in the next few days. A litany of tests were awaiting me starting in the morning, "But your lunch is here now, and nothing is planned for this afternoon, so just relax for today." I sat on the edge of the bed and pulled over the rolling hospital table to prepare for the arrival of my lunch.

A Hispanic man carried a tray with a covered plate. He greeted me and placed the tray on the table in front of me. He smiled, turned and left the room. I lifted the cover off the plate to see a very large serving of disappointment. Ice cream scoops of brown and ivory masses sat in the center of the plate. Before I ventured a taste of the mounds, I read the menu to find that they were ground roast beef and mashed potatoes. I replaced the cover onto the untouched plate and then took the cover off of the cup of soup. Although the soup smelled horrible, it tasted even worse. I was content to enjoy the prepackaged ice cream and pudding along with the surprisingly pleasant tasting coffee. Although the physical pain from the broken jaw was not severe, the residual effects were beginning to cause major discomfort.

Nancy laughed at the fine cuisine being served to me. "You have to eat more than that," Nancy chuckled. "Would you like me to go get you something?" For some reason or another, what would usually be at most a snack for me seemed to have satisfied my appetite; at least for the moment. "Thanks, but I'm all set," I responded.

On the tray was also a menu for the evening meal. The items listed sounded so appetizing, but so did the menu they served with the lunch. I decided that rather than look for a protein I was sure would be served like the dinner of a regurgitated bird, I had better go right to the dessert menu. Tonight's dinner would be a bottle of Ensure for an appetizer, leading to the main course of chocolate and vanilla ice cream, followed by a lovely dessert of chocolate and vanilla pudding. I laughed thinking I am probably the only person with a wired jaw that is going to put on weight.

The touch of a nurse's hand awakened me with a start. "Bill, Bill," a soft voice whispered in my ear. After a few blinks and wiping the sleep from my eyes, I saw a young woman in scrubs with a stethoscope around her neck. "I'm here to get some blood and give you some medications before they take you downstairs for some tests," said the woman. "I'm your nurse Haley." I instinctively reached over to my nightstand to grab my eye glasses before I realized that I had broken them in the fall two days earlier. Even though my vision was blurred, I could see Haley's actions as she placed a small bag of medication on my I.V. pole and connect it to my I.V. She then asked me to hold out my arm, looked at my paper wrist band, and wrapped a large rubber band around my arm just above my elbow. She tapped my arm, found a vein, and painlessly inserted a small needle into my arm and let a stream of red fluid fill three test tubes.

As if it was a finely choreographed ballet, the moment Haley finished drawing my blood a gurney pulled up to my room and the transporter stretched a sheet over the thin black mattress. "Your ride is here," announced Haley. "My shift is over in an hour, but I will be back tonight; good luck." "It was a pleasure meeting you, and thank you," I responded as I rose from the bed and made my way to the gurney.

"Mr. Arienti?" asked the transporter with a strong undistinguishable accent. "I was when I came in here," I responded. The transporter laughed and asked to check my wristband. I laid back on the gurney, the rails were put in place, and my day of testing had begun.

For someone who just had to lie there, stand up a few times just to lie back down, and wait for the next test to be prepared, by the end of the day I was exhausted. When they finally returned me to my room, I happily got into my own bed, laid my head atop the plastic pillow, and nodded off about two o'clock.

Cathy's voice called me out of what seemed to be a nice ten-minute nap, although when I looked at the clock, it was a quarter past four. "Can I just get a set of vitals from you please?" I rolled over and reached out my right arm, allowing her access to wrap the blood pressure cuff around my bicep. She then placed a clothespin-like device onto my left index finger to measure my oxygen level as well as my heartrate. "Looking good" said Cathy as she entered the information into the computer. "Cathy, can I take a shower, I feel like such a grub," I inquired. "Sure you can, I will bring in everything you need, and new johnny tops and bottoms as well" responded Cathy.

Cathy was as good as her word, as within ten minutes she returned with a pink basin, bottles of shampoo, mouthwash, body lotion, a tooth brush, tooth paste, a comb (which would go unused!) some lip balm, facecloths, towels and a new fresh johnny ensemble. She then disconnected me from the intravenous and covered the remaining section of the IV with a plastic adhesive bandage, and told me if I needed anything else just call her.

I made my way to the bathroom and looked in the mirror. Three days of beard along with numerous open wounds, scrapes, abrasions and the ever present swelling combined, to put it mildly, into a very unflattering picture. I undressed, turned the water on in the shower, and as the hot water made its way up to my showerhead, I brushed my teeth. Having a bar and multiple wires securing it in my mouth, I was careful not to disturb the dental work. I then stepped into the tiny shower stall and began to wash myself. As I bent over to wash my feet, I began to feel lightheaded. When I quickly stood up, I almost passed out. This was not my normal, everyday shower routine.

I shut off the water, wrapped a towel around my waist and quickly made my way back to my bed. The last thing that I wanted to happen was to fall again, further injuring other parts of my body in the process. I pushed the nurses call button and did not have to wait long before Cathy came running into my room. Seeing me soaking wet on the bed without clothes she provided knew something was not right. "Are you ok?" she asked, with actual concern in her voice. "I got light headed and almost passed out in the shower," I responded to her. Cathy immediately sprang into action. She reached into a basket on the wall and pulled out a strip of electrodes. She then began to attach the electrodes to my chest in various yet specific places, then attached a series of wires to each one. Then, without a word, she reached into a cabinet and pulled out a small plastic bag that contained an adult nasal cannula (a long plastic hose with a loop at one end complete with two tiny air ducts to allow oxygen to freely flow into my nostrils). "Take some deep breaths in through your nose now, and blow them out of your mouth," instructed Cathy. Knowing that I am a firefighter and EMT, Cathy surmised that I deduced what was happening, and began to give me the information she just acquired. "Well, your EKG showed that you have an abnormality, an additional blip. Your blood pressure is higher than it was a little while ago; your pulse is higher, but your oxygen saturation level is lower. Keep taking in some deep breaths through your nose and out of your mouth."

I followed Cathy's instructions, and in about ten minutes my oxygen saturation level increased to 96%, while my heartrate dropped to 82. Throughout the whole ordeal, Cathy stood next to my bed monitoring my every change. Once she had connected me to all the machines, she called the cardiac team for further instructions; nothing additional was forthcoming.

As I was just beginning to relax again, I once again heard footsteps coming towards my room. They were not the footprints of expensive shoes, but rather the squeak of sneakers on a highly waxed linoleum floor. Nancy then walked in with a bag in her hand; and following her by a few minutes were my sister Marie and my cousin Virginia. "I found your other set of glasses," Nancy said with excitement in her voice. "Oh, and I have the contract you wanted Charlie (my oldest brother) to print out."

Both items were essential to my psychological well-being. Having very limited vision for a person with sight is frustrating; especially when you are confined to a hospital. Without my glasses I could neither read nor watch

TV. My days were spent making up little mind and memory games in my head. Once I put the glasses on my nose and over my ears, a new world had materialized. I could see everything, even if a tiny bit blurry, as these were my older glasses.

"Can I have the contract, please?" I asked of Marie. She reached into a bag and pulled out a green folder. I opened the folder to see two copies of a contract with my name on it, as well as Kharis publishing, the two parties of concern. This was it! My fifteen years of writing was finally paying dividends, as my first book, The Gift is in the Giving, was going to be published. I had to sign the contract by that day to ensure its validity, and scan and email the contract back to Kharis that day. I initialed each page, and then signed the contract on the last page. Having no scanner available, I used my cell phone to snap a picture of each page and emailed them back to Kharis. This was it; an accumulation of all my work was about to be recognized by the world. I got on Facebook and notified all my friends and family that I was now under contract to be a published, and hopefully, my first work will be on store shelves by September 2016. I said nothing however, about my medical situation; the last thing I wanted to do was to heap more worry and concern onto to my friends and family who, at that time, had enough of their own.

After ensuring my stability, Cathy informed me that according to the directive from the cardiac team, I was now confined to bedrest. I could go to the bathroom and sit up in a chair for my meals; otherwise I was not to be vertical. The only saving grace was that the Red Sox season was just about to begin, and with this directive in place I had the unhindered ability to view baseball without any of the interruptions I would normally experience if watching it at home; or so I thought.

The bottom of the first inning was interrupted by an aid taking my vitals. The top of the fourth brought the phlebotomist to take more vials of blood. Two outs in the sixth inning brought my evening medications, one of which put me to sleep by the end of the eighth. But the positive side is that the broadcast was going to be replayed the next day. Unfortunately, during the third inning on the replay of the previous night's game the herd of doctors that make up the cardiac unit arrived for a briefing. We discussed the events of the day before and what the potential consequences involved. When the briefing was complete, the lead doctor said after conferring with the staff, it was determined to be in my best interest's not to release me from the hospital, and rather than wait for my jaw to heal, they would schedule surgery as soon as possible.

My mouth began to dry out. I was fine about the surgery when it was weeks away, but knowing that it was impending brought a different level of apprehension to my psyche; in other words, I was scared shitless! I took a deep breath, blew it out, and said "OK". "Oh, I forgot to tell you, I've been in contact with Dr. MacGillivray, and he is going to perform the surgery" I explained to the team. "So why are we here then?" said the lead doctor. He turned to the left and began to walk away, then abruptly halted, turned back and smiled at me. "Only kidding," laughed the doctor. "I've already been in touch with Doctor MacGillivray, and everything is under control."

"Doctor MacGillivray's assistant will be coming in to brief you on all the details; but until then, just relax as best you can." Recommended the doctor. Each person in the group took a turn listening to my heart, back and neck, then shook my hand. The gaggle of physicians left the room at the top of the seventh inning.

Cathy then came in and began to perform her duties, which included taking vital signs, giving me a variety of medications, making me wash my mouth with an antibiotic, and documenting all the information into the computer. It was then that I discovered how nice a person she was.

I began some small talk, and little by little the conversation between us deepened into personal and professional issues. I had told her that I had written a few children's books that I had self-published, and just signed a contract with a publisher for a non-fiction book. Cathy then informed me that she also had done some writing, but never finished her work. I told her how important it is to complete a writing project, especially if it is non-fiction. "It's like stopping a life half way through," I joked. Her bedside manner was impeccable, as she showed a genuine concern for every aspect of my wellbeing. It was not long before we became very close and developed a deep mutual respect for each other.

Once Cathy left the room, I again turned on the television to catch the end of the game. When I found the correct channel the broadcast of the game was over. I started flipping through the different stations and settled for Family Feud. That selection was also short lived, as Nancy entered the room.

Knowing my loathing of the diet that the hospital prescribed for me, Nancy walked into the room with a large red cup with the word Friendly's written down the side. "I brought you a black and white milkshake," she said in a very joyful tone. "That's the kind you like, right?" As much as I loved Nancy for more than half of my life, for the first time in my life I saw the devotion and love she had for me that all these years I had taken for granted. Each day she would maintain the house, go into work, then make her way to see me, riding on the subway which she so detested. After visiting, she would once again walk to the MGH subway station, and ride back to her car in Quincy. She would then drive another twenty minutes to reach our home, let the dog out for a few minutes, finish the housework that the time did not allow earlier that morning. Exhausted, she would climb into bed and sleep until the morning alarm would wake her at seven o'clock, and again the cycle would repeat.

Nancy has never been a strong, sturdy woman; but more ladylike and demure. She is not athletic, but loves being a spectator of all sports. She is a woman committed to her family with as much fervor as a mother bear with her cubs. She is honest to a fault, and would never utter a bad word behind anyone's back. Each time she entered my room I resented myself for perceiving her love and devotion as commonplace, and not recognizing how exceptional her dedication to our son and to me actually is. I swore to all I held holy that day that I would never again discount how much this beautiful woman does.

Nancy placed her bag on the floor and kissed me as she handed me the milkshake. She pulled a chair close to the bed and began to tell me the out of the ordinary events that she witnessed on her subway rides. As she related one incident to me, she could not help but laugh from her recollection. Although the stories were humorous, it was her way of telling them integrated with breaks of her laughter that I found more amusing, and had to join her in laughter.

I then told Nancy of the day's big event, the decisions of the cardiac staff, and how I would not be coming home. Her disappointment was combined with anxiety and was evident on her face. She was more afraid of what was about to happen than I was. "Have you decided what type of valve you are going to choose?" she asked with a slight tremble in her voice. Knowing that the mechanical valve mandated I stay on a blood thinner for the rest of my life, and I would have to be monitored on a regular basis, I understood that regimented lifestyle did not fit my personality. "I'm going with the tissue valve, it may only last ten years, but that is a lifetime in medicine, and hopefully by then they can adjust things with a less invasive procedure."

The words had just left my lips when a woman in a white lab coat walked into my room. "Mr. Arienti?" she asked. I had not yet encountered this woman, but I assumed that this was Doctor MacGillivray physician's assistant. "That's me," I replied. "Please, call me Bill" I instructed her, as the more formally we addressed each other, the less comfortable I felt. "OK, Bill, you can call me Janet.

"Well Bill, it looks like you are going to get a new aortic valve" announced Janet with a lift in her voice as if I had just won a new car on *The Price is Right*. Although I was more nervous at this moment than I had been since I regained consciousness, I tried to lessen the tension, not as much for myself, but for Nancy. "Looks like I hit the lottery!" I answered as I chuckled. Nancy shook her head and smiled like I have seen her do a thousand times before when I say something unexpected. "I spoke to Dr. MacGillivray, and he told me that he had explained the difference between the mechanical valve and the tissue valve to you; have you made a decision which way you want to go?" Asked Janet. "I think I am going to go with the tissue heart" I responded. "I don't want to be on Coumadin for the rest of my life, so the tissue valve is the way for me."

Janet took out a small notebook and began writing down the information.

"Did Dr. MacGillivray discuss the potential hazards that are inherent in this procedure?" I knew right then and there that no cutting up or quick one liner was going to protect Nancy from the barrage of negative possibilities that I was facing. "No, not yet" I answered in a more serious tone.

"Well, they do thousands of this type of procedure a day across this country without any problems, but I have to make you aware of the possibilities." Janet began. "First, there is always a chance of infection, another organ could be accidently cut which would require further treatment. While placing the breathing tube there is the slight chance that we could puncture your trachea, cause excessive bleeding, an abnormal heart rhythm, damage your heart from and interruption of blood flow, blood clot and cardiac tamponade, a chance of stroke and death." She read these things off the same way a waitress in a diner tells you the daily breakfast specials. "Do you have any questions?" "Well," I smiled, "I think I could have done without the last risk." Again, Nancy began shaking her head. "Well, I had to tell you all the risks, but very few of these risks actually happen," apologized Janet. "I completely understand," was my response.

"Do you have any other questions?" posed Janet. I had recalled many of the questions that Nancy and I discussed the day before, and felt this was the ideal time to get them answered. "Where do I go after the surgery?" was my first question. "Immediately after surgery you will go to the cardiac intensive care unit for one or two days, then you will go to the cardiac care unit on the eighth floor for a few days." Janet replied; Nancy nodded in understanding.

"How long is the recuperation period?"

"We recommend three months before you are able to resume your regular work schedule."

"I'm a firefighter, is three months sufficient for me to completely recover and return to work?"

"You might have to wait four months, but you should be alright."

"When I get discharged, do I go home or to a rehab hospital?"

"You will go home, but you won't go home until we think you are ready to go home. We may recommend you participate in a cardiac rehab outpatient program. Six weeks after the surgery Dr. MacGillivray will want to have a follow up visit just to make sure everything healed properly." Janet took a breath. "We will give you a date and time before you leave for an appointment. In the meantime, we strongly recommend you contact a cardiologist to monitor your progress once you return home."

I took in a deep breath through my nose and blew it out my mouth. "I guess that's all I have." I looked over to Nancy and asked her if she had anything that I may have forgotten. "Did you want to ask her about October?" Responded Nancy.

"Oh, yeah, I forgot." I said as I looked at Nancy. "Janet, we have a trip to Italy planned for October. Am I going to be able to go on that trip?" Nodding her head, Janet replied "What is this, April? September is six months away. You should be fine by October."

"Well, I'll be in and out over the next few days; if anything comes to mind just ask me." Janet slowly rose from her chair. "Well Mist…Bill, it was a pleasure meeting you; Nancy you too. Try to get some rest and good luck." I thanked her and Nancy and I watched her leave the room. "What do you think?" I quizzed Nancy. "You're ah... You're going to be alright," answered Nancy as she took my hand in hers. "I know I am, as they say, only the good die young!" I said to break the tension.

I knew that Nancy and I had to make provisions if things went south during the surgery, but this was not the time. Nancy already had too much to digest with everything she just heard; I could not add another layer of anxiety onto her. We had a few more days before the surgery; that would leave us plenty of time to get things in order.

Over the next few days, a number of relatives and friends visited, helping the time go by. Through that time, my day nurse Cathy and night nurse Mary, another wonderful woman who treated me with the utmost of care, both kept me hydrated with intravenous, medicated me, helped me clean myself, took my vital signs, took blood and were able to take the time to visit me between their other duties. Their professionalism combined with their compassion helped me relax and relieved my angst. Over the week I spent in their care, I felt like I was their only concern on the floor, and I greatly appreciated it. The last day there, after informing them that I had just contracted with a company to publish my book, I asked them individually if they would like me to give them a reading of one chapter that detailed the turbulent hospital stay of an elderly woman. They both were very responsive, and after hearing the story, both nurses were filled with emotion. They asked when they could buy the book, and I told them that I will bring some in when they are published.

On the morning of Tuesday, April 12, Dr. MacGillivray came into my room. Gone were the finely fitted suit and stylish shoes, and in its place was a pair of hospital scrubs covered by a lab coat. "How are we feeling this morning?" His unmistakable voice asked. "I'm as good as I can be, Doc," I replied as I reached out my right hand in friendship. "Well, I've got news for you," he said as he shook my hand. "It looks like we are going to take you in on Thursday, is that ok?" Since I had already spent almost a week in the hospital, the idea of hurrying the procedure along by any means that would get me home quicker was more than acceptable. "I'll be waiting with bells on," I joked. "OK then, Janet will be in as will the anesthesiologist to go over a few things either today or tomorrow, and I will see you on Thursday," He then turned and began to leave the room.

"Sounds good," was my answer. "And Doctor, thank you for everything you've already done for me." Dr. MacGillivray, turned and smiled; "My pleasure."

At about eleven o'clock, Janet appeared as foretold by Dr. MacGillivray. "Hi Bill, looks like everything is all set for you to have the procedure done the day after tomorrow." I nodded in anticipation. "I can't wait for this to be all over and go home," I responded.

Janet pulled from a large brown folder a smaller colored folder. I just have to get a couple of things done before you go. Opening the folder, Janet took a pen from the breast pocket of her lab coat and began to ask me a number of questions that I had already answered a hundred times before. With each answer she made a check mark on the papers in the folder. After the last question, Janet asked me to initial the first two pages, and then sign at the bottom of the third page. "You have a great signature," noticed Janet. "Ten years of Catholic school," I laughed. "Do you have a power of attorney and a comfort care form in there?" I asked. "You know, just in case anything does happen." Janet nodded, "I understand, the floor nurses have those here; I will tell them to bring then in for you." "Great, thank you," I said.

"Has the anesthesiologist been in to see you yet?" asked Janet. "No, not yet, but I am sure he'll be here shortly," I joked. "He will be here either today or tomorrow," explained Janet. "And just so you know, all the questions that I asked you today, he will ask you again." I nodded my head and smiled, "It figures."

About noontime, Nancy made her way into the room with her usual dietary supplement for me. She kissed me and handed me the large Friendly's cup. I took the cup and as quickly as possible, stripped the paper off the long straw, inserted into the perpendicular slit on the lid of the cup, and began sucking in the shake with the force of a Hoover vacuum cleaner. "Wow," Nancy laughed. "You must have been hungry," said Nancy. "What did they give you for breakfast today?"

Having to remain on the soft diet, my breakfast options were extremely limited. Being tired of eating oatmeal and cream of wheat, seeing a new item available appealed to me. I have always liked French toast, and immediately checked the corresponding box the day before. That morning, when my breakfast tray was delivered, I picked up the menu and recalled the choice I made for that morning's breakfast. Even this tiny change brought about a feeling of excitement within me.

As I lifted the cover of the main course, the aroma of cinnamon wafted from the plate. The smile began to form on my lips, until I saw the abomination sitting under that cover. Two pieces of bread, regurgitated and reformed into unrecognizable shapes, sat in the center of the plate. Sprinkled atop the mass was a little powdered sugar, most of which had already melted, inadvertently but fittingly in the shape of a frowning face. "I know how you feel" I said to whatever it was that sat on that plate. I recovered the plate and drank the coffee and juice.

As I explained my morning adventure to Nancy, she laughed and punctuated her response with a number of "awe's" and "oh's". Once I finished the shake, and Nancy had made herself comfortable, I decided that it was time to break the news to her. Rather than just blurt it out, I felt breaking it to her in a gentler manner would be more appropriate. "I can't wait until this whole thing is over and behind us," I began. "Oh, me too; I want you home." Responded Nancy. "Well, that's good, you feel that way too, Doctor MacGillivray was in the room earlier and told me that the surgery was set for Thursday morning." I explained.

What was once a phantom event, an unspecified time in the future now had definite date and time. It made the abstract real; the future now. I saw Nancy bite her bottom lip; a habit of hers that I recognized after thirty years together as a signal of stress. "Well… that's good, it will finally be done," said Nancy in a hesitant fashion. She reached down and took my hand in hers. I could feel a slight tremble in her grasp as she sat down on the bed next to me. "Nancy, I'm in the best hospital in the world with the best surgeon in the hospital. If something happens, it's not going to happen because of some fluke. No matter what, when my number is up, my number is up," I reassured her. "If it was my time, I would have died the other night on the ground. The world is not done with me, and I have something else to accomplish before I go."

As if the moment was already not melodramatic enough, what happened next brought the scene to the level of a Greek tragedy. As Nancy began to accept the news of my procedure, the cardiac unit's coordinator entered the room with a number of papers in her hand. "Mr. Arienti, did you request the power of attorney and DNR order?" I felt my eyes uncontrollably rolled into the back of my head. My first concern was Nancy, and she seemed to be fine. "Yes, are those them?" I asked. The coordinator put the papers on the rolling table and informed us that we had to fill out the papers and then we both had to sign them in front of a witness.

Nancy hurriedly began to fill out the papers when her already strained nerves began to manifest. Usually quite meticulous when it came to paperwork, Nancy made a number of errors, and wrote over them. "Relax," I said, "It's just paperwork." My instruction fell on deaf ears because Nancy and I had already discussed what I wanted if I were to be on life support. Being a firefighter, as morbidly as it sounds, having an understanding such as this between a husband and wife is prudent.

When she had finished, I told her that we needed another copy of the paperwork because this was a legal document and should be written with unmistakable accuracy. I didn't mean to make Nancy feel bad but having dealt with more of these documents than I care to remember, it was almost instinctual. The coordinator assured us that it was fine and asked us to sign them. Nancy signed her name first, and I placed my signature on the line after her. The coordinator then signed the paper in the witness section and dated it. She took the papers, left the room only to return a moment later with copies of the documents for our records.

Nancy and I tried to put the issue behind us by discussing the upcoming Presidential election. I was sure that this would distract her, as even though we are both died in the wool Democrats, she was supporting Hillary Clinton and I was a Bernie Sanders fan. The debate got a little heated, but cool heads prevailed.

Once we put politics aside, Nancy told me about the religious zealot who shared the same train as her last night. "I know Jesus loves me, but how many times do I have to hear it!" she laughed. "The worst part about it is that he rode the subway all the way back to my stop." Nancy again made me laugh and relieved my stress. Situations like this seem to happen to Nancy all the time, and I told her she was something of a "nut magnet."

As we laughed, a man dressed in blue hospital scrubs, along with a blue hat and face mask hanging around his neck came into my room. His stylish ensemble was completed with paper covers on his shoes. It seemed to me that he wanted people to know that he just came out of surgery.

"Mr. Arienti?" the man in blue asked. "That's me" I answered. "I'm Dr. Kayem, the anesthesiologist," he announced. "I have to ask you some questions." I began to feel like Ebenezer Scrooge from Dickens Christmas Carol being visited by the ghosts. Dr. Kayem first asked to see my wristband to assure I actually was William Arienti. The slew of questions then began delving into my medical, family and personal history. Dr. Kayem must have asked these question a hundred times that day. His voice and demeanor was dry, and his delivery was more robotic than human. After he finished one of his lists of questions, I interrupted the Doctor. "I have a question." My abrupt interjection into the physician's litany of questions seemed to have taken him by surprise. "Ah, ah, yeah, go ahead," he said. It was obvious that he was not accustomed to either being interrupted or having a question returned back to him. "Do you ever smile?" I inquired, more in an attempt to break the tension in the room for Nancy and for me, but it was also an attempt to bring some warmth and humanity to the Doctor's delivery.

A very nervous and forced smile appeared on the Doctor's face for a moment, and then he went back to his mechanic droll. I looked over to Nancy to see her holding back a laugh and again shaking her head side to side. Upon finishing his list, Dr. Kayem decided it was time to tell me all the risks I faced by being sedated with anesthesia. This is what I did not want Nancy to have to witness, but she had heard the same risk factors the times she had medical procedures performed, so she did not seem fazed.

"Have you been washing with the antibacterial soap?" was the Doctors final question. I replied in the affirmative to which he replied, "OK then, see you Thursday." He turned without saying goodbye to Nancy and left the room. Once out of ear shot, Nancy looked at me, shaking her head again saying, "I can't believe you, do you ever smile?" She began to laugh upon completing her sentence.

As the day went by, I looked closely at Nancy. Although she would deny it until the day she died, it was clear to me that she was exhausted. I felt horrible that I was not only causing her worry, but physically draining her as well as she had to work, take care of the house and then rush back and forth here every day to see me. My sister Marie had driven her in numerous times, but even with the pressure of driving removed, it was a grueling routine she was performing. She refused to stay home, even when I asked her to.

I was afraid she was going to wear herself down to the point of illness. Not being the most robust of people, when overtired, Nancy was susceptible to illness more than others. I have never experienced such undying love and devotion as she was showering on me.

When my lunch was delivered the both of us were anxious to see what gastric abomination was set before me. As I lifted the cover, I began to laugh; not at the food, but comparing myself to a contestant on "*Let's Make a Deal*", praying that there was not a "zonk" behind the curtain. Once revealed, I could hear the "Wa wa wa" sound that is played when someone on the show loses. I knew what sat on my plate only from the description on the menu, as it resembled nothing that I had seen before. As was my normal routine, I drank the coffee and Ensure, ate the ice cream and pudding, and pushed the table away.

When the meal delivery person returned to take the tray back to the kitchen, the cover was still on the main course. "How did you like it?" the woman with a strong Hispanic accent inquired. "It was nothing less than superb" I responded. "It's almost like the chef found the perfect blend between Alpo and Chuck Wagon," I said sarcastically, knowing that she most likely did not understand what I was saying. The eye roll from Nancy followed my comment as it usually did, although this time she did not admonish me.

My brother Ernie then came in to see how I was doing. We talked, joked, and laughed. Although Nancy could make me laugh, she was quite proper in her sense of humor, and did not appreciate my cruder jokes usually enjoyed by less sophisticated men. This was what I needed. Even though it was for a short period of time, the off-color exchanges between us took my mind completely off the impending operation.

I was also happy that Ernie came in because I wanted Nancy not to have to take the train home. A relaxing ride would give her a little time to decompress from the constant barrage of tension which she was enduring. Before leaving, Nancy went down to the cafeteria for a cup of tea, and returned not only with the tea, but with an ice cream sundae for me. It was a welcome surprise, as I was certain that the disappointment of lunch would continue upon the arrival of dinner.

I told them to go home, relax. Nancy wanted to stay, but Ernie had appointments to keep. "Nancy, go home with Ernie, I'm fine. I'm going to read my book and watch TV, that's all." Although she was not satisfied with the arrangement, she acquiesced, kissed me goodbye and left with Ernie.

Against medical directives, I climbed out of bed and walked to the window that overlooked the Charles River. I could see sculling teams practicing in the water, children playing baseball on the baseball diamond, people strolling down the walkway beside the river. It was a beautiful warm and sunny spring day, and here I was sitting on the tenth floor of a hospital. I would have given almost anything to be done with this and join all those people, but then that little voice of reason which had taken residence up in my head reminded me, "Everything happens for a reason." I turned around and got back into bed just in time, as Cathy walked into my room to measure my vital signs yet again.

"I have to tell you something" announced Cathy. "You have inspired me so much that I took an old book that I was writing years ago out of storage and began to finish it. I smiled with genuine happiness. I am someone who loves to see people who not only realize their goals, but also overcome the fear or apathy to reach for them. It takes courage and commitment to reach for a goal, and those attributes are not found in everyone. I was proud for Cathy, and in no uncertain words, I let her know of my excitement. "That is fantastic! I am so proud of you Cathy. You have no deadlines except for the ones you put on yourself. You are a brilliant woman, and I am positive that you will accomplish anything that you put your mind to. The most important thing is not to be too critical of yourself; have fun with your project."

I attempted to give her a congratulatory hug, but just outside the room were a number of hospital administrators having an impromptu meeting. Cathy walked just out of their sight and we hugged. I was very honored that she used me and my experiences as a vehicle to achieving her own goal.

Later that evening Mary's shift began. Although not as close as I was with Cathy, Mary and I had forged a bond as well. As she took my vitals, gave me my meds and began to ready me for Thursday, she asked me when my book was coming out. I informed her that hopefully it will be out in the fall, and if not this year, it would certainly be out next year. Mary promised that she would buy the book once it comes out. I then asked her if she would like to hear a portion of it. "Oh, God, I would love that," she exclaimed. "I have to go do my rounds; can we do this around ten?" "Whenever you are available" I chuckled; and off she went to perform her duties and bring that happy feeling she has to other patients.

Around ten, Mary returned to my room. She took my vital signs again, attached the antibiotic to my intravenous and then gave me my other meds. Once finished, she sat down on a chair, stretched out her legs and said "OK, I've been waiting for this all night. I picked up my phone and scrolled to the documents section. I found the file that I kept my book under and then paged down to chapter five. I began to read my story to her complete with voice inflections to emphasize the story. When I finished, Mary wiped her eyes with a tissue and thanked me. "This is my last night working as a floor nurse, and I couldn't have asked for a more wonderful way to end my shift." I was surprised by her declaration, "I had no idea that you were leaving" I responded incredulously. "Where are you going?" I asked. "I'm going to the cardiac outpatient clinic. It's a much less hectic schedule," she explained. "Well, thank you for everything you've done for me, I truly appreciated all of it," I said trying my best to bestow my gratitude to her.

"Please tell me when the book comes out" requested Mary. "You can even come in here and sell some, I will tell everyone how good it is." Her excitement caused me to smile. "I'll do that" I answered. Mary lifted herself from the chair, put her hand over mine and wished me good luck, told me to take care and assured me that everything was going to be alright. She then left the room and it was not a long time after that that I fell asleep.

"Mr. Arienti, Mr. Arienti" whispered an unfamiliar voice as I felt a small hand gently shake my shoulder. "I'm sorry to wake you, but I have to take your vitals." I groggily rolled onto my side to see a very petite woman standing at the computer. If I had seen her on the street I would have taken her for no older than seventeen.

"What is your name?" I asked the girl as I wiped the sleep from my eyes. "I'm Kristin" she said as she scanned my wrist band to confirm my identity. The tiny nurse stood on her tiptoes to attach the I.V. bag to the tall pole. "How are you feeling?" she asked. "I'm OK, how about you?" I responded instinctively. Kristin smiled and chuckled, "I'm fine, thank you...but that is not important." After taking my vital signs, Kristin entered them into the computer. "Hit the call button if you need anything, OK?" Kristin explained. "Are you comfortable? Are you warm enough?" inquired the nurse. "I'm fine, thank you. I'm just tired" I retorted, hoping that she understood the hint. "I'll let you sleep" she responded. "Your meds aren't due until seven in the morning. Good night now." I don't think she reached the door before I fell back to sleep.

Five-thirty brought an early wake-up call from Kristin. Although she did not mean to wake me, her best intentions fell short of her goal. In her attempt to change the bag on the IV pole, she again stood on her tiptoes, and accidently pushed the pole against the bars on my bed. After thirty one years on the fire department, my sleeping habits had become keenly acute of the slightest sound; this sound was not that slight.

I sat up in the bed with a start, waiting for the next noise. "I'm so sorry Mr. Arienti." Kristin's apology was accepted without hesitation. "I was just reaching to add your meds on the pole." Already suffering from a case of sleep deficiency, two more hours was not going to make a difference.

As the sun was coming up, I climbed out of bed, walked to the window that overlooked the Charles River, and took in a deep breath. I knew that this procedure had been done countless times before with an astronomical success rate. I knew the hospital I was in was the best in the United States. I knew the Doctor I had was the top one in his field, but even being armed with these facts, I still was nervous. The fear was not for me, after all, I already died once, and it wasn't as bad as I had always imagined. I was afraid for my family, my wife, my son. I had lost my father when I was 19 and he was 55; my son was now 20 and I was 54. I recalled the anguish and absolute uncertainty I felt then and that continued even to this day because of his death. These feelings were not the feelings and legacy that I wanted to pass on to Mark.

The morning sun was now reflecting off the calm Charles River. Looking upstream, I could see the cobblestone bridge stretched over the river connecting Boston to Cambridge. I was a sight fit for an artist to recreate on canvas. I thought to myself how beautiful a city Boston is, and how fortunate I was to have experienced it all my life. I closed my eyes, took another deep breath in through my nose, held it in my lungs, rolled my eyes back into my head and expelled the air. I was ready for anything. Life will do to me what it desires, and I will have no decision in the matter. Every problem has a solution, therefore, if there is no solution, there is no problem. I had no solution; hence, this event was not my problem. I climbed back into bed, adjusted the controls on my bed to the most comfortable position, laid on my back and began a session of self-hypnosis.

Wednesday was full of doctor visits, signing papers, texting and phone calls. The ringtone on my phone alerting me of texts was a bell sound. After an hour of constant bells, I turned the alert off and just let it vibrate when someone contacted me. I received visits from the anesthesiologist, his supervisor, the oral surgeon, the nutritionist, the surgeon, the cardiac liaison, the physician's assistant and the ecumenical minister. Nancy and my sister Marie came in sometime between the others. The two women took in all the information recited by whoever the visitor was, and once that person had left, they each repeated the information that the last person had explained. Although somewhat nerve wracking, I felt compelled to listen to them, if not for anything else, I felt it gave them comfort to think they were helping me, and in some small way my listening was a way to thank them for all they had done to insure my comfort and safety.

As the hours slipped by, the visitors stopped, the phone calls and texts slowed. My surgery was scheduled for 10:30 the next morning, which allowed Nancy and Marie to come in and see me before the procedure. Enjoying a nice black and white shake in place of my rather putrid dinner, Nancy and Marie said their goodbyes and left.

When I finished the drink, I began another session of self-hypnosis and continued it with a guided meditation. By the time the nurses aid came in to shave me and give me a bath in medicated, anti-bacterial soap, my mind was enjoying the white sands and salty turquois water of the Caribbean. Although more potent tranquilizers would soon be administered, I was in the greatest state of relaxation that the human body could attain.

"Mr. Arienti?" Although she butchered the pronunciation of my name, I responded to the soft, Hispanic voice. "That's me." The woman appeared from behind the curtain dividing the room. She looked like she was no more than 18, very petite. Her skin was naturally tanned which complemented perfectly her black hair that she twirled into a bun. "I have to shave you for your surgery, then wash you with the medicated soap." She announced. "Could you please get out of bed so that I can prepare it?" I followed her instructions. Leaving on my johnny bottoms, then removed my johnny top exposing my chest to the young woman.

"What is your name? I inquired. "I am Sophia," responded the woman. "I know a Sophia back home; she is a beautiful woman too. It must have something to do with the name," I joked in somewhat of a flirtatious way. "Oh, you're too kind," laughed Sophia as she stretched a sheet over the bed. "I'm going to step out of the room, can you please get undressed?" Sophia continued, "there are a bunch of towels, feel free to cover up with them.

Preparing for heart surgery, I thought that having my chest and torso shaved would be sufficient. "I am undressed Sophia" I replied. Sophia then informed me, in a sheepish smiling way, "No, Mr. Arienti. I have to shave all of you, front and back." Well, this was news to me, but whatever. Sophia left the room and I removed all my clothes and covered parts of my body with towels.

A few minutes later, I heard Sophia's voice calling to me. "Are you all ready?" She asked. Feeling a little embarrassed, I answered "ready as I'll ever be". Now, to be honest, I have absolutely no problem with nudity, myself or others. We are all human, and nudity had just never caused me any discomfort. However, being unclothed in front of a very young woman made me uneasy. I thought to myself that this girl was young enough to be my daughter. Before she made her way into the room, I adjusted the towels to ensure sufficient "coverage."

Sophia came in with a basin of warm water and placed it on the rolling table. She then took a towel from the chair behind her and submerged it into the warm water. She then removed the towel from the warm water, wrung it out in her hands, unfolded it and laid it upon my chest. She continued the practice with both legs and both arms. Once the covering was complete, she removed the chest towel and with a safety razor began to shave my chest and torso. By warming my skin with the damp towels, she relaxed my skin and enabled her to remove all the hair from my body. The legs were next, then the arms. As she was readying me for surgery, I began some small talk with

Sophia. She revealed to me that she was just finishing up nursing school and had taken a few years off after high school to earn enough money to pay for nursing school. Life happened, and things got delayed, but now, at thirty, she was about to reach her lifelong dream of being a nurse.

Her story was both inspiring, as well as a relief. I was impressed by her undying dedication and commitment to achieve her ultimate goal; something very few people accomplish. I was also relieved that she was closer to thirty than seventeen. It just seemed more comfortable in a way.

When she completed my arms, she allowed me to position the towel so it would give her access while allowing me sufficient privacy. I did what was requested of me, and by the time I was finished, I resembled a six foot, two hundred fifty pound baby. "OK," said the soon to be nurse, "roll over, I have to shave your back now." This was much less nerve wracking and was actually soothing.

Upon her finishing the removal of all my body hair, Sophia gave me a robe to wear and asked me to once again get out of the bed. Simultaneously, a nurse entered the room, one whom I'd never seen before. She was around 45, red hair, a little overweight, but very pretty none the less. "Hi, I'm Karen," said the new nurse. She walked over to the white board, erased the name of the day nurse and replaced it with hers. "Can I get a set of vitals from you?" asked Nurse Karen. "Sure" I replied as I sat down in the chair beside the window. It was dark out now, and the streetlights reflected as circles of light in the Charles River. Karen tightly wrapped the blood pressure cuff around my left arm and connected the Velcro. She then placed the device to measure my oxygen level and pulse on the index finger of my right hand. She then turned and pushed the button on a machine and the blood pressure cuff began to expand, tightening around my arm.

Karen made her way over to the computer and began documenting the medications that she was about to give me. "You're getting an Ambien tonight I see." Reported Karen. "Yes," I retorted. "I asked Doctor MacGillivray this afternoon if I could have one to help me sleep tonight." Karen then hung a small bag of fluid on the IV pole, handed me a small wax paper cup with four pills in it, and poured me a cup of cold water to flush them down.

Karen then checked the numbers on the machine and entered them into the computer as well. "Are you all set with him?" Sophia asked Karen. Karen, with a surprised look on her face responded with "Oh, I'm sorry, I thought you had finished already." Shaking her head Sophia said "No, I just shaved him, I didn't give him his medicated bath yet." While Karen had performed her duties, Sophia had removed the sheets containing all the hair that she had shaved off me. In its place were a series of bed chucks, the thick padded squares designed to keep the sheets clean and dry. "You can lay down now," said Sophia as she pulled the curtain around my bed to offer my privacy. She again gave me a towel for privacy, and asked me to get undressed. "I'll be right back." Said Sophia as she left the room with the pink basin in her hand. I could not help but overhear the two women talking to each other as they left my room. The moment I was alone I readjusted my bed and began another round of self-administered hypnosis. By the time Sophia had returned with the basin, I again was lying on that Caribbean beach, white sand and all. When Sophia returned, she again called my name, however, this time she pronounced it correctly. Although it was rude, I did not open my eyes, but instead I stayed on that island as long as I could while she began to wash my body with a sudsy water laden with a microbial disinfectant. It was the most relaxing moment I had experienced in a week.

CHAPTER 6

I find in the spring, summer and fall, when the world seems to get the best of me, the one way to shrug off the burden is to go fishing. There is something about being next to the ocean or a lake that in itself is relaxing. But just sitting next to that body of water in time becomes somewhat boring before your body and mind can fully decompress. Fishing gives you some sort of diversion from the monotony to remain by the water for longer periods of time. The longer you remain in a serene environment, the greater the feeling of inner peace.

When I fish, I put a worm on the hook, cast the line in the water and find a nice shady spot to sit where I can read without disturbance. Every once in a while, I look up to see if the tip of the fishing rod is twitching, then go back to my book.

The only company I enjoy during these times is my dog Zeus. This four year old golden Labrador retriever loves to run free in the field next to the lake. After a few minutes of running full speed, Zeus makes his way down to the water where he wades in up to his body and then begins to spread the pads of his paws and swims in the cool water. Consistent with his breed, Zeus is as comfortable in the water as he is on land. For some unknown reason just watching him swim through the water, his yellow head cutting the calm surface like the bow of a boat makes me smile.

The funny thing about fishing to relax is that it doesn't matter whether or not you catch any fish. Just the smell of the grass, the shade of the tree, the sound of the water, the taste of cold lemonade on a hot day, or coffee on a cool day, it is a treat for all the senses. If the tip of the rod never moves, it means you had a great day of reading. If you catch fish, the excitement of the moment adds to the experience.

In short, fishing is not about fishing. To me, fishing is sitting in nature without the disturbance of television, radio, cell phones or traffic. Fishing allows you to experience a natural, undisturbed area to infiltrate your entire being. Fishing is conversing with no one but yourself, talking out your problems and visualizing the potential outcomes of your decisions.

With Zeus swimming around in the water, the chances of my catching any fish was slim to none. In actuality, I was much more likely to catch Zeus in my line than a trout. On occasions like this, although I enjoy the delight and exhilaration of catching a fish, I would rather see the line remain slacked and the rod stay steady. The act of fishing is just a tool to keep me in a natural environment for an extended period of time until nature fully permeates my mind and soul with peace and tranquility.

CHAPTER 7

The combination of the self-hypnosis, the Ambien and the warm water bath reacted together to create an irresistible sedative for all my senses. When I rolled over for Sophia to wash my back, I must have fallen asleep because I the next morning when I awoke I was wearing a johnny that I had no recollection of donning the night before.

The morning sun had fully illuminated my hospital room and roused me from the most restful night of sleep I had in ages. I sat up in bed and reached across the table for my glasses. When the room came into focus, I saw that it was already 8:30, and this was the big day. Still groggy from the tranquilizing drug, I attempted to get out of bed, but when I sat up the brightly lit room began to spin. I didn't know if the cause of this lightheadedness was from the medication or some other reason. I decided it was best to lay back in bed and let the uncomfortable feeling pass. As I placed my head on the pillow a nurse walked into the room with two bags of saline. "Good morning" she said in a cheerful voice. "You were asleep when I gave you your antibiotic, and I didn't want to wake you to take your vital signs." I looked up at the IV pole to see a small bag of antibiotic fluid emptying into my arm.

"I'm Meghan, by the way," said the nurse. "Hi Meghan," I replied with an inadvertent yawn. Meghan once again took my vital signs and documented them into the computer. She then put the two bags of saline on the hooks of the IV pole and hooked them into my line. "We have to over hydrate you before the surgery," said Meghan. She then adjusted the drip control mechanism to allow for full flow. "I'll be back in a few minutes to give you some medications."

At 9 AM Nancy and Marie entered my room. Marie sat in the chair at the foot of my bed, and Nancy sat on my bed. "How are you doing, Bill" asked Nancy. Her face, as beautiful as it is, was enveloped of worry. "I'm fine. Are you ok?" I returned. Nancy tried to smile, "Oh yeah, I'm ok," She assured me. Meghan then re-entered the room with a small wax-paper cup and two hypodermics. "Here are your meds" announced Meghan. I swallowed the meds with as little water as possible. She then took one hypodermic needle and injected it into the rubber fitting on the IV. She then took the other hypodermic and said, "I have your Heparin." Heparin is a medication that helps to prevent blood clots. Since I was immobilized for an extended time, I was susceptible to blood clots.

I pulled up my johnny and folded down my sheets to expose my abdomen to Meghan. She pinched my skin to make a fold and quickly inserted the needle, administered the medication and removed the needle. She then disconnected the near empty bag of saline and connected the full one to my line. "They should be coming for you shortly," said Meghan. "You might feel a little groggy in a few minutes." It was ten o'clock already.

I began to tell Nancy a few things that she needed to know, and in front of my sister I made her promise that if anything happened that I do not want to be kept alive by alternative methods. Nancy begrudgingly agreed to my wishes, but declared, without a doubt, "Nothing is going to happen, Bill."

As we were speaking, a middle-aged man wheeled a gurney to the door of my room. I watched as he walked into the room wearing hospital scrubs and carrying a plastic bag. "Are you Mr. Arienti?" he asked. I answered in the affirmative. "I'm here to take you down to surgery, my name is Jerry." He was tall and in addition to wearing hospital scrubs, he also wore a brimless cap, and had a mask hanging around his neck. "Can I please check your nametag?" he asked. I lifted my left arm, as I had done countless times before to prove I was me. "Please sit on the edge of the bed, I have to prep you."

Jerry opened the plastic bag that he carried in with him and asked my wife and sister to please wait outside the room. Once they were gone, Jerry took a pair of latex gloves out of the bag and put them on. He then removed a sealed package from the already opened one. He opened the second package and took out a pile of what looked like oversized baby wipes. "Please remove the johnny," Jerry requested, and I immediately complied. Grabbing one the wipes and unfolding it he began to wash my neck and shoulders, then discarded the wipe in the trash. Jerry repeated the process all the way down my body to my feet. When he finished, Jerry once again reached into the bag and removed a new johnny and a pair of hospital socks and helped me put them on.

"Do you think you can walk to the stretcher?" he asked. "Only one way to find out," I joked. Jerry's sense of humor, if he had any at all, did not extend to his professional life. "If you cannot make it to the stretcher, don't tell me you can," He scolded, his voice betrayed his less than pleasant bedside manner. Thoughts of Sister Honorius from Saint John's Grammar School came rushing back to me. What a great thought to have just before going in for open heart surgery. (For some reason or another, saying heart surgery does not denote quite as urgent a level as saying open heart surgery. It seems the word "open" elevates heart surgery to a higher realm.)

"I will bring the stretcher in here," he said shaking his head. The idea of reciting a line from the movie "Stripes" came to mind, and I had to stop myself from blurting out "Lighten up Francis," but thought better of it. I did not want to aggravate someone who might be assisting in my "open heart surgery."

Jerry walked out of the room and returned pushing a gurney with a black worn mattress. I began to stand from my seated position at the edge of the bed until Jerry ordered me not to move. I returned to my position watching Jerry remove a white sheet from a plastic bag he had earlier laid on the gurney. He stretched the sheet across the black mattress and tucked in the extra material at the head and the foot. Jerry then made his way over to me, assisted me to stand up and escorted me to the stretcher like a prom date. Once on the stretcher, he removed another clean sheet from the plastic and draped it over me. He then allowed my wife and sister to return.

Marie reached me first. "OK, good luck, everything is going to be alright." She kissed me and stepped away. Nancy then kissed me. Since Jerry had already removed my glasses, the fear in Nancy's face became more evident as she got closer to me. "I love you, don't worry, it will be alright, you're going to be fine," she whispered, assuring herself as much as she was reassuring me. She kissed me twice and again said "I love you". I smiled, "I love you too, thank you for everything." I know a thank you was a strange thing to say at a time like this, but if anything did go wrong, I wanted Nancy to know how much I appreciated having her as my partner, my friend and my wife.

Jerry then positioned the IV pole at the head of the stretcher and off I went. Both Nancy and Marie stayed behind, wiping tears of worry from their eyes. At this point, I cannot say that I was worrying. I like to use the phrase that every problem has a solution, if there is no solution, there is no problem. Plus, if there is a supreme being, why would it kill me here instead of just letting me die in that parking lot? Whatever the scenario that was about to play out, it was out of my hands, and I had made peace with myself, ready to accept any outcome that might befall me.

The gurney traveled down a maze of hallways. Although Jerry didn't seem too deep in the personality aspect, he sure was a good stretcher driver. We went through a double door that required a badge for entrance, then through another set of double doors to reach our destination; the cardiac surgery waiting room. Jerry pushed my stretcher back into a stall and locked the wheels. "Thanks Jerry, I really appreciate the ride," I said, actually meaning to thank him, but just adding that little jab at the end, he not knowing if I was being serious or sarcastic.

The medications were slightly sedating as I waited to be taken into the operating theater. One by one, nurses came out to talk to me and tell me virtually the same information. What the hospital scrubs, hats and masks everyone was wearing, and me in a stupor, it might very well have been the same nurse on one visit that ran over and over again in my mind.

After a long wait, I was wheeled into the operating room. With only a vague recollection, I remember the room being somewhat small with huge adjustable white lights hanging from the ceiling. There were a number of TV monitors around the perimeter of the room, metal tables and pumps. Once in the room, my stretcher was brought over to the operating table. One of the nurses then pulled the trigger to drop the rail on the right side of the gurney. I attempted to wiggle over from the stretcher to the table, but was met by orders to stop. "We will take care of that, let us put you on the table," came a voice from behind one of the masks.

A moment later someone began to count "one, two," and on "three" I felt myself being slid from the stretcher onto the table. Looking straight up I saw a masked face staring down at me at the head of the table. "OK Mr. Arienti, I'm the anesthesiologist, (he did say his name, but at that point I was less than fully coherent and don't remember it). "I'm going to put you to sleep now" he stated. "Hold on a minute, please!" I requested. The voice from behind the mask asked what was wrong. I responded by saying "Nothing is wrong, but I probably won't see any of you again, and before I go to sleep, I just want to thank all of you for what you are doing for me."

The anesthesiologist muttered, "Well, that's a first". The nurse to my left said "Oh, isn't that nice," and in unison with a nurse standing next to her replied "You are very welcome." The anesthesiologist then asked if it was OK to go on. I retorted with "Carry on."

CHAPTER 8

S omeone once said "We are all born to die." Although it is quite a morbid way to look at life, it is in fact true. No matter how well you take care of your body, how healthy your diet is, the complete avoidance of tobacco and alcohol, there is no avoiding the cessation of life. We, like every other living organism, are all temporary inhabitants of this world.

I look at existence as a war between life and death. Ultimately death will be the victor, however, it is up to each individual to fight that war with the utmost ferocity. Each day that an event occurs which brings you joy, happiness or satisfaction is a victorious battle you have claimed against the forces of death. The ultimate goal in life is to win as many battles as possible in the war we wage with death.

The victories are not very difficult to achieve. All one has to do to grasp a victory over death is to bring happiness into to your soul. This can happen when someone tells you that they love you. It happens when you tell a loved one how much you appreciate them. It happens when you hold a small child in your arms and when you hug your grown child. It happens when you Journey to a place that brings you joy, or when you treat yourself to an indulgence. It happens when you complete an undertaking that has sat on your shelf for much too long a time. There will be challenges to overcome, but none are insurmountable. People will act as soldiers of death, causing you unrest; the actions of these people must be put into perspective as temporary setbacks, for as the wise man once said, "This too shall pass."

I truly believe that all people are inherently good, and it is their failure to emerge victorious in battles against death which causes them to become agents of death. When a person hates their life, wakes each day dreading what lies before them, sees the faults in others rather than the virtues they extol; that is when death wins!

People who follow paths such as these become the obstacles death puts before us. They cause anxiety, timidity and resentment. They make you question your every action, create doubt in your own abilities, instigate dissention among your friends and family. These are the weapons of death, and the soldiers that wield them. They fight for the cause of death because their jealous being cannot tolerate anyone enjoying the gifts of life.

Battles like these are the toughest to win, but with the exception of the very last battle, death is not undefeatable. All must find within themselves the ability to put aside such efforts without the use of extraneous aids such as alcohol or self-medicating. Within each of us is the power to heal ourselves. If learned at an early age, each of us can understand not only how to eliminate the stressors caused by agents of deaths, but the ability to use the negative forces of those agents against them to achieve your own personal serenity.

The first, and most important thing in overcoming negative forces is to believe in one's self, and then remember, as I stated earlier, all things do pass. One also needs to accept Karma as a legitimate power of the universe, and daily meditation or self-hypnosis are the only weapons necessary to taste victory in virtually every battle.

However, to the contrary, one must also take into account the double edge sword wielded by Karma. If one creates turmoil, then one must expect it to be returned to them in some way. Creating darkness in others shall cause darkness within you. To deny acceptance of this cosmic retribution will only cause further barrages of Karma to inject itself into your life. This will continue until you realize the damage your actions have created and fully accept the responsibility and request forgiveness from the universe. If you take nothing else from this chapter, remember this; it is never too late to say I'm sorry. It is never too late to offer forgiveness.

CHAPTER 9

I t was a cough that first woke me. I was lying in a room that I had never seen, complete with a nurse on each side of my bed. "Good, cough again!" cheered on my nurse. I realized that I had made it through the surgery, either that or heaven was not the paradise they make it out to be. I was more machine than human at this time, with tubes down my throat, in my neck and more wires connected to me than in a pinball machine. My chest felt like a piñata at a child's birthday party. Every cough felt like that child was hitting me fiercely with a baseball bat expecting me to explode and deliver a treasure trove of candy.

Another cough caused me enough pain to return me to full consciousness. The nurse on my left took a small heart shaped pillow and put it against my chest. "Hold on to this tight when you cough," she said. "It will help a lot." I took her advice just in time to catch the next cough; she was right, it did help.

After a few more coughs, I began to bring up the fluid left in my lungs from the surgery. The nurses caught the liquid in a small pink, kidney shaped container. After a few minutes of this condition the coughing stopped, and the nurse on my right explained that it was time to remove the tubes that went down my throat. These tubes were the only way air had reached my lungs since I was sedated.

The nurse removed the thin strips of adhesive tape that held the blue tube in place. "OK, now I want you to open your mouth as wide as you can, and when I pull, try to empty out your lungs," directed the nurse. "Ready?" Whether I was ready or not it was time. The nurse began to pull the tube

46

from my mouth and it felt like she was pulling my windpipe out of my mouth as well. Once out, the nurse apologized for the pain which she caused. I would have said it's ok, but the trauma from the intubation temporarily damaged my vocal cords, rendering me speechless.

It was at that moment that a thirst such as I had never experienced before overcame me. I felt like I had run a 10K race in 100-degree heat with a pile of sand in my mouth. We have all been thirsty, but this thirst was immeasurable. Although I could not ask, one of the nurses knew from experience how bad I was suffering, and without prompting placed a spoonful of ice chips into my parched mouth. The ice quickly melted and the tiny amount of water it produced felt divine. It was barely enough to moisten my tongue, but it was welcomed with all my heart.

The moment it took the ice to melt, the nurse was readied with another spoonful to sooth my throat. We repeated this dance a few more times before the nurse informed me that I had enough and could not have any more for now. Although the pain in my chest was excruciating, the thirst caused it to pale in comparison. As she stood next to me adjusting wires and tubes, I summoned up all my strength, and with what little air I had in my lungs, in a raspy whisper I said my first word, "More."

I know it doesn't sound like much, but it took all the strength and energy I had in my body to accomplish it. Unfortunately, the nurse was not impressed or moved from her position, "Sorry, you can have some in a little while." The other nurse then placed a rubber bulb in my hand right hand. "This is a morphine pump." Explained the nurse. "Whenever you feel pain, squeeze this and you will get your medication. Don't worry, you can't overdose on this, it will only release the medication when the green light is on." Needless to say, I pumped that bulb like I was taking someone's blood pressure.

It was only a few minutes of languishing in dryness before the nurse once again presented me with a small spoonful of ice chips. Still too weak to speak, I had hoped she saw how grateful I was by the way I looked at her. My face was still messed up from the fall, so I was not sure if she understood my gesture. The pleasure was short lived again, as after the fourth spoonful of ice chips, I was again shut off. At this point I would have given two years of my life for a huge glass of water; but it wasn't to be. The ice chip feedings came every ten minutes, but it was always four spoonfuls only.

The medication was doing its job, at least it was taking the edge off the pain. The aching in my chest and shoulders was still there, but it wasn't anywhere near as sharp it was earlier. I squeezed the bulb every time the green light came on in an attempt to stay ahead of the pain, and it seemed to be working…until I fell asleep.

I don't know for how long I had been asleep, but it was long enough for the two young nurses who had escorted me back into the world of the living to go off shift, and be replaced by one older nurse. She introduced herself as Josie, (Josie was not her real name, but I do not want to embarrass her.) It was the pain that woke me up this time. I don't know what time I had fallen asleep, but it was nine-thirty in the morning now.

I pumped the bulb and received my partial allotment of morphine. The effect of the drug was negligible, as the practice of staying ahead of the pain was discontinued when I fell asleep. Josie adjusted my pillow, examined my wires and tubes, and gave me a spoonful of ice chips. I know ice has no flavor, but it seemed more enjoyable when delivered by someone who looked like they had at least a modicum of compassion. This was not good ice. She shoveled in the four spoonfuls and turned away without saying anything.

My pain was building faster than the morphine could accommodate it. I pressed it every time the green light came on, but I needed more. I have always had a high threshold for pain, so for me to request additional medication was truly out of the ordinary. Once again I, in that raspy voice, whispered,

"My chest and shoulders are killing me; can I have more meds?" "You have the morphine pump there, why don't you try that," was the response I received. For me to emote that last sentence was a feat in and of itself. I did not answer her right away because I needed to collect enough air in me to push the words out. "I have been, but the pain is too intense," I informed her a few moments later.

I have a couple of friends who are cardiac care nurses. To reach that level of health care provider a person needs to be intelligent, experienced and good at their job. With the exceptions of emergency room and pediatrics nurse, cardiac care is probably the most stressful job in nursing. There is a high burn out rate in these positions, and I think that Josie was giving off the last sparks of her sparkler.

Josie sighed. It seemed her hope of an easy Friday was vanishing before her eyes. "Let me check what the doctor ordered for you. She walked over to the new computer and attempted to sign in, again and again and again. There was agitation in her voice now as she began to argue with the inanimate computer. On every failed attempt came another loud sigh that seemed to increase in volume every time she failed.

It was nine forty-five when I requested the pain medication. Since I was still immobilized, watching the clock on the wall directly in front of my bed became my only source of entertainment. It was now ten, and she still was not signed in to the system. The sighs began to resemble the sound made by horses when they are in the paddocks before a race. Josie then turned and walked out the door. At 10:05 she returned to the room with a younger nurse that appeared to be of Asian descent. "Do you know your password?" asked the younger nurse. "It is a new password; you were supposed to change it from your old one during the training given on this new computer system."

Josie's eyes rolled into the back of her head as she tilted it towards the ceiling. "That's right, OK, I got it now. Thank you" said Josie and the younger woman walked away. Josie then entered the password into the computer, and a large sigh once again escaped her lips. I know this seems difficult to believe, but it was only the beginning, as it was literally 10:55 when she finally brought my meds. Although the throbbing in my chest was unceasing, I decided that when Jessie apologized, I would say don't worry about it, or forget about it. However, because my words were predicated as a reply to Nurse Jessie's apologizes, they were never said, as no apology was forthcoming.

Immediately after I was administered the medication, Nurse Jessie's phone began to ring. She answered the phone, turned to me, and asked "You have family members here, do you want them to come it?" Nodding my head the best I could to show an affirmative response, my physical reply was not sufficient, and again Jessie asked if it was alright to admit my family. I then pushed the word "Yes" from my arid mouth. "Let them in," Jessie ordered the unit coordinator.

My sister Marie's was the first face I saw, immediately followed by the face of my wife. Never were the sight of two faces more welcome and relieving to my eyes. "How are you doing?" Nancy asked. Her voice was like a Mozart symphony, sweet and soothing. I don't know if it was my love for Nancy or my respect for her, but her voice had the power to somehow reassure me in times of tumult. I tried to respond with a witty answer, but all I could emit was "Hi". Although the aching in my chest did not subside in the least with their arrival, the two of them just being there made me not care.

Nurse Jesse remained at the computer while Nancy and Marie visited. Nancy asked, "how are they treating you?" Nancy saw the demeanor of my face change to more of a scowl. As she looked into my eyes, I motioned to Nancy with my eyes that the Nurse's bedside manner left much to be desired. When two people are together for as long as Nancy and me, a language of small gestures or motions develops to such a degree that words are not essential.

"Ice chips," I whispered, trying to tell Nancy that I was in dire need of some moisture in my mouth. "What did you say?" responded Nancy. I guess my voice was still not strong enough for normal conversation. Nancy leaned over the bed and placed her ear next to my lips. "Ice chips," I again whispered. Nancy stood up, "What did he say?" asked Marie. "He said that he wants ice chips.

The moment Nancy said ice chips, Jessie completely abandoned the computer, and spun around like a gun slinger out of the old west. "He just had ice chips, he can't have any more for fifteen minutes," barked the nurse. Nancy, ever sweet and polite looked at the nurse and said, "I don't think we were introduced, I'm Bill's wife Nancy and this is his sister Marie." Jessie

49

looked at them both and responded, "Hi, I'm Jesse." Not the warmest response, but it was acceptable.

The new computer system got the best of Jessie, and she abruptly left the room to find someone more experienced with the new programs. It was then that I saw my chance and took it. "She is terrible," I said in an audible voice. The pain from expanding my lungs made it difficult, but I continued. "I told her that I needed pain meds, she checked and said that I was due for them. She started playing on that computer and I didn't get meds for almost an hour. I was squeezing on that Morphine drip bulb in rhythm with my pulse.

Nancy is the most non-confrontational person I have ever known. Her demeanor allows her to accept things others would never permit. I knew that Nancy would not criticize the nurse, but I had to fume to someone. "We're here now, don't worry, we will take care of you," assured Nancy as she stroked my forehead. "Are you in pain now?" questioned Nancy. "Nothing major," I answered.

"Do you know why you had to wait so long to go into surgery yesterday?" inquired Marie. I looked at her with bewilderment. I had no idea how long I waited. I was so doped up that I was at the point that I wish it never ended. "I was waiting a long time?" answering a question with a question. "You were supposed to go into surgery at eleven, but they had an emergency come in early this morning, and Dr. MacGillivray had to work on him." Marie continued, "I was talking to his family in the waiting room and he was at two hospitals before they flew him in a helicopter here." This had to be something greater than a valve replacement to necessitate a Med-Flight transport. "What did he have?" I asked her. "Something to do with his aorta, like yours," recalled Marie.

Having worked in the medical field for over thirty years, I have had my share of medical emergencies. The single most threatening one is an acute aortic aneurysm. Basically, it is when the aortic artery is about to burst in your chest, denying a flow of blood to the heart. If the artery ruptures, death is almost instantaneously. In the most ideal situation, someone who experiences an acute aortic aneurysm has at best, a 40% chance at survival. In the field, the survival rate drastically decreases because of time, distance, and the condition of the road. An unnoticed pothole or an ill placed speed bump may cause just enough trauma to sever the artery. For this man to be transported to hospitals and a helicopter ride is unheard of.

"His family was so nice, they were so worried about him," Marie sighed. "I hope he made it; he was so young." I had neither the heart nor the voice to tell her that his chances were quite slim, but there is always hope.

It was not long before Nurse Jessie returned, this time with reinforcements. A short Asian girl accompanied Jessie to the computer. Jessie showed her the problem, the Asian girl nodded, pushed three buttons and said, "That should do it." Although the problem was resolved, Jessie seemed just as frustrated as she had been before.

"Ice chips, please" I implored once more. Nancy looked at Jessie and asked if she could give me some ice chips. "Go ahead," she said to Nancy, "but not too much". Nancy picked up the Styrofoam cup and filled a plastic spoon with small ice chips. Once the chips hit my tongue they vaporized almost instantly. I again opened my mouth, almost like Oliver Twist asking for more. Nancy granted my request and placed another spoonful of ice chips into my mouth. This time, my mouth being cooled by the first spoonful, the ice seemed to melt nicely into droplets of water trickling down my throat.

"One more," said Nancy as she again filled the spoon with ice. I felt like I could drink a gallon of water right down, but for now the ice chips would be my only source of moisture, so I had better get used to it. I took the third serving, held all the ice on my tongue until it all melted, then swallowed the one larger drop created by all the smaller ones.

Jessie walked over to the IV pole to check my medication levels. She had two hypodermics that she dispensed into my intravenous system without saying a word. I thought she might have picked up on the negative energy she helped foster within me.

Completing my medication delivery, Jessie announced, "It's time for you to get up," and called for a nursing assistant to assist her. I was exhausted, in pain and groggy from meds, and this woman wanted me to get out of bed now? "Alright," I whispered. "Let's give it a try."

Nancy and Marie left the room, and Jessie pushed a large reclining chair next to my bed. The assistant began to raise the head of my bed, slowly. Each degree the head of my bed rose was agonizing. Once finally at its maximum height, the assistant removed the sheets from my bed, and coordinated the spiders nest of wires and tubes I had connected to my body. "This is what we are going to do," exclaimed Jessie. "First you are going to put your legs over this side of the bed, as that happens Jim will help you sit up and turn your body to the side. You will stay in that position for a little while, then we will help you stand and turn you so that you can sit in the chair."

Following her orders, I began to put my legs over the right side of the bed until I heard Jessie shout "Stop! I will help you with your legs." I was happy to hear that piece of news, because just lifting my legs was one hell of a chore. Jessie then took her position at the foot of the bed, looked at her assistant and said "Ready". Jim must have nodded because I did not hear a response. Suddenly I felt my legs and hips being pulled to one side while my torso was being positioned directly behind them. I know it wasn't much of a task, but just that much exertion sapped all of my energy. I sat on the edge of the bed, and with as little effort as possible, tried to regain my breath.

Jim bent down in front of me and once again arranged my wires and tubes to prevent tripping, or worse yet, accidental removal. A few minutes had passed, and Jim looked at me, "Are you ready?" he asked. I nodded my head and answered with my usual "Yup", and with one of Jim's arms under my left arm and one of Jessie's under my right, I stood up, turned forty-five degrees, and sat in the large padded chair. Upon my positioning in the chair, I emitted a loud sigh, again out of breath.

Nancy and Marie then returned to the room to see me sitting before them. "Oh, you look great!" Nancy said in a cheerful voice. I knew it was a lie, I looked something like the cat coughed up, run through a meat grinder and left outside to rot; but none the less it was nice to hear her say that. "Your lunch is here." Announced Jessie. I looked at Nancy and joked "Aren't I in enough pain already?" Nancy smiled, "Never a dull moment with you around." Marie pulled the mobile table in front of me, and to my pleasant surprise, it was all packaged juices and ice cream.

I ate, or rather, drank my lunch, and remained sitting up for a while. Nancy and Marie sat with me and kept a conversation going. Jessie again went to the computer, pressed some buttons on the keyboard, and scanned my wristband. She then inserted another hypodermic into my IV, and announced that she was going to lunch. "If you need anything ask Sarah, she's in the next room." Jessie turned and retreated out of the room.

We kept talking for about an hour when I began to nod off. Still sitting in the padded reclining chair, I knew it was time for me to get back in bed. Nancy pushed the call button mechanism for the nurse, and we began to wait. About a minute later a voice came over a cheap speaker on the wall of my room. "Can I help you?" the voice was distorted, but audible. "My husband just had open heart surgery," Nancy informed the bodiless voice. Since this was the cardiac intensive care unit, I am sure they were familiar with my situation, but it was a nice touch. "He is sitting in a chair and is tired and wants to get back in bed." "Be right with you" came the response.

After waiting about ten minutes, Nancy walked into the next room to look for Sarah, the covering nurse. Sarah came into the room, saw me sitting there and said, "I can't put him back in bed. Your nurse has to do that." A deep groan seeped from my lips. "I will get her, she's at lunch." Sarah left the room and walked towards the nurse's station.

What tiny amount of energy I used to get up, sit down and stay in the chair had taken quite a toll on me. I was not used to having absolutely no stamina, and began an attempt to stand on my own, but weakness and two women yelling at me aborted my efforts. For the next ten minutes I sat, straining myself to stay awake.

"What's wrong?" barked Jessie upon entering the room. It was a bitter sweet moment for me. It was sweet because Nancy finally saw the side of Jessie I had come to know. It was bitter because she was my damn nurse!

The attempted solo journey from chair to bed had exhausted all of the little energy I had amassed, to the point that I could not even expand my lungs sufficiently to push the words "I'm tired" from my mouth. "He is tired and should be back in bed," stated Nancy. To truly understand Nancy is to realize that she is a dichotomy of emotions. To almost everyone she is the demure, somewhat shy woman who avoids confrontation as much as possible. Then there's Mamma Bear Nancy with all the ferociousness of a grizzly, save the fur coat.

"Well, he is fine there," Jessie retorted with a tone that was less than proper bedside manner. "I still had five minutes left on my lunch." At that moment, all I could think of was watching a lit fuse make its way into a firecracker. With what little strength I had, I opened my eyes just wide enough to watch Ali/Frazier redux. "Well, maybe you should have helped him back in bed before you went to lunch," snapped Nancy. "You told us that Sarah would take care of him while you were away, maybe you should have informed Sarah of that fact." Suddenly the tone from Nurse Jessie softened; "I'll get the aid, hold on," she mumbled as she left the room. I half expected to see Nancy raising both hands in the air shouting "I'm the Greatest!" but it was not to be, as the second the incident was resolved, my loving and demure wife Nancy was back at my side. I laughed to myself, if only she could calm down that quick when I get her mad, but some things are better off unsaid.

Jessie returned with Jim for my return voyage to my bed. Just as we had worked together to bring me to the chair, we united our strengths to place me back from whence I came. I don't think I got the word "you" out of "thank you" before I was asleep. This was a fortuitous moment for all of us; I slept, Nancy and Marie went to the cafeteria for a lunch break, and Nurse Jessie got a little "Me time" to decompress.

"Your dinner's here," a phrase I once loved, but had since grown to hate. The call woke me from my well-earned nap and brought me back to my alternative reality. This would be the moment that I would usually come up with some sarcastic remark, but it wasn't to be. The Hispanic girl had the cutest smile as she placed the tray on my table. Visible were a container of cranberry juice, a container of milk, a Hoodsie cup (a euphemism in Massachusetts for a small cup of ice cream) and a plate covered with a dome. Although I felt comfortable with the items out in the open, I began to feel like Joan Crawford in the classic movie, "Whatever Happened to Baby Jane?" when an evil sister delivers meals to her bedridden sister, often with sinister surprises under the dome. Nancy lifted the dome, and to my pleasant surprise, chocolate pudding was my entre. As hospital food goes, chocolate pudding is the equivalent of Beluga caviar.

Nancy assisted me with my dinner, holding the containers while placing the bended straw in my mouth. She then fed me some of the ice cream and the pudding. Even though I was still very thirsty, my fluids were closely monitored, as prior to surgery I had been pumped up with almost a gallon of fluid. It was not until I had rid myself of the added fluid and return to my pre-surgery weight that I could drink without restrictions. This meant that I had to always ask for ice water or ice with my juices so that I could get additional residual moisture, as little as it was, down my arid throat.

Just the act of taking nourishment was exhausting. Once Nancy had finished feeding me, it took all the effort I had just to keep my eyes open. As I would nod off, I would be awakened by a conversation between my wife and my sister. They both realized that I would be better off without any interruptions to my sleep, and decided to leave for home. They kissed me goodbye and quietly left the room to drive home in rush hour traffic.

Once they had left, I closed my eyes for what seemed like just a moment when I heard the steel ball bearings on the room curtain slide in their track. I opened my eyes to see a close friend and neighbor standing by my side. Karen Doremus and her family lived one street over from us. She was a person with whom sharing time was always a pleasurable experience. I had forgotten that she worked as a cardiac care nurse in the Mass General, and seeing her smiling face brought a smile to mine. "How are you doing Bill?" Karen said as she squeezed my hand in hers. Still finding it difficult to speak, I whispered "I'm OK." Karen nodded in approval. I did not want to criticize Jessie for her shortcomings to Karen, feeling that my words could cause more of a problem than resolve anything. Karen then kissed my head and instructed me to let her know if I needed anything. She turned, and I think I fell asleep before she left the room.

Jessie made one or two cursory visits to check my meds and ask if everything was alright. I am probably making more of what the situation was, but at the time it was occurring, it was all too real.

CHAPTER 10

In New England, the first day of every season brings with it excitement, refreshment and anticipation. Unlike some other parts of the country, each one of New England's seasons has a distinction all its own. These characteristics tremendously affect the world around us.

The beauty and the grandeur of the mountains covered in snow begin the year. If you look up at the slopes at the right angle, and the right time of day, the snow changes from pure white to a hue of light blue, and then to a flaming orange as it reflects the sun that slowly sets behind its peaks. Spring erases the white mantel, painting it with the light green splotches of the budding trees. The summer brings life to the mountains, as plants fully bloom, trees grow their canopy of green, hiding the slopes from the spectators at ground level. Unless far away, the peaks merely disappear from view. As beautiful as the preceding seasons are, the mountains reserve their majesty for autumn. Nature spares no color of the spectrum as the once green trees experience a magical transformation, as the leaves prepare to separate from the tree, an array of reds, yellows, purples, oranges meld into one masterpiece one can only describe as breathtaking.

Like the mountains, the forests and the meadows join together to produce their own displays of magnificence, as both flora and fauna together dance their ballet. The branches of trees, once bountiful with leaves, now bare, reach out towards the sun as if begging for warmth. The forest's dried leaves and the meadow's once tall grass now lie on the ground, covered with a blanket of snow. With each step taken, they announce their presence with an audible crunching sound. There is no greater kingdom of solace than a winter's forest. Silence surrounds you. The cold wind bites deeply into your face. It is a place that other than the fragrance of pine, there is no smell.

The warmest boots seem futile against ice and snow that encapsulate them. If you are fortunate enough, a wandering deer or rabbit may pass you on their search for food. One can only imagine this level of isolation by experiencing it.

Spring's warmer temperatures cause the snow to melt into the once frozen ground, creating a labyrinth of muddy paths. The scent of pine is now joined by the pungent odor of saturated dirt and rotting wood. Animals, like the porcupine, who spend the winter huddled tightly with their family in a tiny hutch now begin to emerge, searching for anything edible to fill their empty bellies. Summer brings new life to the forest and meadows. Grass grows side by side with wildflowers. Paths through woods are now dry and solid as the trees and undergrowth has absorbed all the water from the once muddy trails. Food is plentiful for the animals as they over-nourish themselves and their new offspring to prepare for the next winter. As lonely as the forest is in the dead of winter, it is fully reincarnated every summer.

As fall cascades into the forest, no words I can find that can honestly pay sufficient tribute to a New England autumn forest. The forest is nothing less than nature's most ornate cathedral. Pictures of this splendor cannot show the depth of intensity, the vivid explosion of color, the welcoming smell that is like no other in the natural world. If you have not yet experienced this phenomenon first hand, do whatever you need to do so you can personally bear witness to this masterpiece of nature. Plan the weekend of Columbus Day to visit the Berkshires, the White Mountains, Down East Maine or the Green Mountains of Vermont. Drive the Kancamagus Highway in New Hampshire, hike the Mohegan Trail in Massachusetts, spend the day with the family apple picking in Vermont, or go to the Fryeburg Fair in Maine. You will be amazed at the beauty that still exists in this world.

The oceans are the mightiest forces in nature, and like everything else, they too change with the seasons. With the exception of temperature, their transformations are more subtle, but they exist none the less. Winter's cold turns the sea to a field of thick ice. The large blocks begin at the shore and slowly work their way out to the horizon. The powerful salt-laden winds cut deeply into your face. In winter the ocean has great fury and little sympathy for those brave enough to venture across its surface. Crushing waves of tons of water lift themselves out of the sea and crash without remorse against anything that happens to stand in their way. Few manmade structures can repel these forces except the lighthouses, which stand in defiance of all the power nature can produce.

With the spring and summer, the viciousness subsides. The waters warm and the colossal waves diminish. It is the time when the ocean offers itself to all who wish to partake. It offers relaxation, exploration, recreation, and for someone like me, it earns admiration. The ocean gives nothing to no one, and is as heartless as it is vast. Its creatures are both beautiful and dangerous, as is the ocean itself.

Autumn is a contrarian time for the ocean. While temperatures begin their decline, the oceans reach their highest temperatures. It is a short-lived gain, however, for as quickly as the oceans tranquility and warmth are available, the cool fall air returns them to their most impressive and undeniable fury. Of all the powers on earth, it is the oceans that rein with undaunted sovereignty.

The world is a very funny place. The only constant on which we can always depend is change.

CHAPTER 11

T he first night that I was conscious brought with it incoherency the likes of which I had never experienced. Although the night started quite somberly, it was not long before I woke. I knew that I was in a hospital and had surgery, but I felt that I was being confined. The myriad of wires and tubes seemed to imprison me, as if I was caught in a large net. In my delusional state, I decided that I needed to escape. I began to pull the wires from the heart monitor from my body, then the nasal cannula oxygen supply from my nose. By the time that I had finished, two nurses and an aid had arrived in my room and rushed to my side.

"What are you doing?" questioned one of the nurses. Because I did not know what I was doing, I kept silent. As one nurse reattached each lead to the electrode, the other nurse began to untangle my sheets which I had twisted into a pile of knots. "Your oxygen saturation is down to 90 percent, you have to keep this oxygen on."

The only saving grace was that I did not attempt to remove the wires connected directly to my heart. These three wires were inserted into my lower abdomen and would be used to restart my heart if any complication occurred. The wires were further down than the monitor wires and were not connected to anything. The nurses left, and I fell back into a very restless sleep.

I don't remember how many times these two nurses had to return for the same reason, but it was at least two times. Once awake, I knew what I did was senseless, but once in the throes of sleep, I seemed to lose all control. At three o'clock in the morning the frustration of trying to sleep was too much to accept, so I decided to just stay awake. The medications relaxed me and took away my pain but were powerless to putting me to sleep.

A few hours later, the day nurse introduced herself as she cheerfully entered the room. "Hi, you're Bill, right?" As tired and weak as I was, I used a head nod to say yes. "I'm Nancy, your nurse for today." I realized that it was Saturday, the weekend, and the regular weekly nursing staff was off, and Jessie would no longer be an annoyance to me, nor I to her. I inhaled as deeply as I could through my nose and in a soft voice, I said "Hi Nancy, that's my wife's name." Again, just the most minute output of energy was enough to exhaust me. "That's a coincidence," said Nancy as she checked the levels of all my medications and took a set of vital signs. She then walked over to the computer, pushed a few buttons, then scanned my wrist band with a scanning gun. "You're due for your pain medication, do you want it now?" I returned to my system of response and nodded. "OK, I'll be right back." Said Nancy as she left the room to fetch the meds. Suddenly, I felt like one of the children in Mary Poppins, with Nancy playing the title role.

Returning with a smile, Nancy began to insert the needle of a hypodermic into my intravenous tube. "You're going to get some of these things off you," explained Nancy. "I heard that you had a tough night last night with all these monitors. Well, we are going to get rid of some this morning." Her voice was cheerful, she was an average woman with a great bedside manner. "Can I have something to drink, please?" I asked. "Sure, what would you like? Water? juice?" responded Nancy. "Water, please" I answered. Within moments, Nancy was turning the bendable straw into my dry mouth. When the straw no longer delivered water into my mouth, I asked Nancy for the Ice chips. Nancy took the cup from my mouth, removed the straw, and returned the cup to my lips. She gently tilted the cup and allowed a small pile of ice chips to slide into my mouth. "Would you like more water?" the nurse asked. "No, thank you", I answered.

I saw the foot of a gurney arrive outside my door, and a man with a very familiar face entered the room. Nancy saw the gurney and informed the transport person that I was to be taken in my bed, not on a gurney. The young Black man agreed and pushed the stretcher at the doorway against the wall away from the doorway. He returned and began to attach all my monitors, intravenous and oxygen directly to my bedrails. He then disconnected the bed from the electrical outlet, unlocked the wheels and pulled my bed from against the wall. He then got behind me and started pushing my bed out of the room. From this angle, I remembered how I knew this gentleman. He had taken me from the cath lab when I had to lay flat. I only knew his face by looking upward and backwards at him.

"Hi Samuel," I said to the young man. The recent drink of water seemed to have saturated my throat enough to allow me to speak at a more normal level. "I remember you, Mr. Aren, Ari, Arn,..." "Arienti," I said, "just spell the word RENT and you pronounce my name." "Hey, that's pretty neat," commented Samuel as he repeated it a few times on our way to the clinic.

Upon our arrival, Samuel pushed the head of the bed against the wall and plugged it back in to the electrical outlet. He locked the wheels and shook my hand. "Good luck to you now Mister R-E-N-T," he chuckled with a wide grin on his face. "You take care."

"Are you William?" a feminine voice asked. Having not slept the night before, I was quite groggy when the words were said. With my eyes, still closed, I answered the question with an informal "Yup." The nurse introduced herself to me, but unfortunately, with my less than attentive level of conciseness, I could not recollect her name. "Your breakfast is here, and I also have to give you two units of blood before you get all these tubes and cables out." I took in a deep breath and released. "OK, I didn't know I needed blood." The nurse, an older woman with a strong build placed the breakfast tray on my table. "You have to sit in the chair for a while too, I will help you." I laughed to myself when she said that she would help me, it took James and Jessie together to put me in and out of a chair yesterday.

The nurse pushed a button which raised the head of the bed to almost 90 degrees. As I sat up in bed, the nurse adjusted all my tubes and cables. She then took my hand in hers, and put her other hand under my knees. "On the count of three, I'm going to twist you to the side, OK?" I nodded with affirmation and when she got to three, I was twisted into the perfect position to leave the bed. I was impressed.

"Now we're going to stand up, turn and sit, OK?" With the success of her first maneuver, I had no doubt whatsoever of her ability to get me into the chair. "I'm ready whenever you are," I informed her. She squatted down a little, told me to put my hands around her neck, then she put her hands under my arms. "One, two, three," she grunted on the three as she straightened out her legs which began to raise me. I pressed my feet onto the floor and straightened my legs out as best I could. I was standing. Although she had her hands under my arms, they were there only to steady me. I took two steps to the chair and sat; this maneuver required a little help though.

"Wow, you're doing great!" she said. The nurse then brought the tray with my breakfast to the table and asked me if I needed any help. "I think I can do this" I responded as I lifted the dome off my main course revealing a small bowl of cream of wheat. I began to prepare my coffee when the nurse placed two small bags of what looked like thick burgundy wine on my I.V. pole. As I ate my breakfast, the nurse stretched a long tube from the wine bags to my intravenous. "This goes really slow," said the nurse as she adjusted the speed control on the tube. With my mouth full of Cream of Wheat, I nodded as if to say I understand. "If you need anything just push the button, you still have the morphine drip as well if you are in pain," she advised me as she left the room. With the exception of feeling tired, I could not believe how good I felt. I was amazed until I coughed, then back to the morphine.

His voice filled the room with "How are you doing?" I didn't remember falling asleep in the chair, but I certainly remember how startled I was when I woke up. Gone was the memory of heart surgery, the machines that I was hooked up to, the blood coursing into me from a bag. For one second, I was the old Bill, trying to jump out of the chair in the same fashion that I had become accustomed to after 30 years at the fire department. This, however, was short lived, as by the time I was only one quarter out of the chair, those lost memories came back like an old friend, and this time, they brought their buddy, unmitigated pain. I don't know how much morphine I immediately pumped into myself, but I think I blew up basketballs with fewer pumps.

Dr. MacGillivray quickly stepped over to my chair to ensure that I was not going to take another spill. "Whoa big guy," he chuckled as he realized that I had barely enough energy to lift a spoon to my mouth. "How are you feeling, Bill?" he asked again. "Well, other than the spasms of excruciating pain, tremendous thirst and complete lethargy, I think I'm doing pretty good." I responded, trying to muster the best smirk I could on my face. As he stood in front of me, wearing a long white lab coat over his surgical scrubs, Dr. MacGillivray crossed his arms and smiled. "Well, you didn't lose your sense of humor, that's a plus" he said as he smirked back at me.

"Today we are going to take these three tubes out of you and disconnect the machine." His eyes looked down at the machine attached to the two tubes to which I was tethered. "We have to leave these other two wires in place because they go directly into your heart in case we have to shock you. We will take them out a little later." I nodded my head in understanding, but then realized that I had only two tubes in me. Looking down at the machine to which I was hooked, I said "Where is the third tube?" "Your catheter, we're going to take that out too today." Since I was asleep when they inserted the tube into my bladder through my urethra and into a large bag, and I hadn't had the urge to urinate for a long time, I had forgotten all about it.

At that moment the nurse came back into the room to investigate how the two bags of blood were progressing. "You ate all your breakfast!" she said as I nodded my head. "It looks like you have another 10 minutes before they're empty." I looked up at the two bags and both were almost completely flat. "You may feel a little better, not as tired after today," said Dr. MacGillivray. "But that doesn't mean you can exert yourself; I want you to rest until the cardio-physical therapist works with you before you do anything."

Even though I now had two units of new blood coursing through my body, I did not feel any different. Physical exhaustion had me in its grasp, and it felt like it had no intention of letting me go for a while. "I'll stop in later," stated Dr. MacGillivray as he turned to exit the room. "Things look good, keep it up." I did not know what to do, or how to do it, but I said "OK" anyway.

As he left the room, I could hear the murmurs of a conversation between my doctor and my nurse. The only thing I could gather was that after I was disconnected from all the apparatus that I would be transferred out of the intensive care unit and brought to the cardiac care unit.

The nurse came into the room and disconnected me from the two empty bags of blood. She then stood in front of me and informed me that I had to return to my bed. I began to sit up on my own only to hear shouts of "wait, wait, I have to help you," emanating from the nurse's mouth. As I sat back into the chair, I noticed that my strength and energy level, although still just a fraction of what I had pre-surgery, had increased. I don't know if it was the breakfast, the blood or the rest, or a combination of them all that made me feel noticeably better.

The nurse took her position in front of my chair leaned over me. She put her arms around my back and said "OK, on three. One, two," and the moment she said three, I summoned all the power I had to reduce the amount of effort required to lift me. As I stood up in her embrace, I could not help but to see the surprise in her eyes. "Take it easy, let me do this for you. You shouldn't be pushing your limits at all right now!" I began to nod my head, "alright, alright, I just didn't want you to have to lift me, the petite flower that I am." The nurse laughed, "A petite flower, huh?" she asked in an incredulous tone. "Let's get you in bed now," she continued. This was an opportunity that I could not let pass without a comment. "If I had a nickel for every time a woman said that to me, I would be a rich man!", I joked. "I guess I left myself open for that one," laughed the young woman. The woman then attempted to say turn towards me, but laughed out loud after the only saying tur...

Her face, red with embarrassment, looked up to me, and through her laughter said, "I guess they didn't remove your sense of humor." She took a deep breath, blew it out and again attempted to state her intentions. "OK Mr. funnyman, turn to me and take two steps." I obliged her commands, and in the matter of a few seconds, I was in my freshly made bed.

Once settled, the nurse walked over to the counter by the sink and took a hypodermic needle she had placed there earlier. As she walked back over to me, she placed the cap shielding the needle between her teeth and pulled the hypodermic away, exposing the needle. "This is going to make you a little groggy" said the nurse, as she inserted the needle into the I.V. port. "No problem," I assured her. "When I was a teenager, I used to pay good money to feel this way!" The smile returned to the nurse's face and her eyes rolled back into her head. I thought to myself, this woman doesn't even know me, but has the exact same reactions to my jokes that my wife does. "Maybe it's me?" I thought; then reason returned to me and I thought "Nahhh, can't be."

The drug worked fast, and my head began to spin. The last thing I remember after this feeling began was, if the nurse thought I was nuts before

I took this stuff, wait until I start talking under the effect of this stuff. Fortunately, because of my altered level of consciousness, I didn't have to apologize to anyone for any colorful comments I may have articulated.

As the drug began to wear off, and cognizance slowly replaced confusion, I opened my eyes and immediately began to search for the morphine drip bulb. The pain was a severe burning sensation at the base of my abdomen. Although the pain killer takes a few minutes for me to notice any effect, the psychological relief of knowing that the pain would soon be gone was in and of itself cathartic.

"How are you feeling Bill?" asked the nurse. "Are you in pain?" I assumed that she saw the little green activation light on the morphine pump. "Yeah, a little, but I just took some morphine." I informed her. "That's good, once that kicks in I'll remove your catheter." Even though I was still not completely conscious, I could not let this comment go by without a response, and I still had the plausible deniability afforded me by the medications. "First you want to get me into bed, now you can't wait to get your hands on my junk. Is this a hospital or a bordello?" Her reaction was predictable, eyes roll in the back of her head, with a little giggle. Again, I thought "I wonder if it's me?" But this time, I put more thought into it and realized, "No way, this is funny stuff."

Over the years I have had the good fortune of never being awake when a catheter was placed inside me. I never knew how fortunate I was to be able to say this. I bring this up because after being loaded with Propofol with a morphine chaser, having a catheter removed was still tremendously painful. The only saving grace is that the procedure was done quickly, and once complete, the pain is as well.

CHAPTER 12

O ver the years, when people share a story of tragic events, I would invariably try to offer comfort to them by saying "I can just imagine what you went through." I never actually tried to imagine what they went through, but I hoped my saying those words would offer some level of solace to a person experiencing emotional pain, and having them know that there are people out there who would take the effort to put themselves in another person's shoes to share their pain.

A while ago Nancy and I went to visit a friend of ours who, at a comparatively young age, suffered a stroke. He was admitted to a rehabilitation hospital for an extended stay in an attempt to give him the ability to regain his physical capabilities. As we walked into my friend's room, we discovered that we were not the only ones who chose to visit him that day. The room was full of people all hovering around my friend Bobby's bed. The loud voices and laughter that could be heard all the way to the nurse's station caused the nurses to intervene and ask people to leave. Unfortunately, as people left, more came to take their place, and the cycle continued.

As I made my way to the other side of the room, I noticed the curtain room divider was fully extended. I looked behind the curtain to see a man lying alone in his hospital bed. He had no visitors, no flowers, just a U.S. Army hat that sat on the counter by the window. He sat there quietly reading a book, blocking out the noise of the party that was taking place only a few feet away.

"Hi, good book?" I asked, even though I had never seen this man before.

"My friend Bobby is in the next bed, sorry If we are too loud for you. The man looked up and removed his black framed glasses. He placed both his book and glasses on his lap and squirmed this way up the mattress into more of a sitting position. The man looked at me and in a soft and even-tempered voice said, "It's a little long winded and takes a lot of poetic license, but it is entertaining.

I looked down at the book and read the bold words on the cover, "The Tunnel Rats." I recognized the term "Tunnel Rats", but I couldn't remember from where. "I'm sorry about the noise next door, Bobby has a lot of friends, and all of them love to talk." The man chuckled.

"It's no bother," the man said as he adjusted his bed. "Bob and I have had a few conversations; he is one funny guy." I nodded in agreement. "Oh yeah" I replied. "We've known each other since we were kids, he has always been a riot. By the way, I'm Bill Arienti," I said as I stepped closer to him and extended my hand in friendship. "Hi Bill, I'm Johnny Kelly; pleasure to meet you."

As I took his hand, I noticed a number of severe scars on the back of his forearms somewhat disguised under a tattoo of what looked like a cartoon rat wearing a helmet and holding a gun in one hand, a flashlight in the other. The words that circled the tattoo were pretty faded, but I made out the words "Tunnel Rat, Not Worth a Rats Ass." The tattoo of the rat brought back the memory of a "Sixty-Minutes" segment that told the story of an elite group of soldiers in the Army whose duty was to crawl down the tunnels that led to the Viet Cong underground forts. The only protection these soldiers had were a flashlight and a pistol.

The soldiers would crawl down the tunnel head first with their flashlight to light the way. The tunnels were very intricate and could travel hundreds of yards. Once inside the fort, the Viet Cong had constructed cities underground that included hospitals, dormitories, mess halls and armories. There were a number of tunnels that led in and out of the fort to allow for emergency escape.

My curiosity got the best of me, and I asked if the book on Johnny's lap had anything to do with the tattoo inscribed into his forearm. "Yeah, I was a Tunnel Rat a few years back in Nam, sixty-seven and sixty-eight." Johnny finished his sentence and turned his head to look out the window. This man beside me was either one of the bravest men in the world or one of the craziest. I understand how people who have had a traumatic past do not like to discuss the exploits that put them in that frame of mind, but I couldn't help myself, I had to say something. "I saw a Sixty Minutes show about Tunnel Rats, I was amazed."

"Yeah, I saw that one," he responded; "It was actually pretty factual, not like some of the books. You read some of these books and you just have to laugh; there is no way these guys ever crawled through an active hole."

Shaking my head, I repeated an old saying that I thought would fit the situation, "Well, those who tell don't know, those who know don't tell." A smile came across Johnny's face, "You got that right," he replied as he nodded his head.

At that point, Johnny opened up and began telling me some of the experiences he lived through. They went from hilarious to absolutely horrifying. He then told me about his arm. "I got to the bottom of the hole and was waiting until everybody left the room. When I couldn't hear any voices, I began to crawl into the room. I put my left hand holding my flashlight into the room and just as I was about to poke my head out, I felt like my arm was cut off. One of the Cong had stayed behind and when he saw my arm, he hit me with some type of multi blade sword. I fell out of the hole and shot him." I was stunned and amazed, this was unbelievable. Johnny continued, "When I let go of the round, I knew the whole platoon would be on my ass in seconds, so I jumped back into the hole and climbed out and ran my ass off."

This was the scariest story I had ever heard, and the way he told it just heightened the intensity. I wanted to respond in some way to let him know how compassionate I was, but I didn't use my traditional response, instead I replied with a slightly updated one. "I can't imagine what you went through." Johnny looked up at me with a deep stare; "I'm glad you said it that way. People always say that they can just imagine what if felt like, but they can't, nobody who was not there can imagine what it was like." He was right.

Johnny delivered to me an epiphany that I have implemented in my everyday life. Unless I lived an extremely similar experience, I cannot imagine what they felt. This has given me an insight and a better understanding in a variety of ways. If you realize that unless you were under the same pressures, same dangers and same frame of mind, you cannot truly offer judgement on another.

I have employed this logic in criminal activity, socioeconomic discussions, racism, sexism, theology and other topics. Try this for yourself, before you make a full judgement on another's actions, try to imagine that you have their finances, their history, their education, their upbringing. I don't know if this would affect your beliefs, but it just might plant the seed of understanding.

CHAPTER 13

As the effects of the medication slowly dissipated, I began to regain my consciousness, and with it came an uncomfortable pain in my lower abdomen that until then I had never experienced. The pain was not substantial enough to administer pain medications, but enough to know that it was there. I opened my eyes to look down to see that the two tubes there just a short time ago were disconnected and removed. They were replaced with two one-inch square gauze bandages. The two long thin wires that were connected directly to my heart and hung below my johnny still remained.

Lifting my head from the pillow, I turned my head towards the corner of the room and in the seat in the corner of my room to see my sister Marie sitting in the chair. She was thoroughly engrossed in her paperback book and did not notice that I had awakened, nor had she noticed any other goings on inside the room.

"Hi Re," I said in a groggy but much stronger voice than the one she had heard just a few days prior. "You're awake," she exclaimed. "You look and sound much better, how are you feeling?" I lifted my head a little higher off the pillow to face her in a conversation. "I'm ok, just tired" I revealed. "The meds are kicking the hell out of me."

"Relax, put your head down." Instructed Marie. As my head hit squarely on the pillow, my eyes closed. I could hear my sister talking to me, telling me that Nancy would be in a little later that afternoon.

My nurse re-entered the room to find me coherent, but not fully awake. We are going to take you to your room now; it's on the eighth floor. "Can I go with you?" asked Marie. "Well," said the nurse, "If you would like, you can go to his room and we will be there shortly." My sister agreed to do that, stood up and walked out of the room. "See you over there," called Marie as she left the room.

Having injured my back a month or so prior to this incident, I had been prescribed a number of medications for pain and swelling. The Mass General continued with those medications as well as starting me on a new medication regimen. The combination of the old meds with the new meds was quite potent, leaving me in a confused state, and causing a severe state of insomnia.

Waiting alone to be transported to my new room, I lay in my bed and began to run my tongue across my teeth. I could feel the tiny wires that were installed the night I fell. The wires were weaved between my teeth and tied together to stabilize my upper jaw. A few days earlier, the wires had been rubbing against my inner cheek and jaw. What began as an irritation quickly transformed into a pain. After being told by one of the other dental surgeons that there is nothing they can do to relieve the pain or adjust the wires, they gave me wax sticks to force into the voids between the wires and my teeth. I reached back into my open mouth and located the stray end of a wire with my fingers. Under normal circumstances, I would have not touched the wire except to bend it back into the weave. This, however, being anything but normal circumstances, I began to manipulate the wire.

Pinching the piece of metal between my thumb and forefinger, I began to pull. The pulling allowed a tiny bit of slack left in the weave to extend. Once it was long enough, I began to twist in little circles, using the weave as an anchor. A young woman walked into the room wearing hospital scrub pants and a T shirt. "Are you Mr. Arienti?" I quickly took my fingers out of my mouth to respond to her query. "Yes," I said. The nurse then came over to my bed and told the girl what room she was to take me to, and off we went.

By the time I was arrived at my room, Nancy had joined my waiting sister. While we talked, I began to have difficulties comprehending what was being discussed. "Do you mind if I nod off?" I asked the two women. "No, try to sleep said Nancy, it's alright." I closed my eyes and continued to listen to the two women chat. As hard as I tried, I could not fall asleep. Even with the softest of whispers from Nancy and Marie, sleep would not come. Although I knew that there were only single and double rooms in the hospital, looking from side to side I counted three beds. Every time I counted, I seemed to end up with seeing three.

There was suddenly a knock on the open wooden door. "Hello, I'm Roseanne," said a young brunette nurse as she stood in the doorway. "Are you Mr. Arienti?" Before I could answer, I heard my sister say "Yes, he is, but he's sleeping." I opened my eyes and spoke, "I'm awake." "Hello," she said. I could pick up a slight Eastern European accent in her voice. "I will be right back to get some vital signs, give you some meds, and get you anything else you need."

"She seems nice," observed Nancy. "When she gets back, I think we're going to head out, is that OK?" I still was feeling the effects of the medication, and most definitely was not contributing to any conversation between the two women; hell, I could barely keep my eyes open. "Nancy, Re, go now. You don't have to hang around; all I am going to do is sleep anyway."

Nancy, for the first time since this whole ordeal started, looked like she was finally at ease. The surgery was over, I was out of intensive care, the machines had been removed, and the doctor told me I would be home in a couple of days. As physically demanding and draining as these past two weeks had been on me, they were just as demanding and draining mentally on her. Over the years I'd had more than my share of broken bones, cuts, surgeries et al, and through them all, Nancy was there for me. Even something as small as a sprained ankle would bring out a higher level of nurturer within Nancy.

"Alright then, we'll take off now. Do you want me to bring anything in for you tomorrow?" Inquired Nancy. With my eyes closed I just shook my head from side to side, as there was nothing I needed. I felt a kiss on my cheek, and from the essence of the shampoo, I knew it was my sister kissing me goodbye. A few moments later I felt Nancy's lips pressing very softly against mine. "I'll see you tomorrow Bill, I love you," she whispered just before she left.

In the midst of what I can only describe as a dream, two nurses came rushing into my room and returned me to full consciousness. "Are you alright?" asked my nurse, Roseann, in an urgent nature. As I was just roused that very second, I was still somewhat confused; not unlike the feeling that I experienced the night of April 6th.

I looked around the room and did not recognize my environment. "You took your oxygen off, and you disconnected some of the wires to your monitor," said Roseann, as she attempted to once again place the nasal cannula back into my nose. As she worked on that, the other nurse lifted the sheets and started to reconnect the monitor leads to my chest. "You have to keep these on," said Roseann. "Why did you take them off?" I had no answer for her. I remembered tearing the wires and oxygen tube off of me but had no idea why I was doing it.

I was tired, exhausted actually. Even though I had spent most of the last ten days in bed, I could not reach a state of REM or a peaceful night's sleep. When the nurses had finished reconnecting me, I again closed my eyes, but did not fall into sleep; instead I just lingered in flux, halfway between alert and asleep. I could hear every word being said outside my room, but I could not understand. Although I recognized the words, I could not comprehend what was said when they configured the words into a sentence. It was almost as if it was a foreign language, like taking high school French all over again; you can pick out a word here or there but had no idea of the actual dialogue.

I began to run my tongue over the wires that were holding my jaw in place and felt the loose ending of one of the wires. I inserted two fingers into my mouth and began to search for it. It was on the right side of my mouth and was cutting into my cheek and gum. I surmised that the breathing tube that was inserted during my surgery had somehow cause the end of the wire to become dislodged. I began to wiggle the wire, back and forth, hoping that it would just snap off. I was not so fortunate though, as the wire was stronger than I had estimated. In somewhat of a daze, I began to twist, turn and pull the end of the wire to break it from the brace. The twisting and twisting became more fervent as I began to recognize the taste blood. I removed my fingers from my mouth and saw that the wire had punctured my fingertips a number of times, and I was bleeding pretty good. However, the blood did not deter me, as I continued to use all my might to snap that wire. Finally, after twisting it, curling it, pulling it and bending it, the little piece of wire broke from the rest and laid in my hand.

Unfortunately, still in that frame of mind and alertness, I ran my tongue over the left side of my mouth and found a situation similar to that on the right. I again began my attempt to remove that little piece of wire. I had twisted, pulled, bent, yet the wire would not release. Roseann walked into the room with my dinner and saw blood soaked into my sheets. "What happened here?" she asked. I explained the situation to her and showed her my fingertips which were covered with blood. Roseann immediately fetched the disinfectant, bacitracin ointment and band aids. She hurried to return and cleaned and bandaged my fingertips. Roseann then left the room and unbeknownst to me, called the oral surgeon to the room to repair the wires.

The oral surgeon entered my room a few minutes later. "Why are you doing this?" asked the surgeon with a very heavy Indian accent. "I don't know, it was just driving me crazy. I broke the one on the left, but couldn't break this one," I said knowing that my words were at best slurred.

"You could not break these wires. Wires like these hold airplanes together," he continued. I nodded my head, reached onto my bed table next to me and took the little piece of wire I had removed. I then handed the piece of wire to the dentist and said, "Here, go build me a plane." The dentist then pushed a wire cutter into my mouth and snipped the loose end. He then adjusted the cut ends into the weave of the remaining brace. He then inserted some hardened wax into the brace to relieve the friction created by the metal on flesh, and left the room.

"I have your dinner here on your table," announced Roseann. Again, I was less than thrilled with that tidbit of information and wondered what epicurean disaster sat under the dome. The bottle of Ensure, the cup of ice cream, the small bowl of chocolate pudding and a cup of coffee would again be my dinner. Roseann brought the table to my bed and set it before me. As she raised the dome, her expression was much like everyone else who saw what was intended to be my dinner. "Feel free to pick on the entrée if you're hungry," I said with tongue in cheek. Roseann quickly refused. "I just had my dinner before I came in here," she explained. "Oh yeah, sure you did...come on, just a little taste..." I continued. Her look of surprise was being replaced with a look of panic. "I'm just kidding," I laughed; a moment later Roseann began to laugh as well. "If you're still hungry after this, tell me and I will get you some peanut butter or something." She then put the head of my bed into the sitting position and left the room.

The dinner ritual played itself out like it had every other night since I was admitted, with the full plate of entrée returned untouched to the kitchen. I then turned the TV to the relaxation channel and closed my eyes in another attempt to sleep. I began to try self-hypnosis to assist in my endeavor. I had taught myself years earlier how to hypnotize myself, and the greatest benefit of this practice was the feeling of ultimate relaxation that envelopes you once you are finished.

I performed all the steps in order, used the proper breathing techniques and employed the visualization process, but sleep would not come. I could nap, I could relax, but full and proper sleep continued to elude me. My frustration continued to increase proportionally with my lack of sleep. I tried mind exercises, memory exercises, even counting sheep, but to no avail. I finally decided to stop trying, and if sleep came, I would welcome it.

With the exception of a small sliver of light from the hallway sneaking through a slightly ajar door, my room was dark. As it happened earlier, I was neither awake nor asleep, but somewhere in between. Inexplicably, once again in this state of reduced consciousness, I began to remove myself from the wires and oxygen as I had done earlier that day. I was aware of what I was doing even though I did not know why I was doing it. I just pulled whatever I could grab. I then sat up on the edge of the bed when the door quickly opened, and a different nurse entered.

This nurse was older, very friendly. Although somewhat overweight, she was surprisingly quick as she performed the tasks that I made necessary. "What are you doing?" she asked with an elevated volume. "You took all your wires off; your oxygen is off and your SAT (oxygen saturation level) is down to 84." She then repositioned the nasal cannula on my face and instructed me to take a series of deep breaths through my nose. After the fifth breath my SAT increased with every breath I took. Once again, I was up to an acceptable level of 95. Once that emergency had been mitigated, the nurse began re-attaching the heart monitor leads to the small pieces of tape stuck all over my chest.

"You're Bill, right?" asked the nurse. Her voice carried with it a natural laughter, that soothed me and was pleasant to my ears. "That's what they tell me," I said as I was regaining my alertness. "I'm Franny," said the nurse. "What are you doing here, and what are you doing getting out of bed?" Again, I had no explanation for my actions. "I had to go to the bathroom," I stated, giving me at least a modicum of an excuse. "You call me when you need to go to the bathroom. Unless someone is here with you, do not get out of bed. Do you understand?" The intrinsic laughter had disappeared from her voice. The pleasant feeling I felt earlier in my ears had ceased, and was replaced with the tenor of an angry nun. "Yeah…I'm sorry…I'm a little confused." Fran took a breath, and her laughter-infused voice once again returned. "No problem, you're all hooked back up, try to get some sleep." I thanked her and rolled onto my side.

After what seemed just a few minutes, I was again awoken, but this time by a young man named Paul. He had a very soft and friendly voice and apologized the whole time he was waking me. "I have to take your vital signs, and give you your meds," whispered Paul, as if not to wake me. Paul then took my blood pressure, pulse, oxygen saturation level. Once finished, Paul helped me flatten out my sheets, fluffed my pillow and asked if there was anything else I needed. I shook my head side to side and said, "No Paul, thank you very much." He was a little taken aback with my thanks, making me guess that not too many patients show their appreciation for his services. "You are quite welcome," he replied as he walked out of the room and left me once again in darkness.

Fran's angry voice once again startled me. Her admonishment was puzzling to me, but then I realized that I was sitting up on the edge of the bed with my oxygen and my monitor electrodes once again disconnected; an act that I had no recollection of undertaking.

Fran got close and helped me remove the top section of my johnny. One by one she again began to reconnect the leads and the oxygen. "Why did you do this again, and why are you getting out of bed again?" she asked angrily. I looked down at her, thought for a moment and told her the truth, "I don't know, I don't remember doing this." Fran looked up to me and repeated what I had just told her. I just nodded my head in agreement.

I was not comfortable with this occurrence. Although I have had nightmares through my life, like everybody else, I have never been known to sleepwalk. The last thing I recalled was Paul leaving the room. Fran did not seem to share my concern. Although not as friendly as it was originally, her tone of voice was no longer one of anger. "Well, this happens sometimes right after surgery."

As she completed reattaching me to the monitors, she again warned me about the two wires emanating from my lower abdomen. "Whatever you do, do not pull these wires, they go directly into your heart." This warning did not sit well with me. I had memory of my actions, and if an incident like this was to happen again, how would I know enough not to pull these wires while pulling all the rest? "I might as well give you your meds now that you are already up," reasoned Fran, and left the room to fetch a small IV bag and some other sundry medications.

As I waited for the drugs, I began to question what was happening to me. Until then, I had never not been in control of my body or mind. The idea that I could hurt myself or maybe even hurt others without any reason or recollection of the event was more frightening to me than having the surgery. Upon her return, Fran informed me that she was going to put the alarm on my bed to rouse me if I again attempted to exit my bed. This revelation gave me a little more peace, as now, knowing just how loud a bed alarm is, the chances of me doing anything while unconscious were greatly reduced. Fran then left the room as the medication slowly made its way through my IV and into my body. "I'll be back," Fran called. "This med takes a while to finish." I looked at the clock, it was 4:30. I adjusted my head on the soft pillow and laid on my back, hoping for the best.

My eyes slowly opened to the whispered calling of my name, it at 7:05. The voice of a younger, new nurse was soft and sweet. When she saw that I was awake, she gave me a big welcoming "Hi." As I put my glasses on, I saw the cute face that went with the sweet voice. "I'm Morgan, your nurse for the day." I thought to myself that I must be getting really old, because the nurses looked younger and younger. If I had not known that she was a college graduate, I would have sworn that she could be no more than 17.

"It's Sunday, if you want to receive Communion today I will have to let the hospital ministry know," Morgan informed me. I let her know that I was not interested but thanked her for her concern. Morgan then took my vital signs and asked me if I had been up earlier. I told her what had happened earlier and let her know that these actions while asleep worried me. "Well, you are tachycardic at 120. This information was not welcomed whatsoever. Tachycardia is the clinical term for a racing heart. The average adult's heartbeat is around 60 to 80; mine was almost double. "What is causing that?" I asked. Morgan did not answer right away as she surveyed my chart and medical history on the computer. Turning back to me, Morgan explained, "This happens a lot, it's nothing to worry about. They will get it back into range."

"I'm going to get you out of bed today for a short walk, OK?" Morgan said cheerfully. "I'll give it a try," I responded. "I will be right back with your meds," said Morgan. "Dr. MacGillivray's physician's assistant Haley, will be in a little later as well. Morgan left the room and returned with my meds almost immediately. A couple of pills, an IV bag and a small bottle with a wire attached at the bottom were all about to make their way into my body. As she readied my meds, Sanjay entered the room. "Hello, Mr. Arienti," he said with a bright happy greeting. "How are you feeling today, my friend?"

Before I had the chance to answer Sanjay, Morgan informed him that I was Tachycardia. Sanjay put the pulse oximeter on the tip of my finger and watched for the results on the monitor.

Standing back for a minute, Sanjay took my wrist in his hand and placed two fingers where my hand meets my wrist. He held it there for a full minute. He put my hand back onto my bed, and then placed the same two fingers on my neck at the location of the carotid artery. Again, he left his fingers there for a full minute. He inserted the ear tips of his stethoscope into his ear canals, and then placed the diaphragm against my carotid artery and listened intently.

Sanjay again stood back and began to speak. "What you have is what is called A-flutter causing your tachycardia." Being aware of my history in the medical field, Sanjay spoke in a more clinical sense with me than he would have with other patients. "A-flutter is an arrhythmia of the heart where the atrium pumps blood at an accelerated rate. The rest of the heart pumps at the usual speed. This high-speed pumping does not allow the heart to fill with a sufficient amount of blood before it is pumped into the body for perfusion. It is not uncommon for this to occur after a surgery like yours, and very often it corrects itself. In the meantime, we will give you a beta blocker designed to slow your heartbeat down so your heart can adequately fill and then you will be able to pump blood out to your whole body."

As Sanjay was just finishing his explanation, a young girl walked into my room with my breakfast tray. Breakfast was the meal that I used to nourish me for the rest of the day. I would order scrambled eggs, oatmeal, fruit, Cream of Wheat, Ensure, coffee and juice. This was essentially going to have to sustain me for the whole day, so I was determined to finish it. The expression on Sanjay's face was that of incredulity when he saw the amount of food on my tray. "Are all your meals like this?" asked Sanjay. I began to laugh and explained my meal plan to Sanjay. His response was "Well, I guess you gotta do what you gotta do!" and smiled. "I will notify Dr. MacGillivray about your arrhythmia. I will see you tomorrow."

Morgan finished administering my medication, helped me out of bed to use the bathroom, sat me in a chair for a while and changed the sheets on my bed. "After breakfast, would you like to take a shower?" asked Morgan. Although I heard her words in my ears, they penetrated no further. I could not comprehend her comments and had no desire to do so. As someone who never seems to daydream, I felt that I was just existing, not thriving; at least mentally. "Bill, Bill? Did you hear me?" inquired Morgan. Calling my named seemed to summon my attention back to the issue at hand. "What, sorry Morgan, I didn't catch what you said." "I just wanted to know if you wanted to take a shower this morning," she repeated as she tucked the corners of the fitted sheets under the mattress. "Yeah, that would feel good," I responded. "Okay then, I will be back in about an hour, and we will walk to the shower, we can kill two birds with one stone this way," she said. "Let me get you into bed for now." Morgan took my hands in hers and told me not to use my abdomen as I stood. Using only the muscles in my thighs and calves, I pushed myself up out of the reclining chair, Morgan's hands holding mine. We pivoted so that my back was towards the bed, and then I sat back down. I laid down and Morgan left the room. As I laid there, I took a deep breath and sighed, the worst part was finally over; boy, was I wrong.

CHAPTER 14

I n 1967 I was only five years old. It was a time of change in the United States that affected people of all ages. We were mired in a war in Southeast Asia as well as a Civil Rights Marches throughout the country, a very contentious presidential election was developing, and China acquired nuclear capability. It was called the Summer of Love, but for a kid in the Boston area, the Summer of 1967 meant only one thing, the Boston Red Sox were having a great year, and Carl Yastzremski was quickly becoming another Boston sports legend.

A sports team having a great year in most other parts of the country wouldn't be big news, but these were the Red Sox, a team known for breaking more hearts than Casanova. Every year the Sox would start out strong and by July 1st they would be out of contention. However, this year was different. The Sox had Yaz in left field, a great center fielder named Reggie Smith, and a young local phenom named Tony Conigliaro was setting the league, as well as the hearts of Massachusetts girls on fire with his on-field talent as well as off field antics. The rest of the nation knew it as the Summer of Love, but if you were in Boston, it was the Year of the Impossible Dream.

Although five is a little young to understand the sport of baseball, two older brothers and a father who loved the Sox introduced me into our national pastime. I remember my brother Charlie quizzing me on who played what position, and to this day, I can still recite those names and the positions they played.

Most of the games in 1967 were on the radio. Everyone knew the voices of Ken Coleman and Ned Martin calling the game on their AM radio, scratchy with lots of static. Unlike today, all the games were not on television, just a selected few midweek and all weekend games; but there was something romantic about listening to the game on the radio, visualizing the action as Ken called it.

We were not poor, not rich, but somewhere in between. Our television at that time was what everyone else seemed to have, a black and white RCA that received only five channels. It was the advent of colored TV, so the prices were somewhat prohibitive for a growing middle-class family. It didn't really matter though, watching baseball was always a treat for me.

Having never been to Fenway Park, my only idea of how it looked was through still pictures and black and white television. On television the grass was medium gray, the uniforms were light gray, the dirt was a little darker gray and the legendary left field wall was dark gray. Sometimes it was very difficult to differentiate between the teams, as their uniforms looked quite similar from a distance.

Once a year the Mayor of Quincy, Jim McIntyre, would use some of his campaign funds to buy a bunch of tickets to Fenway to watch the Red Sox on a Saturday afternoon. The day became known as "McIntyre Day", and was quite a shrewd campaign trick to attract young voters when they turned 18. At the time the tickets to the bleacher seats were only fifty cents each, so it was not uncommon to see ten or so Quincy School Department busses filled with children from 5 or 6 to 17. There were also a few chaperones, parents of some of the kids who didn't mind having a hectic, nerve wracking day trying to keep their eyes on fifteen kids in a ballpark that holds 25,000.

My brothers had gone for a number of years, and always came home with exciting stories and souvenirs. When the announcement came notifying the city what date McIntyre day would be, my brothers ran to my father and asked him for money for their tickets. So, the story goes, I was standing there watching, and I too asked to go. Charlie and Ernie both laughed, telling me that I was just a kid, too young to go on such a trip. My father smiled and told me that he would do what he could. My mother was adamant though, "You're not going to let them take Billy to the ballgame alone." Disappointment was coming to me in baskets, first my brothers, then my mother. Going to Fenway is what I wanted to do more than anything. Disneyland or Paragon Park held no draw for me, as I found Fenway Park to be like my Emerald City from the Wizard of Oz.

"Well, it says here that they need chaperones," said my father as he read the announcement in the newspaper. "Maybe I will go and take care of all of them." The celebration among we three boys then began. Charlie tested me numerous times a day by shouting out a name or a position and I had to name the corresponding player. Ernie put his pennant from the previous year up on the wall over his bed. Although it was weeks away, I was counting down the days, asking my mother each morning, "Is it today?"

The day finally came. We got out of bed and quickly put on our clothes. Being too excited to eat, we skipped breakfast knowing that we would be eating hotdogs, popcorn, peanuts and ice cream at Fenway. Charlie and Ernie had their baseball caps from the little league teams they played for, and I had a brand-new Red Sox hat that my mother had bought for me.

The three of us then waited outside for what seemed an eternity, pretending to be Red Sox players ourselves. Charlie and Ernie argued who was going to be Yaz, but I was happy being anyone on the team. My mother would call out of the house, "don't get dirty now," which was one of my mother's pet peeves. She took pride in how clean and neatly pressed our clothes, especially our school clothes, looked every day.

Around 10 o'clock, my father drove into the yard and asked if we were ready to go. He didn't have to ask a second time, as we were all in the car before he had finished his question. This still being the 1960's, seat belts and child safety seats were not mandatory, so Charlie sat in the front seat and I sat in the back seat with Ernie. Today if they could see the way we traveled, the head of the highway safety bureau would have a stroke. The kid in the front seat would always turn around, kneel down and talk to the kids in the back seat. The kids in the back seat would be jumping up and down on the seat and crawling on the floor; and if you were lucky enough to have a station wagon in your family, wrestling would commence in the far back where the seats were folded down.

When we arrived in the parking lot of Quincy High School, we all got out of the car. Hearing a call for chaperones, my father, with me in tow, began to walk towards the chaperone gathering point. My two brothers were ordered to stay by the car until my father got back.

There were hundreds of kids standing there waiting to load the busses on a hot July day. Once in, the busses had no air conditioners, and the summer sun caused heat waves to appear on top of each bus. Slowly at first, the sweat began to pour from our faces, until the lighter dry colors of our shirts had totally disappeared and had been replaced with somewhat darker shades, as they soaked through with young people's perspiration. Bottled water was not sold readily available as it is today, but no one seemed to get dehydrated. Once we were all aboard, we formed a caravan with ten or so buses and made our way into Fenway Park, Boston.

The excitement within me was palpable. The chant of "Here we go Red Sox, here we go!" rebounded off the metal walls of the bus as the yellow caravan reached the expressway. Sitting next to my father as the bus bounced from the holes and bumps on obsolete road was like a carnival ride. "Is Yaz going to be there today? How about Tony C.? George Scott?..." My father smiled and responded, "I think so, I don't see why they wouldn't be."

We finally reached our destination, Fenway Park. As we made our way off the bus, I was less than enthralled. In front of me stood a large brick warehouse adorned with a few pennants. The access points were nothing more than large green garage doors. The asphalt was hot and seemed to stick to the bottom of my sneakers as we walked from the bus to the gated entrances. This was not what I had envisioned, in fact it was a disappointment. Suddenly, the black, white and gray images which were the only hues which I saw Fenway Park on television were even less vivid in person. Once we entered the gate, we walked down a dingy ramp to a dimly lit concrete concourse lined on one side with food and beer concessions, and on the other with bathrooms.

With my hand held securely in my fathers, we walked down the concourse until we reached a small tunnel accessible by a slight upward ramp. As we exited the darkness and entered the tunnel, a bright stream of sunlight caused me to squint my eyes. My father stopped for a moment to scan the stadium for our assigned seats, and then it happened. This was the moment in time that affected me so much that it still makes my heart pound a little faster and a small lump to form in my throat just like I am that little boy all over again. We entered a small tunnel with a slight incline and the dingy darkness of the concourse began to give way to a sunlight bright enough to make a small boy close his eyes. As I slowly opened my eyes, I can only compare what I witnessed to the feeling Dorothy must have experienced upon landing in the land of Oz. Gone was the dark gray grass, the light gray baselines, the medium gray wall and scoreboard. There, before my very eyes stood the Emerald City! The vibrant green of the perfectly manicured lawn. The rich russet brown of the infield and warning track accented with the bright white chalk of the baselines. The muted dull green hue that adorns the walls and the "Green Monster" in left field made the bright fluorescent yellow of the foul poles stand out like two giant spires.

Okay, as I write this, I am wiping tears from my eyes.

I looked down to the field and there was Yaz, Reggie Smith, Tony Conigliaro and a number of other Red Sox players wearing immaculate white uniforms with the words Red Sox written across the chests and a large red number adorned each of their backs. The players were stretching and playing catch in the field as throngs of kids hung over the wall calling to the players for them to throw a ball into the crowd, or even just a quick wave to show recognition.

This was my Disneyland. As my father walked towards our seats, he had no choice but to drag me through the crowd as I stood wide eyed, mouth agape in absolute awe of the Temple of America's pastime. My head was turning back and forth in an attempt to take in all I possibly could; the smells of hotdogs, popcorn, beer wafting throughout the park; the sound of the crowd, the organ music, the announcer blaring in my ears; and the feeling of being pulled, pushed, and squeezed by the horde. It was beautiful chaos, a symphony of pandemonium, a cacophony of excitement. I had never been so overwhelmed with euphoria, and save for a few special events since that day, it has not been equaled.

The sensory overload was so consuming that I do not remember who won the game, who they were playing, or if there were any spectacular plays. Although we were surrounded by 23,000 people, it was a moment I shared alone with my father.

Once the game was over and we left the park, I had discovered my Mecca. Each subsequent pilgrimage I would make to this holy place would instantly give me the excitement only a five-year-old boy can express. Seeing the sun reflect off the bright green grass, the grandeur of the left field wall, and the red and blue seats, I feel my hand in my father's once more, and only hope that my son enjoys moments together like these much as I do.

CHAPTER 15

As I opened my eyes from a short nap I was confused. When I went to sleep, I was lying in a hospital bed in the Massachusetts General Hospital. I was on the eighth floor, the cardiac care unit. How did I end up in the lobby of a movie theater? As I lay in my bed, I can see the long red drapery decorating the walls, people walking past my bed to both enter and exit the theater. In an attempt to speak to the patrons, I realized that they were translucent, traveling through space without moving any body part. Although they took somewhat of a human form, their transparency caused me some disquiet.

Somehow, I began to recollect the plot of the movie playing in the theater where my bed was located. It was a teenage horror movie which dealt with people dying, but not knowing they are dead until they reach into their pocket and produce a movie ticket to this particular movie.

I lifted my hand to see if I was as transparent as all those people who were passing my bed, but I was opaque, encased in my natural skin. The voices these figures produced was, for the most part, muted; but the sound of crying was quite audible. Looking in all directions, I noticed that those figures who were crying had just removed a movie ticket stub from their pockets.

I began to wonder if I too was just a figure as these beings were. Was I alive? Did I pass? Do these figures see me as I see them? I reached under my sheets and began to feel for a movie ticket. I had already momentarily left the confines of this world only to return; did I cross over completely? Unlike the feeling of peace I had when I regained consciousness, lying in a pool of blood in the parking lot, at this moment I was less relaxed, not frightened but terribly confused.

I was unsure if I was awake or asleep. Were these figures and scenes truly appearing right in front of me or were they merely figments of an unconscious state? At this point I realized that I was at the whim of the world around me. If I was asleep, then this was nothing but a dream. But, using that logic, if I had died, then this surreal environment would be my eternity. I came to the conclusion that the only thing I could do was let the world dictate to me in what dimension I now resided. I closed my eyes, laid back and exhaled a deep breath that produced an audible sigh with its release. Motionless, I laid there. I don't know how much time had passed, but I opened my eyes, and to my relief, I had been transported back into my hospital room. I was alive; but did I pass and return? Or was this all a strange dream brought on by a combination of trauma and exhaustion.

It was around that time that Nancy arrived for her visit. I was awake when she entered the room and told her about the strange dream. "That sounds strange," answered Nancy. As someone who never remembers my dreams, I am amazed by people like Nancy who not only remembers her dreams but tries to interpret them to find their real meanings. Her penchant for interpreting dreams had become valuable to me, as having suffered some fairly substantial psychological trauma prior to this epic, I was plagued with reoccurring nightmares. The bad dreams were so intense that almost nightly I would thrash in my sleep, swing my arms and scream out unrecognizable rants. Nancy would wake me and let me know what I was doing. The dreams would be so intense that it was not unusual for Nancy, for her own safety, to get up and sleep in the spare bedroom.

"You'll never guess who is coming in to see you today," Nancy blurted out with excitement in her voice. "Mimi and Andy are coming in from Dalton to see you, and I think A.J. is coming as well." Mimi and Andy were very close friends from Nancy's home town. Nancy grew up and went to college with Mimi, and they have remained close ever since. Their eldest son, A.J. had always excelled in his studies. He became a teacher after graduating college and went to impoverished communities across the country to help the less fortunate among us achieve their potential. After doing that work for a few years, A.J.'s path led him to the medical field. He applied, was accepted, attended and graduated medical school, and as fate would have it, he was a resident at the Mass General.

Even though I was both physically and mentally exhausted, true rest came only in short spurts. Since April 6th, I had not had what I could call a restful sleep, and this was April 17th. My mind began to wander to greater and greater levels and the feeling had me concerned. I did not want Nancy to hear any news of my disorientation because she already had enough on her plate. When I felt that I was breaking with reality, I would close my eyes and pretend to be asleep until I returned to reason. It was in the middle of the Mimi and Andy visit that another one of these hallucinations commenced.

While sitting in the reclining chair, Mimi's, Andy's, A.J.'s and Nancy's voice began to fade into the distance, as they were walking away. The lower their voices sounded, I began to hear what sounded like the rotating blades of a helicopter. I closed my eyes and let my head rest on the high-backed chair. Soon the voices were completely drowned out by what I perceived was a Med-Flight helicopter. The medical staff, dressed in blue jumpsuits, rushed in and lifted me onto a stretcher. They secured me with the straps and rolled my down the hallway. As we exited the Mass General, the rear door of a blue and silver helicopter opened, and we raced to it at full speed. The medics collapsed the legs of the stretcher as they slid me into the air ambulance, closing the door all in one synchronized movement.

The sounds of the blades cutting the air became louder and louder until I suddenly felt a thump, then a feeling of unsteady as the helicopter slowly began to break its bond with the ground and become air borne. I laid motionless, as only my pupils darted back and forth to see what procedures the medics were performing on me. Where were they taking me? I was in one of the greatest hospitals in the world, where would they take me? The medics had to shout orders to each other to overcome the noise of the engine and blades, but I did not understand the terminology of the instructions.

"OK Bill," came a voice from behind me. This voice was very different. First it was not being shouted like all the other ones, instead it was a soft woman's voice. The voice spoke without the interruption of others, nor in competition with the noisy helicopters.

"Bill, you get some rest, we're going to get going." Suddenly, the helicopter, medics and stretcher were gone. The familiar soft voice I heard calling me was Mimi, whispering to me as they recognized my inability to properly make guests welcome. "Mimi, Andy, A.J., I'm sorry." My apologies were sincere even though it seemed I no longer had control over my body or mind. "Bill, don't worry!" laughed Andy, a good-hearted man who you could always count on for a chuckle or laugh. I reached out with my left hand to hold Mimi's and shook Andy's hand with my right. "Thank you guys for coming, this meant so much to me…thank you." I was genuinely grateful for their visit. They drove three hours to Boston and now had a three-hour return trip. "Get some rest, Bill," instructed the recently appointed Dr. Piper. "If you need something, let me know." It was a bittersweet moment for me, someone who I had held in my arms as an infant was now giving me medical advice as a doctor. A feeling of pride for my young, brilliant friend filled my heart, and the feeling of the premature old age filled my mind.

"Bill, why don't I help you get into bed so you can rest for a while. I'm going to the café for tea with Mimi and Andy." I agreed with Nancy and together she and I worked together to return me to my bed, tucked me in and raised the bed guard to prevent me from falling out. "I'll be back in a few minutes; do you need anything?" Just from the effort of getting into bed, I was again fatigued. I could feel my heart beating faster than normal in my chest. I put two fingers against the carotid artery in my neck and began to count as I watched the clock. The rate was fast, too fast to feel for 15 seconds and multiply by 4. After the full minute had passed, my heart rate was 128. My God, I thought to myself, am I that out of shape?

I began to put a rhythm to the pace of my pulse, making each beat feel like that of a beat of a subwoofer. The R.E.M. song "It's the End of the World as we Know it" seemed to sync perfectly with my heart rate, as well as having an appropriate name for what was transpiring in my own life. I don't know how long I was keeping pace with the music before I a voice informed me that I needed an X-ray, and the one in the hospital was not the type capable to perform the procedure I required. "Just rest, we will handle everything," said the voice. I opened my eyes to see a tall, thin, handsome Black man preparing my bed for the trip. I felt that I was in good hands, and again closed my eyes to rest. What seemed to be a second later, I opened my eyes to see that I was in a post office. I saw the posters on the wall, the glass doors to the parking lot, the post office boxes, a scale and an x-ray machine. I chuckled to myself, thinking how could the post office have an x-ray machine that had greater abilities than the Mass General?

The machine did not need any personnel to operate, and the film was quickly exposed while I laid in my bed. I again closed my eyes for the return trip, and within the speed of light, I was back in my room in the Mass General. I slowly opened my eyes and turned my head to the right, and there in my recliner sat my wife Nancy. "Did you get some sleep hon?" asked Nancy in a sweet voice. "I just got back, how long have you been waiting for me?" I questioned. "You got back from where?" returned Nancy. "I had to get an x-ray, but they did it at the post office instead of doing it here." "What are you talking about?" said Nancy with a skeptical voice. A look of disbelief and concern washed over her face.

At this point, I no longer was certain what was real and what was imagined, so I began to inform Nancy of the excursions that I had taken that morning. "So far I've been at the movies, in a helicopter and to the post office, and I always end up right back here." Nancy's look of concern graduated into a look of full panic. "You went to a movie theater and the post office?" she repeated. "Yeah, and I went in the helicopter too," I added as I shook my head. "I'm going to see when your lunch is coming, I'll be right back," stated Nancy as she rose from the chair and made her way out the door and into the hallway.

Although I did not notice it at the time, Nancy was terrified that something bad had happened to me. I later found out that when she went out of the room, rather than check on my food, she called my brother Ernie and sister Marie on her cell phone and told them that something was wrong, and they better get in there. Nancy then went to discuss my situation with my nurse and physician's assistant; but leaving me alone was not in my best interest.

Alone in my room, with no mental stimulation, I was left to my own devices. It began to feel like "The Nightmare on Elm Street", but there was no Freddy Krueger, no horror nor murders, just every time I closed my eyes, I was immediately transported to another dimension. I began to almost expect Rod Serling to step out from behind the curtain and say, "Imagine if you will...".

Trying to stay awake is ironically the most tiring of activities. I did not want to close my eyes again, and was engaged in a battle of wills between different parts of my body. The scariest part is the moment when you lose consciousness and enter your sub consciousness. For me, the beginning of my dreams, at least the ones that I remember, seem like I am in a normal situation. There is nothing out of the ordinary, no scary people, nothing menacing, just a non-threatening environment. What happens next is anybody's guess.

My eyes lost the battle of wills and despite all my efforts closed again. I looked around, I was still in a hospital, still in a bed, but the hospital and the bed were not the ones in which I had spent the last two weeks. The semi-private room was now a long hospital ward, on my nightstand was a white enamel basin. Curtains created a series of rooms, and pipes created a pergola over each bed. There were no other patients, but a number of World War II uniforms were hanging on hooks on the wall. The light fixtures on the ceiling were contemporary with the rest of the scene, pendant lights hanging down from a pipe with three chains. The three lit lightbulbs could be seen through the opaque white glass. Everything appeared as it should for a veteran's hospital of the late 1940's.

My immaculate white sheets were now a dark gray wool, and the heavy plastic rails were now square metal pipes. Something was wrong, very wrong. The earlier dreamlike sabbaticals were light, somewhat engaging, with some precise details among a vaguely recognizable environment. This was different, everything I saw was so specific to what I thought an infirmary of this era would contain. For the first time confusion was replaced with fear. I was beginning to wonder if maybe I had passed and was encountering those who had passed before me in the Massachusetts General Hospital. Although I was still confined to bed, and only was to get up with assistance, I could no longer lie idle. If I was dead, damn it I wanted to know it!

Unable to use my primary muscles to exit my bed, I had to depend on my auxiliary muscles to complete my attempt at escape. Once again I disconnected my electronic leads that kept me confined, much like a floating balloon at the Macy's Thanksgiving Day Parade. Once free of all the leads, I rolled onto my stomach and began to curl my legs up under my abdomen. My breath became labored as this was my first real attempt at exercise since my surgery. I pressed on, and once my knees were in place, I pushed my torso up to a vertical position with my hands which enabled me to twist myself off the mattress and place my feet solidly upon the linoleum tile floor.

Once standing, I began to shuffle my feet forward in an attempt to walk. As I reached the door that led to the hallway, my perception of my environment immediately changed. Gone was the militaristic infirmary, and in its stead was what looked somewhat like a rest home. I got the impression that it was a clinic designed for retired healthcare professionals and run on a voluntary basis by off duty nurses. Again, the environment was as specific as it could possibly be. There were bookcases full of books on all subjects; lots of wicker furniture with oversized pillows, a number of green plants growing in dirty plastic pots and a basket full of magazines. Although this atmosphere was much more comfortable than the military infirmary, the fact that I could not control nor understand my location was growing more and more distressing.

Having left my glasses on the nightstand, my vision was extremely limited. Everything in eyeshot was either blurry or unrecognizable. The only thing that I could detect with any specificity was movement, unfortunately I was not able to determine what it was that was moving.

A figure dressed all in a burgundy hospital scrubs quickly approached me. "What are you doing out of bed?" came a voice from the figure. To my relief, I recognized the voice as it filled the hallway, it was Morgan, my nurse. I was about to answer her question when she again spoke, this time her voice seemed to have increased in anger. "You are not supposed to be standing or walking on your own!" Her admonishment was quick and sharp taking me somewhat aback, but then to my surprise, I was once again in the Mass General at the proper place in time.

"I don't know what's going on," I said to Morgan. "I feel like I'm traveling through time and space, over and over again." Morgan took my hand, turned me around, and began to escort me back into my room. When we reached my bed, she once again reconnected my EKG leads to my chest, listened to my heart, took my vital signs and helped me get back into bed. Morgan's voice changed back to a calm, measured tone. "What do you mean traveling?" asked Morgan. I was about to inform Morgan of the unsettling experiences that I had been undergoing when Nancy returned with my P.A. Haley. The three women listened intently as I, in detail, gave an account of events that I knew could not be true. When I finished, Haley spoke first; "Can I ask you a few questions?" she began. "Yeah," I said, hoping that she would somehow have a greater insight into my condition. "Do you know who the President is?" asked Haley. "Obama," I shot back. The questions continued on a quick pace as I delivered immediate and correct responses. "Do you know where you are right now?" asked Haley. "Mass General hospital," I responded. "Do you know where in the hospital?" I nodded my head, "The cardiac care unit." Haley nodded her head with approval to all of my answers. I then asked Haley, "Can I ask you a question now?" Haley responded, "Sure," to which I asked, "Are you sure that I'm not in a psych hospital?" Haley, Nancy and Morgan all began to chuckle at my inquiry. "No, not at all," replied Haley. "Why, do you think that you are in a psych hospital?" I looked directly into the young woman's eyes and answered with all candor, "I don't know what's going on."

Morgan made her way over to the computer and pulled up my file. Because I had torn a disc in my back six months earlier, when my recent medical event occurred, I was already on a number of pain relievers, anti-inflammatories and muscle relaxers. The hospital had continued these pharmaceutical dosages and also added a number of cardiac drugs necessary for my new circumstances. "Have you been sleeping well?" asked Morgan. "Not that well at all," I told her.

Morgan looked at Haley for a moment, and Haley joined her at the computer. The two professionals studied the screen, pointing at a number of entries that appeared before them.

Nancy sat in the chair on my left, holding my hand as the interrogation and diagnosis continued. Her concern was palpable as her hand, soft, warm and moist rested in mine. Without any verbal communication occurring, I could sense her trepidation, as sometimes Nancy's silence was as loud as her shouts.

In a voice that broke what I perceived as tension, Haley announced, "I'm going to talk to Doctor MacGillivray." She pivoted from her position at the computer and walked towards the door. "I'll be back in a couple of minutes," she continued as she walked out of the room. Morgan remained and began to explain that I may have been having a reaction from all my medications. "In addition, a lack of sleep will also cause a number of disturbances within the body," Morgan stated these facts with such understanding that she diffused the apprehension that Nancy and I were feeling.

"Ernie's on his way in," said Nancy, hoping to bring some normalcy back into the situation. I was a little hesitant about having more visitors, as I did not want to be seen in a less than coherent state. "Oh, did he call you?" I asked. Nancy shook her head slightly, "No, I called him, he wanted to know how you were doing." I nodded with approval, even though I was not fully comfortable.

Through the doorway I could see Haley returning to my room. Her walk was quick and light, almost whimsical, and her long hair and stethoscope seemed to bounce in synchrony with each step. Just before stepping into my room, she began to explain her dialogue with the Doctor. "Okay," she said as she launched directly into her report. "Dr. MacGillivray is not a big supporter of medications. Once the initial trauma is over, he would rather see you on fewer meds than on too many. Right now, you are on a number of less vital meds that may be interfering with the meds that you really need. They also may be reacting with each other and not allowing you to get the rest that you require." Dr. MacGillivray's words through Haley's intercession were the best news that I had received in days.

I was long past the stage of tired, and at this point, I was even past exhaustion. They say that the insane do not know they are insane, which I kept repeating to myself because at this point, I was beginning to feel insane. My ability to organize and form cognitive thoughts were no longer within my power. Reality was no longer tangible, but rather acted with the same properties as a liquid, taking the shape and size of its container without any stability of its own. Articulating comprehendible sentences became more and more difficult. I never realized the effects created by lack of sleep, but, as I would later find out, my insomnia had become a legitimate threat to my health and my recuperation.

The pain at my surgical site had dramatically diminished to a point that pain relief greater than acetaminophen could provide was unnecessary. My medications, one by one, were to be discontinued per order of Dr. MacGillivray. Gone were the three back injury meds, gone was the surgical pain meds, gone was everything but Metoprolol and Amiodarone, Prilosec and Zoloft. Ambien and melatonin were added to my list, and they were on their way up.

With that news, Morgan took another set of my vital signs, my blood pressure and temperature seemed within reasonable limits, but my heart rate was still accelerated to an unsafe level of 120 beats per minute. If all the other things that I was experiencing had not already been by themselves exhausting enough, this heart rate made me feel like I was running the Boston Marathon in heavy cement boots.

Throughout this whole ordeal, I had been confident and upbeat with an attitude of invincibility. Heart valve replacements? They do dozens of them daily. Dying? If it was in fact my turn to die, I would not have lived past that night. Broken jaw? Hell, I have a close friend whose face some thugs used as a dance floor. His jaw was broken much worse than mine, and if he made it through, so can I. Up until two days after the surgery, I was not just optimistic of my chances of making it, I was God be damned determined that I was going to improve the rate of survival for this procedure. Just within feet of my location there were people in much worse shape and a lesser chance of recovery than me, but they were fighting for their lives, and for me to lose the confidence and courage to battle on would be a slap in the face to them. I used their determination to bolster my own, the same way that I hoped my grit would encourage others.

It was still Sunday, April 17th. It had been eleven days since the incident in the parking lot; and for the first time since I woke up in that sea of blood, I was scared. People equate being afraid or being scared as liabilities, negative traits that only the weak must overcome. Having fear or being scared are the two traits that keep us alive more than any other. I look at bravery as forgetting your fear and doing something that is dangerous just for the sake of doing it. This type of attitude gets people killed. Courage, on the other hand, is when you are intelligent enough to understand the dangers that you face, and your fears are legitimate, but you overcome them to do what is necessary, using the protective power of the instinctive fear to maintain your safety. Running into a condemned building fully involved in flame with no occupants, no salvageable property and no value to the owner might be brave, but it most certainly is not courageous. Conversely, an officer stopping men from entering an inferno to save men who he was certain were lost, trapped and dead inside is the stuff of which courage is made.

It was evident that Nancy was nervous as well, but she was doing her absolute utmost to disguise her true feelings. After being together for 35 years, her body movements and facial expressions betrayed her. I knew that it was up to me to instill that little extra courage that she required to get the both of us through these chaotic moments.

Having already been through the very worst that could possibly happen, and emerged without fear or trepidation, I had a better insight than most people who may face death. In honesty, I was, and still am, more threatened by the possibility of being disabled than I am of being dead. Armed with this knowledge, I could create a façade of confidence hopefully strong enough to bolster Nancy's already high level of courage. One never truly knows the strength of a person until they see them under the most ominous of circumstances. Nancy, time and time again, had proven her mettle to me, and I can say without a doubt that her personal resolution is up there with the best of them.

As Morgan left the room, Nancy and I heard familiar voices saying hello to her, a moment later my brother Ernie and his wife Nancy entered the room. "Hey, Bill, how are you doing?" asked Ernie as he approached to shake my hand. His wife Nancy approached as well saying "Hi Billy," as she bent down to hug and kiss me. "You feeling OK?" said Ernie as he and Nancy sat down on the chairs in the room. I smiled, "Ernie, I've been in five different places today and I haven't even left this room." The words found their target with precision as a laugh was elicited by all three visitors. The ice and tension were now broken, and a regular conversation ensued.

I explained to Ernie and Nancy the troubling visions that I had been experiencing. Their reaction was a combination of concern and humor as they heard the story in its entirety. My wife Nancy then revealed a part of the story that had completely slipped my mind. "When the P.A. asked Bill if he knew where he was, he told them the cardiac unit of the Mass General," began Nancy. "Then Bill said to the P.A., can I ask you a question? And when Haley said yes, Bill asked her, are you sure that I am not in a psych hospital?" The two Nancy's and Ernie began to laugh at the statement, and to be honest, it brought a smile to my face as well.

Almost as if on cue, both Haley and Morgan returned to the room while we were still laughing. "Well, it looks like you're feeling a little better," acknowledged Haley. Nodding my head, I responded "sometimes education and knowledge are the best medicines you can get. Now add in some laughter and you're indestructible." Haley began to laugh at my observation. "See, I bet you're feeling better already yourself, aren't you?" Nodding her head in agreement, Haley said "you always make me feel better Billy." She then gave me a small cup with two pills in it accompanied with a Styrofoam cup filled with water. She then scanned my bracelet and asked me for my date of birth. This protocol had become more of a ritual than a procedure. I took the two pills into my mouth and washed them down with water.

"Maybe we should get going and let you get some rest," suggested Nancy. "Your dinner will be here soon, and then you can go right to sleep." I didn't have to be asked twice. First finding out that I was not insane was in itself cathartic and knowing the sleeping meds would be kicking in at any time, being left alone sounded great to me. "I hope you don't mind," I said, not wanting them to think that I didn't appreciate their company. "Don't be silly," chided Ernie's wife Nancy. "Get some sleep, we will talk to you later on," said Ernie.

Nancy began to straighten out my sheets before she would say her goodbyes. "Ernie, would you mind giving Nancy a ride back to Quincy, so she doesn't have to take the train?" I asked, knowing that he would surely agree to such a request. "Sure, no problem," said Ernie and Nancy in unison. Nancy finished tugging at my sheets and fluffing my pillows. Ernie's wife Nancy bent over, hugged and kissed me. "Bye Billy, I'll see you soon," she said as she stepped back to let Ernie approach. Taking my hand and holding it in his, Ernie looked down and although I do not remember what he said, it was enough to elicit a laugh from me as well as the two Nancys.

It had been only 15 minutes since I took the sleeping aids, and I was already groggy. Nancy asked if I needed anything else before she left, but I was fine and content with what my immediate future held in store. She then bent over and kissed me, running her fingers through what little hair I had left. "I love you," said my wife, and I was suddenly filled with emotion. Although I kept my composure, I could not help but realize just how fortunate I was, and wonderful she was. I whispered back to her that I loved her as well, knowing that if I said it in normal tones, my voice would surely crack. Two deep breaths in through my nose and out of my mouth and I was back to the wise ass to which my wife had become accustomed.

As the trio departed from my room, I waved goodbye and called out "see you later." I immediately took my glasses off my face and placed them on the nightstand. Lowering the head of my bed to just the right angle, I once again employed my ability to hypnotize myself, but only needed the breathing portion, as a welcomed sleep cloaked my mind and body so deeply that I slept through the periodical vital sign checks that occurred throughout the night.

CHAPTER 16

T he movie "Inherit the Wind" told a story based on the events of the Scopes Monkey Trial. In the movie, a teacher in Tennessee was facing criminal charges arising from his teaching of Darwinism to his high school students. Presenting the Theory of Evolution was forbidden in public schools in 1925 Tennessee; however, John T. Scopes believed his vocation as a teacher compelled him to not only present information to his students, but to challenge their developing minds, and encourage them to think for themselves as well.

The movie was insightful, entertaining and drew parallels to McCarthyism, which was dominating the society when the original play was written. The dialogue in the movie was quite detailed and offered an insight not only to the culture of 1925 Tennessee, but to the current day abhorrence of many ultra conservative Christians who still cling to accounts of the Bible rather than accept the findings of science.

In addition, it also includes a discourse on the effects the budding field of technology, and how it so far has improved our way of life, but in the process has diminished our social skills, our ways of interaction and through the anonymity of the internet, has led to a breakdown of societal behavior.

Spencer Tracy played the role of, Henry Drummond, a character based on legendary attorney Clarence Darrow. Drummond's summation to the jury extols the advancements of modern technology, and simultaneously warns of how those advancements may diminish our behaviors and innocence.

> "Progress has never been a bargain.
> You have to pay for it. Sometimes I think
> there's a man who sits behind a counter and
> says, "All right, you can have a telephone,
> but you lose privacy and the charm of
> distance. Madam, you may vote but at a
> price. You lose the right to retreat behind
> the powder puff of your petticoat or your
> mister. You may conquer the air, but the
> birds will lose their wonder and the clouds
> will smell of gasoline."

So prophetic those words be. Today, we have reached levels of technology that were unimaginable just twenty years ago. The stuff that once was created only in the studios of science fiction are now the household items of modern living. But at what price? What have we given up in return for the things we now know as necessities? Are we stripping our planet of natural resources? Are we destroying our ecosystems? Are we depleting our forests, woodlands, swamps and jungles? Have our actions caused the annihilation and extinction of plants and animals that may hold the secret to our ultimate existence? We must begin to look at the world like the Native Americans, we are nothing more than temporary inhabitants; the world is not ours; we are the worlds.

The proliferation of personal computers has caused some schools to no longer teach cursive to their students. The amount of food needed to feed the world today has caused producers to develop genetically engineered foods. The use of abbreviated words and spell check has decreased the next generation's ability to spell and structure sentences properly.

The implementation of modern technology should be integrated in some way to enhance our current abilities, not replace them. A dependency too great on technological advancements that do not expand or advance our current abilities could cause devastating effects if the grid was compromised. Simple mathematics and grammar would have to be re-learned by a society dependent on calculators and word processing computers. Continuation of the technological innovations, under the ideal conditions, could very well be the demise of our society.

A society that relies exclusively on progressive ideals jeopardizes the future of its existence. Conversely, a society that relies exclusively on the ideals of conservatism has no future. Like everything else in life, a delicate balance must be maintained between the goals to which we aspire and the accomplishments that we have already achieved. The existence of a goal in life is necessary to compel one to persevere. Life is not to be endured, but to be lived. Without goals and aspirations, life is just a mundane collection of minutes, hours, days and years.

Set goals, high enough to achieve, but not so high that you lose yourself in your quest to reach them; and not too low that reaching them becomes commonplace. Celebrate each goal once it is achieved, but rest not on your laurels. Set your next goal with the excitement and eagerness which drove you to achieve your previous objective.

CHAPTER 17

It was difficult to open my eyes, almost as if someone had poured glue onto my eyelashes. I reached up to my face with my left hand and gently scratched the remnants of sleep from my eyes. With my right I reached for my glasses and placed them on my face. The room, now in focus, was illuminated by the sunlight pouring through the window. As I surveyed my room, I noticed that it was 8 o'clock; I had been asleep for fourteen hours. I had slept through the administration of my medications as well as the staff taking my vital signs. I had no memory of anything subsequent to my family leaving the day before. My body felt like it had taken its first deep breath in days.

Sanjay entered the room with his usual smile and greeting. He stood next to my bed and shook my hand, welcoming me to the new day. "How are you feeling today Mr. Arienti?" I nodded approvingly to indicate a positive response. "I feel good this morning, thank you Sanjay." Taking the ever-present stethoscope from around his neck, Sanjay asked "May I listen to your chest and lungs please?" I immediately sat up as quickly as I could and gave him access to both my chest and back. Sanjay took my wrist in his hand and closed his eyes. A few moments later he placed the bell of the stethoscope onto my mid back and instructed me to take deep breaths. I followed his directions and inhaled to fully inflate my lungs, then blew it out. I repeated this two or three times while Sanjay moved the stethoscope around to different areas of my back.

He then asked me to lay down and placed the stethoscope against my chest. After listening for a few moments, he retreated with a look that could only be described as pensive. "It sounds like you have what is known as A-flutter. It is a common occurrence after having a surgical procedure like yours."

Although I had thirty years of experience in the medical field, I had never heard of the term A-flutter before. I asked him to explain the condition to me. "Your heart, through the surgery, has sustained trauma. It is now reacting to that trauma by beating at an accelerated rate, not allowing your chambers to fill fully before pumping," he explained. "We will try to correct this with medications; it is not uncommon for this condition to correct itself over a short period of time."

I had noticed that my heart was beating faster than usual but thought nothing of it. I just believed that it was a reaction to the surgery. But, now that he enlightened me on what was happening, the condition was presenting itself with a much greater intensity. I had almost wished that he had not informed me of the situation but handled it by administering an added medication or two.

I will inform Doctor MacGillivray of the situation, but most likely we will put you on a beta blocker like metoprolol. More often than not, this will resolve the condition. Finally, something I understood came from Sanjay. Beta blockers are medications that cause the heart to slow down and allow the chambers to fill with blood, then pump with a stronger force to perfuse the body with blood. It was a very non-invasive treatment with a high success rate. Being enlightened by this course of action once again cloaked my body and mind in serenity.

"Now, if the metoprolol does not work, we will have to do a procedure called a cardiac conversion," explained Sanjay. "Are you familiar with that procedure? Again, the blanket of serenity was stripped from me and exposed me to a cold environment. "I don't think I'm familiar with that," I responded, knowing fully that I had no idea what he was talking about. "It's very common to regulate a patient's heartbeat externally," clarified Sanjay. "First, we put you on blood thinners to eliminate any chance of clotting. Once the risk of clotting is eliminated, we place defibrillator pads on your chest, then one at a time we administer a minor shock to stop your heart and let it reset. If it does not reset, we then increase the charge until your heart goes back into a sinus rhythm. "

I took a deep breath and thought how lucky I was to have slept so well the previous night, because if I had been in the same psychological condition, they would have had to peel me off the ceiling. My heart had stopped the first time a week and half earlier for 15 minutes on its own. It stopped again for a few hours a few days earlier for surgery. Now, they are talking about stopping my heart for a third time. Although not having an extensive medical education, I was somewhat sure that stopping and starting a heart repeatedly was not a recommended practice.

Additionally, I have seen EMS workers accidently shocked by a defibrillating device, and although I didn't feel it, the one thing that was for sure was that I did not want to experience that feeling myself. "If you have to do this procedure, where do you do it?" I asked. "It's a very simple procedure," explained Sanjay. "We first make sure that you are in no danger of blood clots, then you come into the outpatient services in the hospital." Sanjay described the procedure without any emotion or fluctuation in his voice. "We then weigh you, hook you up to an I.V. and bring you into the cardiac cath unit. Once you meet with the doctor, we give you general anesthesia, and while you are under, we administer a series of shocks until your heart goes back into a sinus rhythm."

It all sounded too easy to me, almost like getting a big splinter removed. "So, how long do I stay after the procedure? Am I in pain when it's over?" Sanjay shook his head side to side as I posed my questions. "If it all goes right, you go home right after the procedure, and there should be no pain or lingering effects. You will have to stay on blood thinners for a period of time after the procedure though, the duration will depend upon how your heart and body reacts."

I was not pleased with this revelation. I had made the decision to replace my damaged valve with a fifteen-year tissue valve over a permanent mechanical valve for the sole purpose of not having to be on a blood thinner regiment. Now I have the tissue valve, and still have to take blood thinners. Although until this point I had been able to maintain somewhat of a positive attitude regarding this whole experience, this news felt like a kick in the nuts. My displeasure must have been evident in my face, as Sanjay reassured me that other options were available before the cardiac conversion. "Let's not put the cart before the horse," chuckled Sanjay, "Let's see what the metoprolol does first." Sanjay turned around and began to walk out the door when he stopped and backed up into the room. If the morning wasn't already bad enough, more bad news had just arrived in the form of breakfast.

After choking down the lukewarm Cream of Wheat, and washing it down with Ensure and coffee, I turned the television on and waited to see how the Red Sox won the night before. As the meteorologist predicted the days weather, Morgan sauntered into the room with her usual pleasant demeanor. "Good morning Mr. Arienti, how was your night?"

To be honest, I never felt comfortable with anyone older than 18 calling me Mr. Arienti. I understand it is an act of respect, but it makes me feel uneasy. With all the different staff, nurses, doctors, assistants, I don't know who I informed of this pet peeve, but knowing that Morgan was going to be with me for a while, I figured that if I already told her to call me Bill, I would just have to tell her again. "Well, I finally slept, it felt good." I answered. "Could I ask you for a huge favor, Morgan? I don't know if I told you before, but can you please call me Bill, it's just that it's much more informal, and I am an informal guy."

Morgan smiled and chuckled at the request. "I don't like addressing anyone by Mr., or Mrs.. What are you supposed to do if you have a patient who is an older woman that has never been married? Do you call her Miss, like Driving Miss Daisy?" She had a good point there, one that makes you think. "Wow, I better never have an existential discussion with you, you would kick my ass!" I laughed. Morgan smiled; "As soon as you tell me what existential means, I will give you an answer, Bill." We both smiled with her annunciating my name.

"Well, I see that you enjoyed your five-diamond rated breakfast," knowing full well my opinion of the hospital cuisine was a little less than stellar. "Well, the temperature of the Ensure was intriguing, although I prefer it chilled, serving it like it has been under someone's arm pit for twenty minutes was an interesting dynamic. However, when it's coupled with a lukewarm cup of moist sawdust, it brings the whole meal to a higher level of gastronomical putridity." My attempt to sound like a New York Times food critic must have fallen short because it did not even elicit a smirk from Morgan. Either that or she, like my wife, had quickly learned to ignore my futile efforts at highbrow humor.

The morning ritual of taking my vital signs at the start of the shift was about to commence. As the woman from the housekeeping department strolled into the room with the long handled dry-mop, Morgan came close to my bedside to allow access for the housekeeping woman to sweep the whole floor.

Once the housekeeper completed her work and left, Morgan told me that she had to make a couple of postings in the computer at the nurse's station and she would then return to walk me to the shower room. Her news was very well received by me. I had been up walking a couple of times already, short distances only. It was depressing to be out of breath after only twenty or so steps; even though I was aware of my medical and physical situation, it offered little solace to me, a person so active his whole life. The shower room was further down the hall than I had walked, so this would be a welcomed challenge.

As Morgan left the room, it seemed like someone had installed a revolving door while I was asleep because Dr. MacGillivray immediately entered. "Mr. Arienti, How are you doing today?" I looked up and smiled, "Well Doctor, the day is still very young, but so far I'm doing pretty good." The Doctor smiled back and inquired if I had gotten any rest the previous night. "Oh, yes, I did." I said emphatically. "I think I fell asleep at about 9:30 and just woke up. It felt so good." A sense of relief washed over Dr. MacGillivray's face. "Good, you will notice how much better you feel with a good rest." He continued, "I spoke with Sanjay a few minutes ago, he informed me that your heart rate was too fast. Do you mind if I listen to your chest?" Dr. MacGillivray, not waiting for my response began to remove the stethoscope from around his neck and inserted the earplugs. He placed the cold bell of the scope against the left side of my neck and listened to my carotid artery, then switched sides and listened to the right side. He then listened to my heart and lungs before stepping back and commenting. "This is not uncommon, sometimes it corrects itself, other times we have to convert it back." He explained. "Are you familiar with A flutter?" asked the doctor. "I had a little knowledge of it, but Sanjay filled me in on the details," I responded. "Do you think that this is the reason the nurses have had difficulty getting an accurate blood pressure on me?" Dr. MacGillivray's pupils darted up and to the left of his eye socket; "That is a distinct possibility; I will send up my assistant later on to see if we can get an accurate B.P."

The doctor told me to relax and try to get some more hearty rest. "I will see you soon, if you need anything, have them page me." He then turned and walked out of the room. The remnants of the previous night's sleeping pills began to re-present themselves, as my eyelids began to involuntarily close. It wasn't long before the world around me would continue to spin without any participation or even comprehension on my part.

CHAPTER 18

In my younger days the one event in life of which I had no real fear was death. I looked upon it as just another part of life, something over which I had very little say. My father would always say that when your number is up, that's it, no matter what happens. Two people could be standing side by side, both the same in almost every way when they are both hit by the same bolt of lightning. One lives one dies; one's number was up, the other's wasn't. Although death held no fear for me, I was afraid of the pain involved as well as the dying process.

When my son was born, the fear of death became an issue. Each day I went to work at the fire station I departed my home with a pause, hugging and kissing my son with unbridled devotion. Who would raise him if I were to die? Who would show him to throw a ball, hammer a nail, shave? Who would teach him right from wrong, how to stand up for himself, how to overcome shyness around girls? Moms, as great as they are, do have certain limits, especially when it comes to boys. Although a well-adjusted son of a single mom would be more likely to be more compassionate, more understanding and more caring than that of a single dad, there are certain things that very few moms would be able to fully explain to their son.

From the day he was born until his 20th birthday, I predicated my life more on preservation than on adventure. My tree of life had a very strong trunk, but very few limbs on which to venture out on. I know that sounds funny for a firefighter, but my work was different. Fighting a fire, once you learn how to do it, is not as frightening an experience as you may think. Once you are properly trained, you learn the characteristics and the dynamics, both thermal and physical of fire. With that knowledge comes confidence, and fighting a fire becomes more a challenge than intimidation; more excitement than anxiety.

I believe that if a man hasn't yet grown up, having a child will hasten the advent of his maturity. Those stupid things that you did on a dare or after a few drinks no longer happen; not because their appeal disappears, but because someone else is dependent upon your wellbeing. You suddenly are more concerned with the risks and consequences inherent in the proposal than you are the thrill and excitement that you may derive from it.

As my life proceeded and my son matured, my fear of death became less and less intense. This does not mean that I have the devil-may-care attitude of my youth, as maturity has a way of slapping you on the back of your head when you even consider doing something stupid. But the apprehensions one may have developed to fly in a plane, scuba dive, even rock climb, all in controlled environments, seem to dissolve into a manageable risk.

Having the experience that inspired me to write this book, I came to the realization that my first attitude towards death was not far off. I was here, then I wasn't. Even after returning to consciousness I was engulfed in an atmosphere of absolute serenity. The three broken bones in my face caused no pain. The massive pool of blood in which I laid was of no concern. There was no panic, no sense of dread, just peace.

In the most simplistic of terms, dying can be compared to telling your parents that while playing in the house, you broke an old vase that they really didn't like. The fear associated with the process of telling your parents is much worse than their actual reaction. The fear of the pain, suffering associated with dying is an inverse ratio to the actual event itself.

The event that could have ended my life instead saved it. The malfunction of a critical part of my body caused an even greater danger to be discovered. The diagnosis of a terminal cancer could have crushed me, but instead it gave me hope and confidence to fight on. And the fear of death is no longer a fear, but rather the ultimate peaceful rest that is earned and deserved for all the accomplishments and achievements acquired throughout your lifetime.

CHAPTER 19

It had been two days since I was informed of my A-flutter, and it seemed that the medications which they prescribed had no effect on my heartrate. Each time Sanjay had come into my room he assured me that this was not uncommon for people who had surgery similar to mine. Even though he was an expert in the field and had not pulled any punches so far in my assessment or prognosis, I had no reason not to trust him. I don't know if it was the fact that my heart was beating at 120 beats per minute, or that I had been in the hospital for over two weeks already, but my apprehension to every issue was increasing noticeably.

The arrhythmia now seemed to be causing additional complications, as the electronic blood pressure machine could not adjust the internal pulse sensor to my elevated heart rate. Sanjay was just finishing his paperwork when Dr. MacGillivray entered the room. "How are you feeling?" asked the doctor as he reached out to shake my hand. I sat up and reached out my right hand to meet and grasp his. "I'm sleeping well, but I seem to be tired all the time," I replied. "Well, your heart is working at a pace that is 50% what it should be, so being tired would seem to be a legitimate bodily response," Answered Dr. MacGillivray. "I am going to send my post-op assistant to check out why we can't get a good blood pressure off of you." I just nodded, seemingly without emotion, or so I thought. "Is there something else going on?" Asked the doctor. "Your usual upbeat, joking demeanor isn't as evident today." I didn't intend to be aloof, but maybe things were finally getting to me. "No, just getting antsy being cooped up for so long." MacGillivray smiled, "Well, I guess I can understand that," he replied. "You'll be out of here soon, even if the A-flutter doesn't subside, we can send you home with blood thinners."

I guess the injuries that I sustained in my fall must have reduced the effectiveness of my poker face, because once the Doctor said blood thinner, my face surely betrayed my inner feelings. "Is something the matter?" asked Dr. MacGillivray. I took a deep breath in through my nose and blew it out of my mouth. I did not want to sound angry or upset, but the predominant reason that I had chosen the tissue-based valve over the mechanical valve was that I did not want to be on blood thinners. "I didn't know that I was going to be required to take blood thinners, that's the reason I didn't go with the mechanical valve, I don't like using blood thinners." Dr. MacGillivray shook his head back and forth, "Don't worry, it is only temporary," he explained. "If we have to do what is called a conversion, we have to be sure that there are no blood clots in your system, otherwise they could travel to your heart. It's only a temporary situation until we get your heart beating back in a normal speed and rhythm. You will have to get a cardiologist to monitor your progress and he can also handle your INR levels as well. You might want to think about getting a cardiologist closer to home, coming in to Boston as often as you are going to have to probably would not make the most sense." I agreed by nodding my head and saying OK under my breath.

Sanjay had finished his paperwork when Dr. MacGillivray turned in his direction. "Did I leave anything out?" the senior doctor asked the fellow. "I think you covered just about everything," chuckled Sanjay. "OK then, I'll see you tomorrow, take care," said Dr. MacGillivray as he and Sanjay began to walk out of the room. "Thanks doctor, thanks Sanjay," I called out. Dr. MacGillivray had already exited the room, but Sanjay stopped and responded with "My pleasure," then turned and followed the Dr. as he too walked out of the room.

Morgan, my usual nurse was on her day off. I had become comfortable with Morgan; really, what choice did I have? After all, this 20 something year old woman has seen and bathed every inch of my body. Being my usual self, every time there was an uncomfortable moment, I would make a joke of some sort, often off color. Sometimes it would solicit a smile, other times a laugh, and then on occasion a deer in the headlights gaze. I liked Morgan, and hopefully I made her as comfortable as she made me.

This morning, an older woman, older than me in appearance anyway, wearing hospital scrubs, entered the room. She greeted me with a pleasant "good morning," and proceeded to erase the prior days writings on the white board. As she began to replace Morgan's name with her own, she informed me her name was Janice. "Hi Janice," I responded with a lift in my voice. Janice was tall and slender. Her glasses were rather large for her thin face, and her white hair was pulled back into a ponytail. Her hands, somewhat furrowed by age, had no rings, nor markings that would indicate that she ever wore rings. I did notice that she was left handed, not only by the way she wrote on the white board, but I observed that she wore a watch on her right wrist instead of her left.

"How did you sleep last night?" asked the nurse. Ever since they adjusted my medications and gave me melatonin, my sleeping pattern had a marked improvement. Although sleeping in a hospital is never a tranquil experience, compared to my prior experiences, I was now challenging Rip Van Winkle for downtime. "I slept well, thank you."

Janice was now standing at the head of my bed. She put a plastic sleeve on the probe of the electronic thermometer and inserted it into my mouth. I, having done this to countless patients, noticed the thermometer was not properly reading my temperature, I reached up and adjusted the probe in my mouth without alerting the nurse. Janice then wrapped the maroon blood pressure cuff around my upper arm and pushed the button to activate it. The cuff began to fill with air until it felt like it was stopping the circulation in my arm, then began to release a little air. Suddenly, on its own, the machine once again began to inflate for a moment, only to release the compressed air back into the atmosphere without measuring either systolic or diastolic blood pressure.

This had been happening for a few days now, but I just thought it was a malfunction of the sphygmomanometer (blood pressure machine). The manual machine seemed to work better when they used it. When I informed Janice of this it was not well received. She removed the wide maroon band and reapplied it, pushed the button and the cuff began to once again fill with air, then release, then refill, then release, all without being able to measure my blood pressure. Janice shook her head, again removed the cuff and walked out of the room. It was then that I noticed that unlike all the other nurses that I have ever seen, Janice did not have a stethoscope around her neck.

About a minute later Janice returned with a blue hosed stethoscope in her hand. She reached behind my head and took the manual black blood pressure cuff from the basket hanging on the wall. She wrapped the cuff around my right bicep, slid the bell of the stethoscope under the bottom portion and against my skin, then, repeatedly squeezed the small, black bulb to inflate the cuff. Once the cuff was full, Janice slowly turned the air release knob and the cuff slowly loosened. I could begin to feel my pulse as the pressure of the cuff decreased. Usually, after years of taking vital signs, I can estimate the approximate heart rate pretty accurately by the rhythm; however, my heart was beating so rapidly that I could not even venture a guess as to what my rate was. Julie again pumped the bulb to re-inflate, and then repeated the process.

"Well, your blood pressure is a little on the lower side, which is good," announced Julie, "but your heart rate is high." Nodding my head in agreement I told her that the Doctors had been in earlier today to discuss this situation with me. "They told me that if the heart rate did not slow down on its own that I was going to need a cardiac conversion." Julie, now at the computer documenting my vital signs, nodded her head in agreement. "That is a very common procedure after a valve replacement," she explained.

"Would it be alright if I went to take a shower and change?" I asked Julie. Being in the same flimsy johnny for 24 hours always made me feel grimy. "I'm going to get your meds now, it will take about half hour, but your breakfast just got here." I hadn't noticed, but the silver insulated box that carries the trays to the floors had just arrived outside my room. "That's OK," I replied, "Right now that food is about as bad as it's going to get." Julie smiled and told me to go ahead. "I will get you some towels and a new johnny."

I slowly climbed out of my bed and gingerly stood up straight. Taking baby steps, I walked out of the room and passed the young woman who was delivering my breakfast tray. "¡Hola! Rosa!" I greeted her with a smile. "Buenos días," replied the Hispanic woman. Although the fault was in no way hers, I always felt bad sending back a practically full tray, so I tried to make up with it by being extra friendly towards her. Because I did not know Spanish, my feeble attempts to communicate was always met with a smile. "Hasta luego" I replied as I slowly walked out of the room. "Adios" she called back, laughing at my mispronunciation of goodbye.

By the time I reached the shower room, Julie had already delivered the towels, face cloths and new johnny. I stepped into the shower room, turned on the water, and undressed. I made my way to the bathing area and sat down on the bench under the warm streams of water. I scrubbed my chest wound first, grinding the soapy facecloth against the scar as Morgan had instructed. After that I just relaxed under the therapeutic water, letting it hit my face and run down my body.

Once finished, I walked over the bench outside the shower stall, and dried off. I placed a dry towel on top of the long wooden bench and sat down. I gingerly bent over and carefully placed the hospital supplied non-slip socks on each foot. As I was bending over, I could feel the wound that traveled from just below the base of my throat down to the xiphoid process. Until that moment I had not felt any pain in the incision site since immediately following the surgery. Morgan usually slid the socks onto my feet, but being as impatient a person as I am, I had to perform the duty myself. Once complete, the discomfort disappeared and I was able to don my newly laundered, ill-fitting johnny.

The wet white towels laid atop of the soiled johnny on the shower room floor. I grasped the steel handle protruding from the heavy wooden door and pulled. I exited the room slowly, but refreshed and feeling more energy within my body than I had in any of the past few days. I slowly walked back to my room and sat in the big recliner. Since I had left, my bed had been made with crisp, new linens. The corners of the bed were tightly tucked under the mattress, and the straight creases in the pillowcase were still pronounced even though they were stretched over a foam filled pillow.

I had neglected to tell Julie that this was the first time that I had walked without an escort any further than from my bed to my bathroom. I am someone who does not feel comfortable depending on others to help me perform the most basic of tasks. Reaching the shower room was not that exhausting of a stroll. Undressing was a little more difficult than I thought it would be. Re-dressing was somewhat strenuous, but the walk back to my room took as much strength as I could muster.

As I sat and attempted to regain my vigor, I perused my room and realized that the breakfast tray had not yet been removed from my table. The coffee still being warm smelled so inviting. Instead of adding the small thimble of half and half to the brew, I used the powder creamer so as not to cool it down any further. I lifted the cup to my lips and breathed in through my nose as the warm liquid flowed into my mouth. I not only welcomed the taste, but the aroma was almost intoxicating. Coffee seemed like the only thing the kitchen could make appetizing. Once it saturated my taste buds, my eyes closed, and an air of tranquility washed over my body. I envisioned that it must almost feel like a heroin addict who just got a fix. I took a deep breath, savored the experience, and then took another sip.

As the liquid in the cup slowly diminished, so did the comfort of holding a warm cup in my hands. I put the cup down and reached for the small plastic bottle of Ensure; a dietary supplement drink which flavor brought back memories of grammar school. The taste was a mixture of the small, warm school milk carton mixed with Nestles Quick powder and a healthy dose of chalkboard dust, just to add texture. Ordinarily I would never have ingested this drink after my first experience but seeing that it was the only source of edible sustenance on the tray, I drank it.

The sound of quick paced sneakers approaching my room alerted me that Julie was returning with the morning dosage of my daily meds. The antibiotic regimen that I was taking had really begun to take its toll. Because of my broken jaw, the chance of infection within my body was more of a threat than usual, so to provide me with an extra level of protection they boosted my antibiotics.

Normally, antibiotics have no side effects on me, so I didn't think this would be any different. What I didn't know was that the antibiotics that they were giving me were not only killing all the bad bacteria in my body, they were killing all the good bacteria that keeps me healthy as well. At this point I was more susceptible to MRSA and CDIF than I had ever been. In addition, without the good bacteria in my mouth, my tongue began to develop cankers. In the past, every time I developed a canker, I would dab it with hydrogen peroxide, and it would disappear in a matter of hours.

After taking my meds, I told Julie about the canker situation and asked her for a bottle of hydrogen peroxide. Julie questioned my request saying, "Are you sure? That won't hurt your tongue?" I assured her that I do this all the time when I get a canker and it works great. Julie asked if I was going to swallow it or just wash my mouth with it. I told her that I just rinse and spit. Julie nodded with her permission and left to retrieve the hydrogen peroxide.

As Julie left, Rosa returned to retrieve my tray. "Oh, you didn't eat much, how you expect to get big and strong?" Rosa said with laughter in her voice. "Rosa, I am more than big enough already!" I chuckled. "And strong too!" she responded. Rosa then reached down and lifted the dome off the main dish. Set beneath the dome was a cup of some gray matter. It was too thin to be oatmeal and too thick to be cream of wheat. I looked up to Rosa with a perplexed look on my face and began to laugh when I saw Rosa looking at the dish with the same expression. "You want this?" I asked, doing my best to keep a straight face. Rosa, her expression now more of repulse than bewilderment, slowly shook her head side to side. "We are not allowed to," she responded. With no expression I replied, "Not allowed to eat patients food, or not allowed to eat food that would most certainly make you vomit?" As I finished my sardonic comment, a wry smile appeared on my face, disarming Rosa and creating a burst of laughter among the two of us.

"I say nothing!" laughed Rosa as she lifted the tray from the table. "Mister Bill, you always make me laugh." I smiled and held back from telling Rosa that her deliveries always made me nauseas, just so there would be no misinterpretation. Instead, I replied "Rosa, you always bring a smile to my face and a knot to my stomach." Rosa turned towards the door and carried the tray out of the room. "See you at lunchtime, have a good day," she called back as she slid the sliding door of the lunch wagon closed.

I was now relaxed, and my energy had returned from my exhausting walk. I put my head back against the soft pillow of the recliner and closed my eyes. I don't know how long my eyes were closed, but when I reopened them a small bottle of hydrogen peroxide and a cup were on my table. I took the bottle and removed the cap. There were three cankers in my mouth, and I could feel the advent of a fourth. I poured the peroxide into a cup, put it to my lips and poured the fluid into my mouth. As I began to swirl the liquid around in my mouth, I felt a reaction the likes of which I had never felt before. What I can only explain as the feeling of a forest of Christmas trees began to sprout on my tongue. I could not spit the fluid out fast enough to halt this reaction, and what were once three little annoyances in my mouth had now grown into tiny little volcanoes discharging their burning lava across my tongue.

I reached for the pink water pitcher on my nightstand and not wasting the time to pour the ice water into a cup, I tore off the cover of the pitcher and filled my mouth with a mixture of cold water and ice chips. Swishing the cold water did sooth the immediate burning sensation, but the forest of pines now adorning my tongue did not dissipate. My tongue now felt like one big, continuous cankerous sore. I instinctively attempted to remove the foreign growths from my tongue by scraping the top of my tongue against the bottom of my front teeth, which turned out to be my second bad move.

As I pushed the tip out from my mouth, I placed the middle of my tongue against the bottom of my upper front teeth. I then began to retract it applying pressure through the muscles in my mouth. What I had failed to remember was that the mandible of my jaw was far from healed, and the wires holding it in place were still damaged from my earlier ill-fated attempts to remove them. As the surface of my tongue made contact with my teeth, a shooting pain ran through my entire body. I was once told that the human body can feel pain in only one place at a time; but what they didn't mention was that if you have two injuries in the same spot, it hurts like a motherfucker!

My strategy had backfired with catastrophic results. As I pulled my tongue back in, the end of a small, rogue wire had penetrated through the protective layer of my tongue and had imbedded itself next to one of the original three cankers. No matter what I did to extricate the wire from the flesh, the barb that I had created by twisting the wire just seemed determined to remain. Bracing my body for what I was sure to be an excruciating experience, I grabbed the arms of my recliner, pushed my feet firmly against the floor and pulled my tongue back into my mouth.

My expectation of the level of discomfort that I would feel from performing this action was tremendously underestimated. Although after a very short distance I was able to pull my tongue from the clutches of the barbed wire, the pressure of my tongue against my upper teeth seemed to have dislodged the fractured bone fragment adding yet another dimension to already unbearable agony that I was already experiencing.

Shivering like I had just emerged from an ice bath, my hands were still clutched to the arms of the chair. I was sure the impressions of my fingers were embedded into the wood from my squeezing. I stopped myself from hyperventilating, holding my breath for ten seconds at a time before exhaling. When I finally regained my composure, I looked down at my johnny to see that it was soaked with a mixture of iced water, blood, sweat, and for poetic purposes, maybe even a few tears as well.

It was at this opportune moment Haley, Dr. MacGillivray's physical therapist had arrived to make her rounds. "What the hell happened to you?" she called out as the awful sight she saw. I just lifted my head and looked at her with sheer disbelief. Although I had no way of knowing for certain, I was sure that how I looked was only a fraction of how bad I felt.

As I began to relate the events which brought me to this condition, I immediately noticed that I had developed a distinguishable lisp in my speech.

I hadn't gotten far into the story when Haley stopped me from talking and instructed me to sit still. Hurriedly she left the room and quickly returned with a handful of sterile gauze pads and a container full of ice chips. She donned a pair of gloves, unwrapped a couple of four by four-inch gauze pads and wrapped them around a small pile of ice chips. "Open your mouth," Haley ordered as she approached my chair. I followed her orders to the letter, as she did not seem to be in her usual joyful disposition. She placed the gauze packet onto my tongue; the affect was twofold, as the cold from the ice both soothed the now canker ridden tongue as well as numbed the wound made by the sharp tip of the barbed wire. The gauze also was a useful addition as it absorbed the blood I was not aware of, that was flowing freely from my mouth.

"You're a goddamn mess!" exclaimed Haley as she stood in front of me, her hand on her hips and a look of incredulous disbelief on her face. "Once you stop bleeding, I am going to take you down for a shower." I looked up, took a breath and attempted to speak; "I already took a shower." Speaking with an injured mouth is difficult at best but adding to that a bundle of gauze and ice just worsened the situation by making my words unrecognizable.

"What?" Haley responded. I laughed to myself because I couldn't even discern what I was saying. I took deep breath, removed the bundle of gauze from my mouth and stated with a lisp, "I already took a shower this morning." "Oh, I didn't see Morgan at the desk, when did she take you down to the shower room?" If at this point in the day I had any misconception that this was not going to be my day, the next few minutes would extinguish any doubt. "Morgan isn't in today; Julie is my nurse. I went on my own to the shower room." Haley looked to be no more than thirty years old. Until this moment she always had a smile on her face and a cheerful lift in her voice. "You went to the shower room on your own?"

Not since Sister Catherine Higgins, my high school French teacher, had any woman's tone of voice sent a chill like I now had down my back. This cute little young lady, young enough to be my daughter put the fear of God in me. "Do you realize that just a week ago you were dead? Not sick, not injured, but dead!" She stopped for a moment; however, it was not to regain composure, but to reload. "If that isn't enough, just a few days ago Dr. MacGillivray was up to his elbows in your chest, repairing tissue in your heart so this doesn't happen again and end your life for good? You've been pretty damn lucky up till now, so you think that you are indestructible? I got news for you buddy, it doesn't matter how big you are or how strong you are; sooner or later your luck is going to give out, so you better not push it."

The lump that had formed in my throat during her diatribe made it difficult to swallow. What could I say? She was right in every way. As much as my mouth was hurting, my backside was now aching from the whooping Haley had just administered, and my pride was hurting as well. As difficult as

I have always found it in the past to just shut up and take it, this thrashing left me speechless. Like a disciplined child I lowered my head in submission, took a breath, and then used the muscles in my face to produce two of the saddest puppy dog eyes ever to have been displayed on the face of a six foot, two-hundred-and-fifty-pound man.

"Don't give me tha…" Haley could not finish her statement without laughing. "You're lucky that you're a good guy, I'll tell you. I don't put up with half the crap you have given me from my other patients." Haley was a sweetheart, there was no denying that. She did her job in a professional manner and with a great attitude. I really appreciated everything she had done for me up until this point, and after my less than spectacular morning and her admonishment, I appreciated her even more.

"I'll be right back; I'm going to get you cleaned up." Haley left the room and returned shortly with a couple of towels, a face cloth and a new johnny. The bottom part of my face which had not yet healed from my fall was now once again covered in a new layer of blood. Haley filled the pink basin with warm water and placed it on the table beside me. She then put on a pair of gloves, took the facecloth and saturated it in the warm water. She squeezed the excess water from the cloth and gently wiped the fresh blood from my face. She then rinsed out the cloth in the basin, rubbed a bar of soap into the cloth and began to wash my face, including my neck and head. The warm water felt so good, as I had not been aware that the experience (my oral injury, not Haley's scolding) had caused me to sweat profusely. She then dried me off with the towel and assisted me in changing my johnny top. When I finally saw what my frock looked like, I had an even greater understanding of Haley's concern, as the johnny that I just removed resembled a butcher's apron.

Once I was clean and my bloody top had been replaced, Haley again asked me how this all came to be. I told her about the development of the cankers, my history of curing them, and what actions I took this time. She then asked me to show her my tongue which elicited a rather sickly moan. "Let me get the PA, I think we have to get on top of this right away," advised Haley. She turned towards the door and exited the room. I remained in the chair, my mouth open and my tongue sticking out in an attempt to reduce the continued burning sensation.

Haley returned a moment later with a short, 60ish looking man. He wore glasses and sported what looked like a two-day beard. His button-down shirt was noticeably wrinkled, as well as his khaki pants. A pair of the type of shoes we once called desert boots completed the ensemble. Although he most definitely did not just walk out of the latest issue of GQ, when he greeted me with a warm "Hi, I'm Howie, how's it going?" his soft friendly voice lessened my concern of his style.

To both lessen any unnecessary use of my tongue as well as to offer some comic relief, I shrugged my shoulders and pointed to my mouth. "Let's see what we've got here," Howie said as he bent over and asked me to open my mouth and say ah. I did what Howie asked of me, and when he peered in, he acknowledged the amount of pain and discomfort I must have been in just by the physical appearance of my tongue.

"OK, what we have to do is to get you on a separate antibiotic for your mouth, and we also have to give you a topical mouthwash antiseptic to rinse with. This is something that we have to be proactive with because it could easily evolve into a more serious condition." I knew what was at stake, and the additional dangers I now faced. Julie had entered the room while my attention was directed towards Howie. The P.A. turned to the R.N. and instructed her to get a couple of items. As she turned to leave the room, he then notified Julie that he would put them into the daily medication schedule.

"It's going to take a couple of weeks to resolve this, but it should be OK" said Howie. "This is hopefully the worst it will get; if you feel that it is getting any worse, tell us right away." Howie turned and walked out the door, leaving me with the Haley who had returned to her friendly and caring demeanor. "How about we go for a walk?" asked Haley. With feelings of both energy and fear of being chastised again. I immediately answered "Yes".

Haley assisted me getting to my feet and our walk began. Over the past few days, the distance I could achieve comfortably had lengthened. This seemed to bring Haley a sense of accomplishment. By the time we got back to the room I felt that I could go around again, but Haley was hesitant about allowing me to do this. "Let's call it a day," she said. I returned to my chair and Haley placed the blood pressure cuff on my arm. She pushed the button on the machine and the cuff began to inflate with air. Once full, it automatically began to release the pressure. After a few seconds, the cuff re-inflated, and then began to deflate again. This happened two more times before Haley removed the cuff and tried another automatic cuff on my arm. Unfortunately, the results were the same.

Haley then put the manual cuff on my arm, inflated it, and slowly released the pressure. She placed her stethoscope bell under the cuff and against my skin, and let the pressure decrease more quickly. "They've had a difficult time getting my blood pressure for days now" I informed Haley. Nodding her head in agreement, Haley acknowledged my statement and removed the cuff. She put the items back in the basket from where she took it and turned back to face me. "Are you all set now, no more little walking trips on your own?" Haley joked with a smile on her face. "I will not go for another stroll without holding your hand in mine." I joked back with my lisp more evident than ever before.

Rosa then entered the room again with the full lunch tray. "Mr. Bill, here's your lunch." I smiled. The morning had seemed to melt faster than an ice cream in August. "What putrid concoction of gastronomic abomination have you got for me now?" Although I was somewhat sure that Rosa did not understand my question, she recognized my satirical tone and laughed out loud. "You like lobster?" asked Rosa. I immediately said "Yes!" with a lift in my voice. "Well," she said, "It not lobster." We both laughed at her victorious attempt at sardonic humor. "You're learning pretty fast, Rosa!" Once she stopped laughing, Rosa took a breath and said "Mr. Bill, you are too much fun." She left the tray on the table, turned and said, "I will be back soon." She once again began to laugh at her joke and left the room.

My room began to resemble Grand Central Station with all the comings and goings that were occurring that day. Julie now returned with a small pill cup and a container that looked like a small plastic butter container. Julie first gave me the pill to swallow with a little cup of water. She then opened the plastic container and instructed me to rinse my mouth with it and swallow it. The contents of the container had a consistency of motor oil. It was yellow in color and had a flavor that seemed like someone was trying to make it more palatable by adding an abundance of sugar substitute.

I followed her directions, swished and swallowed. "The reason that you swallow it is because we don't want that condition to make its way down your throat," explained Julie. Her voice had a little bit of an edge to it, which made me wonder if she had been chided by her supervisor for giving me the hydrogen peroxide. Julie began to document on the computer that she administered the medication when a diminutive, blonde, young woman whom I had never before seen entered the room like a whirlwind.

"Dr. MacGillivray asked me to come up and check out your blood pressure," the woman said before she introduced herself. "Hi, I'm Susan, his PA. Can you get in your bed please?" As I greeted her, I slowly stood up from my seated position and turned 90 degrees so that the back of my knees touched the mattress behind me. I gently sat down, laid on my right side and lifted my feet off the floor. Once I was in bed, Susan immediately grabbed my arm and slapped the blood pressure cuff to it. She hit the button on the machine and the cuff started to inflate. The compressor stopped momentarily when it felt like the cuff was fully inflated, then it kicked on again to inflate further. Once the second inflation began, Susan grabbed my opposite shoulder and pulled me sternly onto my left side. My god this little thing is strong, I thought to myself. The compressor stopped and again began to deflate for a couple of seconds when again it kicked back on. Susan immediately pushed me onto my right side with such force that I had to grab the bed rail. The compressor stopped and once again began to deflate. This time the cuff continued to deflate until it was empty, but the readout on the screen flashed "Error" in red LED's.

Susan tore the cuff off of my right arm. The Velcro which secured the cuff in place released with such volume that it sounded like someone had torn a bed sheet in half. She placed it on my left arm and the whole procedure began again, complete with the pushing and pulling that made the first adventure so enjoyable. Once the identical results presented themselves, she once again forcefully removed the cuff and replaced it with a manual blood pressure cuff. This time she began to inflate the cuff with the little black bulb on the second tube. Her hand opened and closed with such speed that it resembled the bobbin on my mother's sewing machine. Although the cuff was full, and I began to feel tingling sensations in my fingers, Susan continued to pump. I thought to myself that she is going to get a blood pressure out of me even if it kills me! By the time she ceased pumping, my arm was a long blue balloon with a small piece of pipe in the middle stuck from the pressure created in the two ends.

Susan then pushed me onto my left side and placed the bell of her stethoscope on the inside of my elbow, just below the cuff. I was quite certain that the placement had more to do with the fact that she could not have fit the blade of a butter knife under that cuff. Slowly she began to allow the air to release from the confined space that secured it. After a few seconds I was once again able to move my fingertips. I heard the young woman mutter under her breath, "There we go". After a few more seconds Susan turned the air chuck on the bulb and released the rest of the air remaining in the cuff. She looked at Julie and announced 110 over 60. She then placed the manual cuff back into the basket from where she took it, turned, and without a word left the room.

I was surprised that within a few seconds from Susan's exit, Nancy and my cousin Laura walked into my room. I must have looked spent because both their faces transitioned from smiles to bewilderment. "Are you OK?" asked Nancy. I took a deep breath, shook my head slowly and replied, "I'm not sure, but I think this little blonde girl came in here and beat the shit out of me." Julie, who was still in the room doing paperwork, let out a loud guffaw. Both Nancy and Laura looked concerned. "I'm not kidding," I rebuked. Julie turned to Nancy and explained what had just occurred. As Julie was relating the series of events, I began to laugh, as the thought suddenly occurred to me that Nancy must have thought that I was hallucinating again.

Nancy and Laura sat in the two semi-comfortable chairs beside my bed. We began to have a nice visit together when Sanjay once again returned to my room. "Hello again Mr. Arienti," he greeted me with his usual uplifting voice. "Hi Sanjay," I responded. "You know my wife Nancy, and this is my cousin, Laura." Sanjay turned to them and greeted them with a gentlemanly hello. "May I speak to you?" ask the doctor, looking at me, but gesturing at my wife and cousin; not knowing if I was comfortable with others knowing my medical situation. "Sure," I responded. "They are fine to hear whatever it is."

Sanjay began, "Well, we got some of your tests back, and Dr. MacGillivray and I both concur that we believe that it would be best to keep you in the hospital until Monday, that way we can schedule you and ready you for the cardiac conversion on your heart. Then you should be able to go home on Tuesday." I must have not looked very happy because Sanjay's usual unrelenting smile turned to a more serious expression. "Is something wrong with that?" he asked. I did not even take a moment to catch my breath; "No, I can't stay," I responded. "I have been in this place two weeks today. I am going crazy. The food is horrible, I can't stand wearing these johnnies, the bed is uncomfortable; I just want to go home."

Both Nancy and Laura saw the frustration grow inside me. I don't think they blamed me for wanting to be discharged and get back to my home, after all, me being in there made life difficult for them as well. Two weeks in the hospital has a way of diminishing someone's patience and good sense. "I want you home too, Bill, but you've gotten this far, a couple more days won't be that bad, and this way you won't have to come back in to get the procedure done." Of the two of us, it has always been me to be the imaginative one, the creative partner. Nancy had been the more grounded, practical one in the relationship. Two weeks in the hospital, although treating my physical infirmities did absolutely nothing for my impulsiveness.

Nancy continued, "I will bring you in some pajamas, I will go out and buy some tonight." I took a deep breath and sighed. Then Laura chimed in as well, "Tell us what you want to eat, we know you cannot have anything hard, but we will make you all your favorites at home and bring them in for you." I know this was not just something to placate me, as Laura and the rest of my family were all outstanding cooks. Sanjay, a look of quizzicality on his face, was awaiting my response. "Alright, fine, I will stay," I sighed with reluctance but also acquiescing to practicality. Sanjay's smile returned to his face before I even finished my sentence. "Good, I will go tell Dr. MacGillivray." He turned to Nancy and Laura, nodded to them both and said, "Nice meeting you, again," and left.

Probably from all the commotion at the time of their arrival, neither Nancy nor Laura had noticed my newly developed speech impediment up until then. "For Christ sake." Is all I had to say once things had calmed down. "Why are you talking like that?" asked Nancy. I explained the sequence of events to Nancy and Laura to see them both shaking their heads. I wasn't sure if it was pity for me or disapproval of my actions, but I was not in the mood to find out.

Noticing the untouched tray on my table, Nancy asked what they had brought me for lunch. "I don't know, I've been too busy to eat, and too afraid to see what it is." Laura lifted the cover from the entre', gasped, and returned the dome quickly. "What's the matter?" asked Nancy. "You don't want to know," replied Laura. I was again reminded of the rat scene in the movie "Whatever Happened to Baby Jane". Nancy gave me the bottle of Ensure and asked me what I wanted for lunch. For the past week or so, my entire menu of sustenance had consisted of Ensure, coffee, yogurt, ice cream and milk shakes. An occasional edible item would appear every once in a while on the tray, but it was not something that was consistent.

"What do you want for lunch?" I laid back and thought for a moment, trying to think of something that I both wanted to eat, and actually could eat. "How about clam chowder?" I suggested. Nancy responded in a positive fashion. "I will go get you some; I will be right back. Laura, do you want to come with me or stay here?" A few years earlier Laura had severely damaged her knee in a skiing accident. After a number of surgeries and years of physical therapy, she still had difficulty walking long distances. "Would you mind if I stayed here?" Laura asked politely. "No, no problem, you can keep Bill company while I'm gone." Nancy now once again turned to me. "Do you want anything else other than the clam chowder?" "No," I answered while drinking down the warm chocolate-like concoction. "OK, I will be right back," assured Nancy, and walked out the door.

As Nancy left, Laura and I began to have a philosophical discussion. I have a number of cousins, all very wonderful people, and greatly talented in their own ways. Laura, however, is the only cousin I have whom I consider to be as adroit in creative endeavors as me. To me, creativity is more than drawing, writing, playing music, cooking or sculpture. In my opinion, creativity is having the ability to think out of the box, seeing things not for what they are, but what they could be, making something everyone else thought trash into a work of art, and being able to put your thoughts into words, music, paint, charcoal, food or whatever your medium, and literally reach in and touch the audience's soul with your creation. Passion is the life sustaining force for creativity, for without passion, creativity would just shrivel up and die on the vine. I know few people in this world with the passion of my cousin Laura.

"So, how are you feeling?" she asked, knowing that I would most likely be more open with her alone than with Nancy present. "I'm OK, just really tired." Laura adjusted her chair, bringing it a little closer, and began to speak. "You know Billy, you are the most positive, must uplifting person I know. When everyone else is falling apart, you are the one who is calm, and able to hold things together. Everybody looks to you for strength, and you always come through." Her words were like a comforting suave on a burning wound. "I just do what I can Laura, it's just who I am, I don't try to be like that, it just happens on its own."

"Billy, I'm going to be honest with you, I don't know if anyone else in this family could go through what you did. Even with Charlie, he told me some of the things you said to him, and how those things made him feel. The times when I call you up to ask how Charlie is doing, I am so sad when I dial your number, but by the time I get off the phone with you, I always feel so much better, so alive, just from your outlook on things. Billy, if anyone can survive this thing it's you; I have no doubt."

I smiled and shook my head, "To be honest with you Laura, it is not me who is going to get through this, it is us who will get through it, together. Without your visits and words, as well as everyone else in this family's good wishes and thoughts, my row would be much harder to hoe. Thank you Laura, you have no idea how much I appreciate what you just said.

"Well, have I got a story for you!" Laura continued, and related an experience she just had where she accidently met the Dali Llama of Thailand while visiting a Thai Temple in southern Massachusetts. He was so taken by her and the fudge she had made to offer as a gift that he invited her back the next day for a cookout the people of that temple were holding in his honor.

As I said earlier, Laura is a very passionate person, and often her passion gets her involved into adventures that are just remarkable. Tom, Laura's husband is a quieter person who seems to not only enjoy the experiences his wife creates, but revels in them. Although less boisterous than Laura, he is quite an engaging and intelligent man. It is not uncommon for an exuberant Laura to tell of a situation the two encountered, and how they managed to experience something new or encounter someone of notoriety in a real-life situation. While she is doing this, Tommy usually injects even more life into the story with commentary, facial expressions and an occasional contradiction.

Before long, Nancy returned with a large container of clam chowder. "I had to walk a mile up the street to get this! Nobody around here has clam chowder, imagine, in the middle of Boston and you can't find a restaurant that has take-out clam chowder!"

Nancy placed the container on the hospital table and removed the cover. She tore open a small plastic bag of oyster crackers and poured them into the chowder. I then took the container of soup along with a soup plastic soup spoon and tasted the chowder. Because Nancy had made such an effort to find and retrieve the meal, I did not have the heart to tell her just how bad it tasted. I slowly ate half of the contents in the container and placed the rest of it back on the table. "I will save the rest for later." I told Nancy. "Thank you, it was delicious." I am quite sure that Nancy knew I was lying but did not let on.

Rosa entered the room with her ever present smile to take my tray back to the kitchen. "Oh, looks like you had something special brought in," Rosa joked. "Shhh, be quiet, I got friends on the outside." I responded to Rosa's comment. Rosa pulled the table back, took the tray in her hands, leaving the half full container of chowder on the table, and left the room.

My face must still have had the look of disgust or dejection on it as I sat up in bed. I had been admitted on April sixth, and her it was, April twenty-first, and now I had another seven days to spend in here. "Bill, you got through this much, you can get through a few more days," consoled Nancy.

Until this point, I had a pretty positive outlook. I considered myself fortunate that all these events occurred just to keep me alive; for what reason, I had no idea. I was more grateful than I was despondent, but facing yet another week in the hospital was just too much more than I could take. "Billy, would you rather go home, have something go wrong and then have to spend another three weeks in here?" explained Laura. I hated the fact that she made sense at I time that I would have preferred to be irrational.

Once I accepted the news, although I was not happy with it, I was able to relax. I put my head back on the pillow and lowered the top part of the bed. "Maybe we should go," said Nancy. "We'll let you get some rest." Laura took my hand in hers and kissed my cheek. "Remember what I told you," she said as she turned to walk out of the room. Nancy kissed my lips, said I love you, and said "I'll bring in some pajamas for you tomorrow."

Nancy turned and joined Laura in the hallway, and the two of them made their way to the exit. I laid my head back and noticed it was now almost 4 o'clock, I closed my eyes and thought to myself, "What a day!"

CHAPTER 20

When we think of philosophers, a number of names immediately come to mind. Aristotle, Socrates, Confucius, Nietzsche and so on. Each spoke and wrote on their views of life, government, politics, existential beliefs, and even everyday situations. Philosophers seem to be fewer and fewer today. Maybe Noam Chomsky and Simon Blackburn are two of a number of today's philosophers, but I believe that philosophy has had a rebirth, not through the traditional means, but by people who offer reasonable explanations of the world around us. These people are not college professors or logicians, although there are still a number of philosophers in these careers. No, today the most listened to philosophers are seen on stage, screen and television. They write books and appear on talk shows. They are not commonly known as philosophers, but by a more comfortable name, a name that is less imposing. Today's philosopher is known as the comedian.

Who better put into words the workings of our society than the late George Carlin? Carlin, in the matter of minutes, could explain virtually every aspect of society today and make you laugh uncontrollably as he did it. He studied people and did so for many years. His studies provided him with insights and an understanding of human beings like few others. His observation that "When we are born in to this world we are given a ticket to a freak show. When you are born in the United States, you are given a ticket in the front row", kind of sums up his view on both life in generalities and specifics.

Carlin even spoke of coincidence and irony, and how the two relate to each other. "Irony deals with opposites; it has nothing to do with coincidence. If two baseball players from the same hometown, on different teams, receive the same uniform number, it is not ironic. It is a coincidence. If Barry Bonds attains lifetime statistics identical to his father's, it will not be ironic. It will be a coincidence. Irony is "a state of affairs that is the reverse of what was to be expected; a result opposite to and in mockery of the appropriate result." For instance: a diabetic, on his way to buy insulin, is killed by a runaway truck. He is the victim of an accident. If the truck was delivering sugar, he is the victim of an oddly poetic coincidence. But if the truck was delivering insulin, ah! Then he is the victim of an irony. If a Kurd, after surviving bloody battle with Saddam Hussein's army and a long, difficult escape through the mountains, is crushed and killed by a parachute drop of humanitarian aid that, my friend, is irony writ large. Darryl Stingley, the pro football player, was paralyzed after a brutal hit by Jack Tatum. Now Darryl Stingley's son plays football, and if the son should become paralyzed while playing, it will not be ironic. It will be coincidental. If Darryl Stingley's son paralyzes someone else, that will be closer to ironic. If he paralyzes Jack Tatum's son, and that will be precisely ironic."

He was a brilliant man who made us laugh at ourselves without insult or degradation. With all due honor and respect to Socrates, Aristotle and Plato, your thoughts and writings will last forever, but George Carlin remains my most favorite philosopher of all times.

As Carlin was to society, Lewis Black is to politics. Black's approach differs from Carlin in many ways, most of all, delivery. Carlin would explain things that resembled a cross between your Grandfather who is teetering on the edge of senility and Mr. Rogers. Conversely, Lewis Black has a delivery more like Howard Beale in the movie Network and Michael Douglas in Falling Down. He's had enough and he is going to make sure that you hear every bit of it. His humor is dark and acerbic. He is loud and sometimes obnoxious. I believe that he is truly an idealist who has been encapsulated by the cynicism that only disappointment and repression can create. He constantly uses hand gestures as he works himself into a full lather before he pauses to take in an elongated breath.

Bill Maher is much like Lewis Black as they are both highly educated, well versed in history and government and are not afraid to state their views of what is going on around us. Their humor and deliveries are legendary, and after seeing them in person, people leave the theater with laughter induced belly pains as well as a better, logical and reasonable understanding of the follies of our nation. They give us examples of ridiculous historical events to create a situational topic, then they explain how the politicians of today are repeating those same stupid events; who are causing them; and why they are doing it. Finally, they offer you options on how to fight it or learn how to fight it harder.

I believe that Lewis Black's most poignant offering concerning

Congressional cooperation is, "The people we elect aren't bipartisan. The American public is bipartisan". His insight on governmental aid is "I am angry that the Democrats don't have the ability to explain to Republicans that we should be able to feed people in this country, and that is not socialism." Black even puts paying taxes into a realistic realm, "It's a privilege to pay taxes. Yeah! It's not a political question, folks. We have to pay for stuff."

In today's society, we have a myriad of outlets to direct our attention away from the daily mundane duties of life. Television, social media, hobbies and many more. Today, philosophy and philosophers are no longer the compelling attraction they once were when man lacked the knowledge and understanding of the world around them. These men replaced ignorance with reason; fear with understanding and created a level of comfort so that the masses could live their lives without the overwhelming fear of the unknown pressing down on them.

Philosophers of today no longer offer reason, but instead offer a diversion to release tension, stress, exhaustion, as well as providing laughter, insight, self-reflection and an opportunity to not take ourselves so seriously. Personally, I believe that today's philosophers are just as important as they were in 400 B.C.

CHAPTER 21

Whoever said no news is good news never spent over two weeks in the hospital. Each morning upon their visits, I would beg Dr. MacGillivray and Sanjay to release me. Thursday it did no good. Friday's results were just the same as Thursday's. I've always been a person who had seen the glass half full, but after 16 days in the hospital I was ready to smash that glass against the wall.

Because I was on blood thinners, I had not been allowed to shave with a razor. With sixteen days of growth on my face, I felt quite sloppy. It seemed every time I saw my reflection in the mirror with a start of a full beard running down my neck, I began to resemble one of the back woods men in the movie Deliverance. I asked Morgan for a razor to no avail. "You have to get an electric shaver," explained Morgan. "If you cut yourself while taking blood thinners it could be a real problem." After my tongue debacle, her words re-enforced the memory of my last unsuccessful attempt at performing self-hygiene.

Having had an electric razor years earlier, I was not impressed with their performance. Nancy had bought me one for a Christmas gift, and I used it for a few weeks, but always had to follow up with a traditional razor to insure a clean shave. I knew that it would be foolhardy to go against Morgan's orders, so I began to research on line what types of electric razor was best for my type of beard.

Once I determined what I thought would work best, I called Nancy and asked her to pick one up for me. I had already checked availability at the department store near my house, and they had the model in stock. Nancy explained how she had to go into work that morning and was not sure that she would be able to get to the store before coming in.

Mark was near Nancy while I was on the phone. He asked Nancy if he could talk to me and she gave him the phone. "Hi Dad, how are you feeling?" Mark's voice sounded somewhat anxious. He had been studying hard at college as well as working part time at South Shore Hospital. I was sure that my illness and extended hospital stay was not conducive to a positive study environment, so I did not want Mark to feel pressured to come into the Mass General. "I'm doing ok," I assured Mark. "What's happening in school and at work?" Mark informed me that everything was status quo, nothing new, nothing exciting. "Do you need anything?" I knew that he felt somewhat helpless, and I know how much I hate having that feeling; so, I figured that I could make us both feel better. "Is there any way that you could get to Target sometime today?" Mark's voice perked up. "Sure, what do you want?" I could hear a little excitement in his voice within his response. I told him about the razor that I needed, gave him the model number and price. I then told him to get the money from his mother. "Don't worry Dad, I got it." A smile appeared on my face with his comment. My son was growing up and showing responsibility. Throughout this whole ordeal, the fall, the surgery, the hospital stay, I can say, without reservation, this was the best moment I had experienced in over two weeks, and actually, probably a lot longer.

When I hung up, Morgan announced that it was time for my walk and shower. The young nurse had heard about my recent solo stroll and was not about to let me do that again. I climbed out of bed and began to take a few steps towards Morgan. "Do you want to try going up stairs today?" She asked. I had been feeling myself getting stronger each day along with an increased level of stamina. "Let's give it a shot," I replied. Morgan grabbed the back of my elbow and we began our stroll; down the hallway, take a right at the gym, down the hallway and then the challenge, the stairs.

Morgan opened the door to the exit door, and we entered the stairway. "How do you feel?" she asked. "I can do this," I stated, and began my trek up the stairs. The first two step were difficult, as my legs had barely been utilized for weeks now. The slow pace soon quickened as I walked up one flight of stairs and began the second. Morgan called for me to stop and return to the starting point. Walking down the stairs, like always, was much easier and although I was not running, I was walking at a speed which I thought was brisk.

"Wow, I'm impressed!" praised Morgan as I reached the stair landing. "Can you make it back to the room?" I smiled and responded, "I can, can you?" Morgan smiled. "OK wise guy, let's hit the showers." Together we continued our walk down the hallway, past my room, and on to the shower room. I entered the room and sat down on the changing bench. Morgan informed me that she was going back to the room to get a clean pair of my pajamas and towels. "Do you need help taking a shower?" I shook my head, "Nah," I said, "I'm fine." I began to disrobe as Morgan closed the door. Once undressed I took a new bar of soap and turned the shower onto hot water. Once the water reached a comfortable temperature I stepped under the stream and scrubbed my wound, then washed the rest of my body. After the extended walk I thought I would be exhausted, but instead I felt exhilarated.

I turned the shower control to off and left the shower area. On the changing bench sat my pajamas, new hospital socks and towels. Beside that pile was a pink basin containing my tooth brush, tooth paste and deodorant. I dried off, groomed and then dressed myself. The only difficulty I had was donning a new pair of socks, but Morgan helped me with that. Once done, Morgan carried my toiletries and we finished our walk as we returned to my room.

Once I sat down in the recliner, I took a deep breath and blew it out. I was not out of breath, I was not tired, I felt I could do another lap around the floor but thought it would be best to stay put. I had not noticed, but Rosa had left the morning meal on my table while I was on my excursion. Seeing Rosa was one of the highlights of my day. She was always ready to spend a few extra minutes joking with me and sharing a story or two. I looked at the tray and saw a bottle of Ensure, a cup of coffee, creamer, sugar, oatmeal, milk and a container of maple syrup. I then looked under the dome and saw a plate of reconstituted French toast. Although I had eaten the French toast before, it's less than appetizing appearance caused me to pass on it that morning. I used the syrup for the oatmeal and drank the Ensure and coffee.

The volume of the television was barely audible when I turned it on. I changed the channel to CNN and increased the volume. The big story was how a ship carrying 500 refugees sank in the Mediterranean with only 50 survivors. A tragedy of extreme proportion, as innocent people just trying to get their families away from the death and destruction of war are killed in their efforts. The images shown on the television were heartbreaking, as men, women and children washed up on the shore. I watched with a lump in my throat. How bad must their home be to take such a risk to bring your family to safety? Of all the things in my life that I cannot understand, and there are many, the one thing that most confuses me is how man can be so inhuman to man.

Towards the end of the report Rosa entered the room. "Mister Bill, I missed you earlier!" Her cheerful greeting was exactly what I needed at that very moment. I quickly turned my head and answered her greeting with one of my own. "Good morning gorgeous!" I responded with a smile on my face. Rosas smile grew brighter. "Oh, I'm not gorgeous, I'm just beautiful," she giggled. Her comeback was great, but her giggle is what brought me to laughter. As Rosa picked up the tray, she stopped. "My, those are stylish pajamas you have on," she observed. "Thank you," I replied. "I have a date with the woman in room 822 in fifteen minutes and I wanted to look nice." Rosa laughed, "Oh, she will be quite impressed!" From our time together and conversations, Rosa had become quite acclimated to my sense of humor.

Rosa then left with her usual laughter. I had never appreciated her visit more than that day as she took my mind off of the news story I had just viewed. When I looked back up to the television, there was another story in the 24-hour news cycle our world has become. I changed the station to a more mindless program, watching people dress up in outlandish costumes in an attempt to get money, CSPAN.

"Bill, Bill, sorry to wake you," whispered Morgan. "I have your medication." Rolling my head in the pillow, I began to return back to consciousness. I slowly opened my eyes but found it difficult from the buildup of small particles of dried tears in the corner of my eyes. When I was finally able to open my eyes, I saw Nancy sitting in the chair beside me. Morgan was standing next to my bed with a scanning gun in her hand to scan my bracelet before administering the medication. I extended my arm towards Morgan who shined the guns red light onto the bar code until it beeped, then handed me a small plastic cup with a collection of pills. I swallowed the pills, then drank a cup of water to wash them down. A small container with a sealed cover was then given to me by Morgan, along with the instructions, "rinse your mouth with this and swallow." I opened the container, poured the thick liquid into my mouth, rinsed for a few seconds and swallowed. The liquid did not taste bad, almost like an unsweetened melted vanilla ice cream.

I greeted Nancy as she rose from the chair to kiss me. I lifted my head as she bent down, meeting somewhere in the middle, our lips met, and a rush of comfort mixed with excitement rushed through my body. "How are you doing?" asked Nancy, now standing next to my bed holding my right hand. "I'm OK," I responded as I reclined my head back onto the pillow, then pressing the button on the rail of the bed to raise the head of the bed.

Nancy reached down into her bag and pulled out a small box. "Mark bought you the electric razor you asked for." She handed me the box, and I took it like an eight-year-old grasping a birthday gift. It was the exact razor for which I had asked. I opened the box, removed the packing Styrofoam and stripped off the plastic bag. I was so looking forward to removing the itchy growth on my face and was ready to jump out of bed to do so. I unfolded the directions and read, much to my despair, "IMPORTANT: Before first use, the razor must be charged for at least six hours." It was like running 99 yards and getting tackled on the one-yard line.

"Well, at least I have something to look forward to tonight," I said to Nancy, trying to make lemonade out of lemons. Again, Nancy reached down into her bag and removed a large red cup. Here is a black and white Fribble for you, (a Fribble is a milkshake made by the Friendly Ice Cream Co.). She tore the paper off of the long plastic straw and inserted it into the top perpendicular slit on the top of the red cup. Nancy wrapped the cup in a napkin and gave it to me to enjoy; it was delicious.

As we sat there talking, Sanjay entered the room again. "Hello Mr. Arienti." "Sanjay!" I said, in a very upbeat tone, "How are you?" It is amazing how sugar and chocolate can raise the spirits of just about anyone. "I am fine, but what is important is how are you?" Sanjay turned and looked at Nancy, "Hello Mrs. Arienti, how is he doing today?" Nancy smiled, "He seems to be doing well," responded Nancy. "I'm fine," I said. "Well, we heard about your walk earlier today, and Dr. MacGillivray decided that you can be released tomorrow. Suddenly it was like the clouds above parted and gave view to the heavens above. I heard the chorus of angelic harmony permeating the entire hospital. I felt the warmth of the first sunbeam of the day heating my face after a cold night. OK, so I'm exaggerating, but after almost three weeks in the hospital, I think I'm entitled.

Sanjay continued to tell me about the practices and procedures that I will have to abide by while I am home. What medications I will have to remain on, what doctors I will have to see, what I can do, what I cannot do, what I could do, what I shouldn't do. By the time he was finished my head was swimming. Nancy, a stickler for details, was trying to remember each and every order. Sanjay finally reached the end of the release orders with the phrase, "You don't have to remember this, we will give you all the information in a discharge report. "OK, that sounds good," I answered. "Can I make one small recommendation to you?" I asked Sanjay. Sanjay smiled and responded in the affirmative. "Just for kicks, next person you give the discharge instructions to, you might want to start off with the ...you don't have to remember this part..." Sanjay and Nancy both laughed. "Dr. MacGillivray will be down to see you before you leave," said Sanjay, and he was off.

"Well, that's good news!" exclaimed Nancy." Zeus will go crazy when he sees you." My smile must have reached from ear to ear as Nancy observed, "I haven't seen you this happy in a long time." I had to admit, I was bordering on ecstasy with the news. I thought back, April 6th until April 24th, 18 days in the hospital; it was something that I never imagined happening to me. "So, I guess you heard the good news!" Haley greeted me as she walked in the door as Morgan followed in right behind. "Feeling pretty good, are you?" asked Haley. I had passed "good" when Nancy brought in the razor, this feeling was only surpassed with the birth of my son. "I can't wait to go, not that you haven't been fantastic, because both of you are." Haley walked to the foot of the bed and began to address Nancy and me. "There are some things that you need to do..." "Hold on," I interrupted. "Is everything that you are about to tell me going to be on my discharge report?" Haley looked at me somewhat confused, "Yeah, why?" Nancy smiled as I began, "Well, not for nothing, but next time, you might want to lead with that little nugget of information." Nancy chuckled, "Sanjay just gave us a whole litany of instructions that we were both trying to remember, and at the end he told us it all would be in the discharge report."

Haley took the recommendation well, and began again, "This will all be in the discharge report, so don't worry if you forget anything…." Nancy, Morgan and I all smiled with Haley's amended version of instructions. "Mr. Bill!" In all the excitement, I had not noticed that Rosa had pulled the metal food container outside my door. "Rosa, I'm going home tomorrow!" I called out to her. Rosa smiled at the good news, "Congratulations," she wished with a Hispanic accent. As she placed the tray on the table, Rosa asked "How did your date go this morning?" chuckling her way through the question. "Oh, I got stood up," I returned. "She went into a coma; it doesn't look good for her." Rosa's smile turned to a look of deep concern, "Oh, that's terrible," she said with genuine concern dripping from her words. "I'm only kidding Rosa," I laughed. Rosa's smile returned. "She died." Rosa's look of concern turned to one of horror. "I'm kidding, I'm kidding, there was no date, it was all a big joke," I could hardly contain my laughter. Rosa looked into my eyes with a stern look, "Mr. Bill, that is not funny," she admonished, but the second she put the tray down she began laughing. "You terrible," she said as the slapped my shoulder. "I'm going to miss you!" I smiled back at her. "I'm going to miss you too Rosa, but I'm not going to miss this stuff you serve me every day for food!" Rosa looked at me sheepishly, "I don't blame you," A smile grew back on her face as she left the room, "See you later on," she said as she left the room.

"What was that all about?" asked Nancy once Rosa was gone. "Oh, it was just an ongoing joke between the two of us." Nancy shook her head side to side. After over 30 years together she knew that I held very few things sacred when it came to making jokes. She had learned not to take anything seriously with me which always maintained a level of mystery and excitement between us.

When we first met, Nancy was beautiful, and as the years went by her beauty only intensified. Although very intelligent, she was somewhat naïve when it came to sarcasm and caustic humor. My sense of humor played perfectly into her innocence; sometimes bordering on mean, but never in a hurtful way, (although Nancy may tend to disagree). In our time together Nancy had sharpened her wit as well. Although it doesn't happen too often, she has pulled a few fast ones on me as well.

Haley had been standing in the background chatting with Morgan during my discussion with Rosa and Nancy. Once Rosa left, and Nancy was satisfied with my explanation, Haley approached me and asked if I was up for another jaunt around the floor. With the rush of energy coursing through my body from the good news, I felt like I could jog around the floor. "Most definitely," I shot back with exhilaration. I slid my legs to the right side of the bed and sat up before Haley had a chance to say hold on. My feet, adorned in non-slip hospital stockings, were already on the floor by the time she took my hand.

We walked out of the room and down the hall. My gate, at least to me, seemed faster and more energetic. The welcomed news of being discharged put a little giddy-up in my get-go. "Well, I guess you are doing better," remarked Haley. "Let's go around the nurse's station and back to the room." As we made the final turn back towards my room, I saw Dr. MacGillivray heading towards my room from the other direction. "Looking pretty good there!" commented the doctor. He stayed in the hallway as I approached, watching my performance. When I reached the room, we walked in together. Nancy had changed her seat from the soft recliner to the hospital visitor chair, leaving the chair vacant for me. I sat down, took a face cloth and wiped the sweat from my forehead.

"Well, I guess you heard the news already," said Dr. MacGillivray. I could feel the smile on my face growing larger by the second. "You have no idea how great those words sound in my ears," I responded. "I've been in here almost three weeks; I am dying to go home." The doctor nodded his head in agreement, "I don't blame you one bit. I believe Sanjay told you all the information that you need to know for your home care; do you have any questions for me?" I looked at Nancy in such a way to ask her if she had any questions and did not receive a response. "I'm just going to need a couple of letters for work, Doctor," was my request. Dr. MacGillivray smiled and assured me not to worry, everything was already in motion.

The doctor then began to approach me to shake my hand. Seeing his intention, I pressed my hands onto the arms of the chair and stood up. "You don't have to get up," observed the doctor. "To do what I want to do I have to," I replied. I took two steps towards him and hugged him like I would a long-lost brother. "Thank you, Doctor, thank you so much for everything that you have done for me." The Doctor hugged me back and responded, "No, it is me that should be thanking you for all that you have done; you have no idea how much I respect you and the job you do." The two of us released our embrace, I sat down, and he started walking towards the door. "I will see you in a few weeks," he said in an assuring voice. "Until then take it easy." Nodding my head, I agreed to his request. "Take care of yourself," I called out as he left the room. "What a nice guy he is," said Nancy. I could not have agreed with her any more.

CHAPTER 22

The most intelligent person in this world at the moment of birth knew absolutely nothing. It is at this moment in time that every person in the world, unless a previously recognized pre-natal condition was diagnosed, is equal in mind, knowledge and understanding of the world around us. This very moment should be celebrated, because for the rest of life, family, friends and society will change the way each infant will view the world as well as those around them.

It has been said that no one is born a racist or a bigot. These, as well as other hateful traits are not innate, not genetically inherited, but learned; maybe beginning even before they leave the hospital. Whether it is overt or covert, demonstrated or latent, extreme or minimal, every person has a level of racism in their mind. Stating that you treat everyone the same, or you treat people just the way you are treated, and make a conscious effort to substantiate these claims, subconsciously there are powers that you have no idea are inside you that prove differently. This is not specific to one race or culture; actually, it is quite to the contrary. I have seen studies that show our society even causes a level of self-resentment towards a person's own race. The studies are both fascinating as well as heartbreaking, and once seen will stay with you for a long time.

A number of children, both black and white were put into a room together to play. They all played well together and got along quite well. After about a half hour of play, one child at a time was separated from the others and brought to a different room. An adult sat across a table from the child, chatted and made them comfortable. Once the two were acquainted, the adult presented the child with two dolls, a black one and a white one. The child was allowed to play with the dolls for a few minutes and name them. The adult then asked the child if she liked both dolls, or one more than the other. Most of the children did not prefer one doll over the other; but when asked which doll is prettier (mind you both dolls were identical with the exception of their color). The children overwhelmingly chose the white doll as prettier than the black doll. The children were then asked which doll was a good doll and which doll was a bad doll. Again, consistent with the first experiment, the children overwhelmingly chose the white doll as the good doll, and the black doll as the bad doll.

Although the experiment went on to show further biases, this part of the exercise revealed somewhat of a troubling current in our culture. Not only are white children directed towards a discriminatory opinion of Black Americans, society itself has instilled the same level of discrimination of Black Americans by Black American children. Now the question begs to be asked, how can it be honestly said that we all have the same starting point in life when in our most formative years one of us has a societal influenced attitude of self-loathing?

What further validates these feelings of inequality is what we introduce our children to in their education. We want to instill a level of national pride in our children, and mandate that every student takes at least one year of American History. For some reason or other, we do not believe our children are intelligent or emotionally stable enough to learn of our countries less than flattering portions of history. Publisher McGraw-Hill as late as 2010 in their American History textbook, slavery was categorized as "affordable labor." In the history textbooks in Virginia, until the 1970's, Francis B. Simkins, Spotswood H. Jones, and Sidman P. Poole claimed that Robert E. Lee freed all the slaves before the beginning of the Civil War, and slaves and slave owners enjoyed a good working relationship. How can we expect Black America to hold White America in high regard when White America has devalued the very worth and existence of the tragic history of Black America? Even today, our children learn about Columbus, but are not exposed to how he enslaved the indigenous people of San Salvador and the Bahamas. They are taught about the Pilgrims, but are not taught how those same Pilgrims slaughtered whole tribal colonies of the Native Americans to expand their own settlement. They are introduced to Andrew Jackson and the battle of New Orleans, but are not informed of his hatred towards the Native Americans and his actions of encampment and attempted genocide of these proud people. Lessons are presented on how we are a nation of laws, and we are innocent until proven guilty, yet few high school students in the United States have been made aware of the Japanese Americans internment camps during World War II when innocent people were taken from their own homes and made to live in a caged city just because during a war with Japan, their ancestors happened to be Japanese.

Ignorance begets fear, fear begets hatred, hatred begets bigotry. We try to protect our children from the bad things in life, like bigotry. But if children are not taught from the very earliest days about different cultures, different people, different religions, the vacuum created from the absence of knowledge will filled with hatred and bigotry. We, as a society and culture must recognize that after the true Americans, the Native Americans, we are a melting pot of eclectic cultures and beginnings. No group of people are any better than any other group of people. No nationality, no color, no point of origin and no religion that promotes love and acceptance is any better than any other of their counterparts.

Bigots are made, not born. Americans are born, not made, (unless you are an immigrant). We must strive to make America free of hate, bigotry, ignorance, intolerance, and discrimination against anyone and everyone. Before you comment anything about anyone because of their demographic, stop and think of the challenges that person had to overcome, the hatred that person has already faced, the discrimination that person has experienced. Think about the head start, no matter how small that you might have had over this person from birth. Put yourself, or better yet, put a loved one in the position of this person. You may have a different outlook and understanding than you had just a moment before.

CHAPTER 23

The tiny green light on the blue electric razor was blinking on and off, notifying me that the razor was fully charged and ready for use. Even though I had not slept well the night before, I was not cranky or the least bit tired. I was going home. I had spent over two weeks in the hospital, and I could not tolerate another day more. I had been poked, prodded, stuck, sliced, eviscerated, drugged, shaved, wired and starved, but it all didn't matter now, I was going home.

At 6:30, Denise, my nurse from the night before entered my room to take my vitals and administer my morning dosage of pharmaceuticals. "I see today is a big day for you!" said Denise with the sound of excitement in her voice. She must have known by the smile on my face that I had been waiting for? My poker face had betrayed me yet again, but with the way I was feeling, I didn't care. "I can't wait!" I answered, as I poured the small cup of pills in my mouth and sipped a little water to help them slide down. Next came the mouthwash for my tongue. "Is it alright if I get washed up?" I asked Denise. I had no intention of taking another solo stroll down to the shower room; I just intended to wash up in my own bathroom this morning. "Sure, I'll go get you some towels. Denise quickly left and returned to the room with a stack of clean towels and face cloths. Upon her return, I climbed out of bed and stood on my feet. I walked into the bathroom with my new razor, toothbrush, toothpaste, deodorant, soap and towels. When I reached the mirror, I could see just how Denise was able to determine that I was being discharged. My eyes were brighter, my wired smile was bigger, and my posture was straight and true. I was going home!

I pushed up a button on the side of the electric razor which allowed a hair clipper to pop up. I began to drag the clippers over my bearded face and trace a path through the hair. The clippers were both cutting and pulling the short hairs out of my face which stung, but the pain was somewhat pleasurable seeing immediate results in the mirror. I trained the razor all over the bottom of my face and neck except for a mustache and goatee, partly because I wanted to cover up my unhealed wounds, and I also thought it looked pretty good.

Once all the longer hair was gone, I cleaned out the clippers and began to use the rotary blades on my face. Little by little the forest that had sprouted on my face was being clear cut. I then washed my face and gave myself a sponge bath in the lavatory. Finally, I brushed my teeth, put on a new set of johnnies and felt absolutely refreshed. I returned to my room after I discarded the used toothbrush, toothpaste, and soap, but retaining the new razor and deodorant in a small vomit basin. I felt great sitting up in the recliner.

I turned the TV on and watched the highlights of the previous night's Red Sox game. Although I tried to watch the game live last night, the meds got the best of me and after the third inning, I was out. Baseball in Boston is difficult in the spring because the early spring temperatures usually do not lend themselves to the summer game. The silver lining of this fact is that Boston is a cold weather team, and warm climate teams have a more difficult time up here.

Denise returned to the room carrying a handful of assorted sterile items, including a roll of white tape hanging off her left pinky finger. She placed all the items on the hospital table and maneuvered her way to a spot next to me. "How about we take your IV out before you go home," said the young nurse with a voice resembling that of Disney's Snow White. I extended my right arm to give her easy access. Denise held my arm down and in a quick motion tore from my skin the clear tape that held the plastic tube in its place.

She then placed a small stack of gauze pads on top of the point where the tube entered my skin and pressed down as she pulled the tube from my vein. "Can you push down on this for a moment?" she asked me. My fingers replaced hers on top of the stack of gauze and I continued to apply pressure. Denise gathered all the papers and medical waste from the table, wrapped it all up in one hand, then with her other hand, turned the glove on the first hand inside-out, bagging hazardous trash in her blue rubber glove. She then removed her other glove and discarded everything in the red hazardous waste container. She then donned another set of gloves and returned to my side. Denise took a couple of the small gauze pads off the top of the stack and wrapped a long piece of tape across my skin and over the gauze. "Let me just get a face cloth and clean you up a little and you will be almost ready to go."

Denise again left the room and my attention once again was captured by the Red Sox highlights, until I felt a drip on my leg. I looked down to see that my johnny was saturated with blood as the IV wound did not adequately clot. The excess of blood had rendered the adhesive on the medical tape useless. I placed my left index and middle fingers on the top of the gauze stack and applied pressure, while simultaneously raising my right arm over my head. Denise had not realized that my regular medication contained a blood thinning drug as well.

Denise returned a few moments later and was incredulous at the scene which appeared before her. She ran to the bed and quickly put on a clean pair of gloves, then took my arm in her hands. She instructed me to let go of the wound, as she replaced my hand with hers. She squeezed tightly and held my arm straight up. I then surveyed my body to see that my side, my arm and my thigh were all covered with blood. "I guess your blood thinner is working pretty good," Denise muttered, as much to inform me as to break the tension in the room.

A few minutes later Denise once again asked me to hold the wound again as she retrieved more gauze, tape and a new facecloth. I sat there, right hand in the air, left hand squeezing my forearm. Denise hurriedly ran back into the room and began to wash my arm with a moist facecloth. She then quickly replaced the old stack of gauze with a new stack and continued pressure. Finally, she wrapped the gauze and my arm tightly with another piece of tape, wrapping it around the circumference of my forearm. "You're a mess!" announced Denise. "If I had a nickel for every time I heard that, I would be a rich man!" was my retort. "Looks like I am going to need that shower now," I chuckled. "Would you mind helping me walk down the hall to the shower room?" Denise was more than pleased to lend me a hand, and together we made our way down the hallway. "Can you do this by yourself?" asked Denise. I assured her that by now I was quite adept at personal hygiene and would be fine. "I will drop off some towels, facecloths and a new set of johnnies." I closed the door separating the changing room from the hallway and entered the shower room, turning it on to allow the warm water to reach the showerhead.

As I walked out of the shower room, Denise was just dropping off the clean linens. "Just leave the dirty johnny on the floor when you finish," directed Denise before she closed the door granting me my privacy. I placed a towel on the top of a plastic chair and placed it under the shower stream. I then sat on the chair and allowed the streams of water shower over me in a deluge of warmth. I looked down to see that the blood had rinsed from my body and dripped to the shower floor, causing a pink tinge to the residual water as it waited to make its way down the drain. I breathed in through my nose and out through my mouth, deep breaths. Any stress that remained in my body was quickly dissipating, and joining the shower water and blood flowing down the drain.

The sound of a loud, squeaky hinge being extended broke the silence in the shower room. The eerie sound was immediately followed by an inquisitive woman's voice, "Mr. Arienti, are you alright?" The sound brought me out of a comfort induced trance and brought me back to an acceptable level of consciousness. "I'm OK," I called back towards the door. The water was still running as warm as when I first turned it on, but I had no way of telling exactly how long I had been sitting in there. My fear was that I would emerge from the shower room and encounter a line of 5 or 6 people sitting in wheelchairs outside the shower room door like a large family in a home with only one bathroom.

As I rose from the chair, I reached out in front of me, grabbed the shower control knob and twisted it in a clockwise position. The streams of water first cooled, then ceased to spray. I turned and gingerly stepped from the shower room to the changing room where I dried off and slipped on new johnny pants, top and a pair of hospital non-slip socks. Clean, refreshed and dressed in a new stylish outfit, I emerged from the shower room and in the company of my nurse, strolled back into my room.

I sat in the reclining chair and was just about to put my feet up when I heard the slam of the door of the food transport cart. Being Saturday, Rosa was not working today. In her place, a short, thin, middle aged man carried in the brown tray of epicurean wonder. I said, "Thank you, what is it?" The man smiled, nodded his head and walked out of the room. I recognized this means of communication. Having grown up in an Italian family with many Italian friends, a number of my relatives spoke limited English. As I do not speak nor understand Italian, I learned how to communicate by listening to the tone of the speaker and respond with corresponding facial expressions. If they laughed while talking, or spoke with a lift to their voice, I would smile and chuckle with them. If they spoke with emotion, I would slightly open my mouth and put on puppy eyes. If they spoke in a short, curt pattern, I would curl my upper lip under and shake my head side to side. Even though I had no idea what they were talking about, they didn't know it.

I was delighted to see that the morning meal included coffee, Ensure, apple sauce, oatmeal, yogurt, milk and maple syrup. A veritable three course meal from the Four Seasons Hotel. I mixed the oatmeal, milk and maple syrup together to create an aroma that actually increased my appetite. I ate my breakfast with great pleasure that morning; not knowing if it was the food, or the fact that I knew this would be my last meal in the Mass General.

I had just finished my last sip of coffee when I heard the laughter of Nancy and my sister Marie approaching from down the hallway. The two walked in, still laughing, and were surprised to see my appearance. "What's going on?" I asked. Nancy shook her head, and Marie began to tell the story. "We got off the elevator, and Nancy was carrying the overnight bag. We were walking down the hallway at a pretty brisk pace, when Nancy's shoe got stuck on a spot on the floor." At this point, Nancy began to laugh again. "Well, once her foot hit that spot, Nancy went flying. She was literally off the ground, her arms spread wide open, and I was in such shock that I couldn't even talk. Then, I don't know how, Nancy was able to get a foot on the floor and balance herself." Nancy, out of breath and laughing could not add anything to the story. "I thought that I was going to be picking you up and dropping Nancy off."

Nancy began to retell the story, punctuated with spurts of laughter. "I thought that I was going to die!" seemed to be the continuing theme throughout Nancy's recollection of the event. Her face, still red through a combination of fright, excitement and over exertion, Nancy sat down on the side of the bed and took a deep breath. Over the thirty-five or so years together, Nancy, although quite shapely, was never adroit at athletics, or balance for that matter. However, whatever she lacked in the physicality department, she made up tenfold with her care, intelligence and love.

Once she caught her breath, Nancy commented on my newly clean-shaven face and grooming. "You look great!" declared Nancy. "Billy, you do look good," added Marie. My face still had the scabs caused from the fall, but most were hidden by my mustache and goatee. "Wait until Zeus sees you," teased Nancy. "He's been waiting to see you." Zeus, my 95-pound yellow lab, golden retriever mix was the friendliest dog anyone could ever want. He obeyed me, for the most part, but had a bad habit of jumping up on people in his excitement to say hello. Ever since I had hurt my back, Zeus had been my constant companion. Being away from him for over two weeks, I was nervous of just how excited he would be to see me. Being in a weakened state, he could easily knock me over, which is one thing that I could not afford to happen.

"Well, I figured that I would bring you into the house and up to the bedroom," explained Nancy. "Once you get all settled in, I'll let Zeus come in and see you." Zeus, although a great dog, is relegated to the kitchen, living room and family room. The limits of his domain were more for his continuous shedding more than any other reason. I'm often amazed that a dog can lose that much hair on a daily basis and not be bald. Fortunately, the area he has to live in is big enough for him to ramble.

After signing more papers than I did to get a mortgage, I was finally released from the hospital. In the overnight bag Nancy had packed a pair of sweat pants, a sweat shirt, underwear, socks, sneakers and a jacket. After changing into them I refilled the bag with pajamas, magazines and a few toiletries, including my new shaver. On top of all that I put the folder with the volume of paperwork that I had been given. I stood up and tried to carry the stuffed bag, but Nancy would have no part of it, as she snatched the bag before I could lift it from the bed. The three of us began to walk from the room when I paused, turned and took one last glimpse of what had been my home for the past 9 days. I took a deep breath, stepped out of the room and sat in the wheelchair an orderly had brought for me. As Nancy and Marie walked down the hallway, I got to ride comfortably down to the lobby.

As I sat in the lobby, I looked through the wall of glass with amazement. The limited view I had from my room was bleak, as my window faced the façade of a brick building about twenty feet away. Sunshine, if any, was in brief spurts only when the sun bounced off the windows of the adjacent building. The blue tinted lobby glass gave the appearance of an overcast sky; but being under any sky would be a drastic improvement over being under the squares of a suspended ceiling.

As Marie pulled up the hill to the hospital doors, I locked the wheels on the wheelchair, flipped up the foot rests, placed my feet on the floor and began to stand. Nancy immediately interrupted, "Aren't you supposed to take the wheelchair to the car?" The orderly had already left leaving me in the hands of my wife. "Nancy, it's only ten feet, I am fine." I continued to ascend to my feet and walked out the glass revolving door into the world.

Never had I tasted air before. Never had I felt a cloud or heard sunshine. I was a newborn taking his first steps into a brand-new world; seeing the earth, people and birds for the first time all over again. It was the strangest of sensations. I had no lingering feelings about dying, none about heart surgery; to be honest, they were inconsequential to me, or so I thought. Never had I been one for melodrama, in fact I have always been the person to not take life seriously. So, to have these emotional sensations was foreign to me. It was not a bad feeling, but almost like a mild electrical shock running through my body.

It was as I entered the car that I first realized that I did not have the strength, the stamina nor the ability of which I had prior to April sixth. I was no longer the grizzly bear, master of the domain. I now felt more like a black bear, rummaging through a garbage dump looking for my next meal. I lifted my legs, one at a time and swung them into the car as Nancy closed the door. I took a deep breath and breathed slowly to hide my exhaustion from Nancy and Marie. Although I had taken many more steps in the hospital hallways, this small jaunt made me feel like I just ran the Boston Marathon.

As we drove down Fruit St. and waited to take a right onto Storrow Drive, I saw what appeared to be a homeless man, dressed in dirty, raggedy clothes, and using a black plastic trash bag for a cloak. Throughout my life, whenever I could, I always tried to help those in need. Maybe the change I had in my pocket, or a dollar in a cup of a homeless person would do more for someone in need than for me. There were times that I even bought food for someone who looked hungry but did not ask for it. Seeing someone who has no other option but to sleep on the street, or eat from peoples discarded food, no matter what the reason might be, has always caused me pause. Seeing this man made me feel different. My pause turned to pain. My sadness never felt any deeper for a fellow man as it did for him. Although I was not in the position to do anything to help this man, I made a promise to myself that anytime, anywhere that I could offer someone comfort in any way, I would do it. To date of me writing this sentence, I have kept that promise.

As we approached my house, it felt so good to see the houses on my street. I was finally home. Marie pulled the car up to the front stairs and Nancy hopped out of the back seat to assist me. She knew that I would have opened the door and climbed out of the car on my own, which I most certainly would have. Before I could pull the door handle, Nancy had already opened the door and stood before me. I slowly spun my butt to allow both my feet to touch the ground simultaneously, then scooted to the edge of my seat. Nancy put her hands out to take mine, and with her assistance, I rose from seat and stood in my driveway. I looked at my house and felt a sense of accomplishment and pride; not because of what I had been through, but because I succeeded in building a home and a secure future for my family, even if I wasn't there to share it.

The few stairs that lead to my front door were not much of a challenge, as I climbed them, slowly, but without much effort. When I reached the door, Nancy unlocked it and I entered silently so as not to alert Zeus that I was home. Proceeding directly to my bedroom, a feeling of comfort washed over my body. I could not wait to get into my own bed, feel the crispness of a new pair of sheets, the cool luxury of my own pillows, and a mattress without a rubber or plastic cover. I immediately changed into a pair of clean pajamas, and as quickly as I could, slid under the covers and into my bed. The contentment and solace that filled me that moment was something that I never had before enjoyed.

The feeling of absolute relaxation was shattered by the sound of a loud thump hitting my bedroom door. The door flung wide open hitting the doorstop on the wall with another thud, and before I could even sit up, a long, soft tongue was licking every inch of bare skin it could find. Zeus welcomed me with greater enthusiasm than that of the father in the bible story The Prodigal Son. His large front paws were placed on the top of my bed, holding the large yellow dog steady. His kisses were interrupted only by a need for him to let out a whine or cry; from which he immediately returned to his show of affection.

Nancy, upon entering the room, scolded Zeus and ordered him to get down. The dog ignored her commands as he would not stop. Nancy walked sternly over to the bed, attached a leash to the dog's collar and pulled him away from the bed, "Don't let him kiss you like that," shouted Nancy. "Your immunities are way down, and you can easily catch something from him." Nancy pulled the blue leash back and Zeus obeyed her command, and he begrudgingly left the room.

As my jaw was still broken and I was relegated to liquids and foods that did not require chewing, both Marie and Nancy had prepared a number of items that I could eat without much effort. So, for the next few days, my menu consisted of oatmeal, grits, and cream of wheat for breakfast; tuna salad, applesauce and soups for lunch; and mashed potatoes mixed with some ground beef, fish and pureed vegetables for dinner. The between meal snacks of pudding and ice cream were the highlights of my days.

My bed and the reclining chair that Nancy and Mark had bought me for my birthday became my realms. Days would consist of answering the phone with calls from family and friends checking in on me, reading political history books, writing, watching TV, and taking small walks inside the house at first, then little by little increasing the distance and pace of my gait. After the first few days, I could actually feel my stamina growing within me. It was barely noticeable at first, but each day I was able to walk further and a little faster. I measured my progress by the houses of people on my street and would sing to myself Meatloaf's song "Paradise by the Dashboard Light".

By the end of two weeks I was up to 4/10 of a mile in four renditions of Paradise. Nancy was very careful about monitoring my progress and keeping me from over exerting myself. I would leave the driveway with a slow meander, and once I hit the street and got out of sight, my shuffle turned into full strides. If she saw me, I would have hell to pay, so I always made sure her line of sight was obscured.

The only problem that I was having was my heartbeat. At rest my heart beat 120 times per minute since the surgery. My normal rate was 80 beats per minute, so my body was working like I was constantly running at a pretty good clip. As long as I was at rest, my pulse was not noticeable, but by the last leg of my daily constitutional, my heart was beating like the drum intro to Van Halen's song "Hot for Teacher." I would sneak up the driveway, sit on my front stairs and wait until my pulse slowed down enough that I could no longer feel it. Only then would I go inside, head right into the bathroom, take the towel off the rack and put it over my head to absorb the sweat.

The interesting thing about my body is that as high as my pulse climbed, my blood pressure stayed stable at 120/80. That was the reason that the Mass General released me, because if my blood pressure rose at a similar rate as my pulse, I was in danger of having a stroke. To prevent this from happening, I was vigilant in taking my vital signs three times a day; morning, noon and after my walk. The doctors had assured me that this condition was temporary, and if it did not fix itself, they would give me a "cardiac conversion" to bring me back into the normal range.

After about a week, I began to experience dizzy spells periodically when I would stand from a seated position. It was not a normal dizzy, not like the feeling one gets from spinning, but more like a feeling of instability, the feeling that I cannot support myself. The feeling was only momentary and passed without any lingering effects. It never happened during or after my walks, and my blood pressure did not show any discernable fluctuation when the spell occurred. At first, I was not concerned with these spells, but when their frequency and intensity began to increase, I knew that I had to do something. Fortunately, I had an appointment with my new cardiologist in two days.

Doctor Berman had been my mother's cardiologist for a number of years before she passed away. He was highly respected in his field, and according to my mother, a very kind man who knew his stuff. Nancy accompanied me to the office and waited in a large, sunlit room to be called. "Are you nervous?" asked Nancy. I hesitated, surveyed the people in the large room, noticing that I was the youngest person there and wondered if I was about to join the ranks of the walking wounded.

The large oaken door began to slowly open into the waiting area. An older, diminutive woman with her white hair arranged in curls used all of her strength to push the heavy door open, until a young nurse rushed up behind her and pushed the door to allow her to exit the examination section. The woman seemed to be somewhere around eighty years old. She walked slowly, without assistance towards an elderly man sitting on the other side of the room. Her back slowly curved as it approached her neck, causing the appearance of a hump on her shoulders. The man, who appeared to be her husband, pushed himself out of his chair, took a cane that was leaning against the wall next to him. Leaning on the cane with his right hand, the gentleman shuffled over to his wife, and when they were in proximity, they both reached out their hand which seemed to fill them both with enough strength to walk hand in hand out of the office and down the hall to the elevator. These people were the epitome of love and independent dependence. One may be able to live without the other, but given the option, would not want to.

As soon as the older woman cleared the open doorway, the nurse who assisted her looked at a clipboard and called out "Bill?" as she scanned the room for anyone who showed any indication that it was their name she called. Upon hearing my name, I surveyed the room, saw no one else make any movement towards the door, and began to stand. By this time, Nancy was already standing and asking me what I was doing.

I joined my wife in standing and together we walked through the open door and into the examination room down the hallway. We sat in the two available chairs, leaving the doctor's stool and the examination table vacant. The nurse pulled a sheet of paper from the long roll behind the exam table. Once done, she asked me to step on the scale. I did so, and moved the counterweights for her, balancing the indicator between the guide. "Looks like you have done this a few times," commented the young nurse. She wrote down 265 on a post-it and then asked me to sit on the paper exam table. Once in place, she placed a pulse oximeter on the middle finger of my right hand and wrapped a blood pressure cuff on my left arm. Although I could not see the blood pressure readout, I could see that my pulse was holding pretty steady at 120 beats per minute. "Is your pulse normally this high?" asked the nurse. I nodded yes, and then asked her what my blood pressure was. "That's normal, 120 over 72," she replied. "Actually, that is better than good, it's pretty great. I will tell the doctor; he'll be right in."

Nancy and I sat in the exam room for what felt like an hour waiting for the doctor to arrive. Suddenly there was a knock on the door as it slowly was pushed open. A rather slight man walked in. He was about 5'6, around mid 60's but very fit. "Mr. Arienti?" he asked as he entered. His voice was soothing, as he spoke with what appeared to be some type of slight British accent. His face was friendly as well, which established a very calm atmosphere in the room.

"I am Doctor Berman, this is my assistant, Gerald." The two men walked in. Gerald was African American, about 6'2, thin and carrying a tablet. I offered my hand in greeting, which Dr. Berman took in his in a firm but friendly handshake; Gerald then shook my hand as well before sitting next to Nancy.

"Well, I read your chart and I see that you've had a tough go of it lately," said the doctor. I nodded in agreement, "Doctor, you don't know the half of it!" I laughed and began to give him an account of the past month's events. The doctor listened intently, and sporadically typed a few words into his desktop computer. After listening to me, the doctor stood up and began to examine me, first checking my ankles for fluid retention, then placing his stethoscope on my back, then chest, then throat. The doctor removed the stethoscope from his ears and draped the stethoscope around his neck. "I can hear the valve, and it sounds like it is working splendidly."

"It's good to finally get some good news." I responded to his explanation. "Well, it's all not good news, but no bad news," continued the doctor. "Your heart is beating at an accelerated rate, 120 beats per minute, and it is causing a slight arrhythmia known as A-flutter. Sometimes this cures itself, other times we have to do what is called a cardiac conversion." This was the same prognosis that I had received from Dr. MacGillivray and Sanjay a week or so earlier. I knew the basics, but I wanted to hear what his views were on it as well. "Are you familiar with a cardiac conversion?" asked Dr. Berman. "I have a basic idea, could you please go over it with me?"

"You do know what a defibrillator is and how it works, don't you?" After 30 years as a firefighter and 27 as an EMT, I was well versed on the workings of a defibrillator. The heart works by electrical impulses. These impulses are created by an interconnected series of cells called pacemakers. When the pacemakers are working correctly, the heart beats in the correct rhythm. However, when they do not work properly, the heart beat is irregular. A defibrillating device shocks the patient, stopping all electrical impulses in the heart, allowing the hearts pacemakers to reset and bring the heart into a proper rhythm. "Yes, I do know how they work," I answered.

"Well then, basically, we just defibrillate your heart until it comes back into rhythm," explained the doctor. Having seen the effects of a defibrillator shocking an unsuspecting EMT, I was quite certain that this was not going to be a pleasant experience. "Am I awake for this?" I asked with trepidation. "Oh, no," answered Dr. Berman. "We put you to sleep for this. You will not feel a thing." This was the biggest nugget of information that I was waiting to hear. Once I am asleep and can't feel anything, I don't care what you do to me.

"When can we do this?" I asked. I guess I sounded a little too anxious for Dr. Berman's comfort. "Well, I want to keep you on blood thinners for at least four weeks to prevent any blood clots," said the Doctor. "We can do this at South Shore Hospital." I nodded, said OK, and looked at Nancy for her thoughts. Nancy never had any medical training or experience, so the perplexed look on her face was expected and understandable. Nancy's concern for me was immeasurable. She had been a supporter, a nurturer, an advocate, a nurse and a friend. Because of her I wanted for nothing, as she seemed to be able to anticipate my needs and fulfill them before a request was even made. I didn't know at the time how much of the particulars the Doctor described were understood by Nancy, but would soon be surprised by just how quick a learner she was.

"Do you have any other Questions?" asked Doctor Berman. I looked at Nancy, swallowed hard, and said, "Lately when I have been rising from a sitting position, the room begins to spin for a moment, then goes away. It doesn't happen all the time, actually there is no rhyme nor reason when it happens." Both the doctor and Nancy looked at me with a little bewilderment. I continued, "After the dizziness goes away, I immediately take my vital signs, but they are consistent with my regular vital signs. I thought that I might be orthostatic, but my blood pressure never changes."

When I finished, I was more concerned with Nancy's reaction than I was with what the doctor had to say. Her eyes showed a look of concern tinted with the slightest bit of rage. "Does the dizziness go away when you close your eyes?" inquired the doctor. "No," I replied. "As a matter of fact, when I close my eyes, I feel like I am going to lose my balance." While nodding his head, the doctor began to document what I assumed were my symptoms into the computer. "Does anything cause the condition to worsen?" he asked. I shook my head and replied in the negative. "No," I answered. "What it sounds like to me is a touch of vertigo. Try to keep track when it occurs the most and exactly what you were doing when it happened, and we will discuss it further at your next visit," instructed Dr. Berman. "In the mean time I am going to keep you on the Metoprolol as well as the Coumadin and give you this other medication to slow your heartbeat a little more. I want to see you next week, and on the way out please stop for a blood test so that we can make sure that you are getting the right dosage of Coumadin. "

Doctor Berman stood up and reached out to shake my hand. "It was a pleasure meeting you, I will see you next week," he said. He then nodded his head at Nancy and wished her well. Gerald followed the doctor's cue, stood up and said goodbye to both Nancy and me. The two left the room and closed the door behind them. As I began to put my shirt back on, the moment that I had been expecting arrived. "Why didn't you tell me how bad those dizzy spells were? You could have had something serious. You can't just keep things quiet; this is your life that you are messing with." Nancy threw out a few more admonitions that I do not recall. As she continued, I nodded my head in agreement and repeated "yup" every time she paused to take a breath. This was a tactic that men must learn to master over time if their goal is a long, happy marriage. As I had mentioned earlier, Nancy is a loving, caring and quiet woman; but like all women, get her angry and she will tear your throat out. Other than the yups and nods, I was silent the rest of the way home.

CHAPTER 24

With all that I had been through, an uneventful day would have been a welcomed event; but an uneventful week was like a Caribbean vacation, and for a number of following days, that is exactly what my life felt like. I had begun to feel better, the pain was subsiding, and I was able to get around much more easily. I could now quickly walk the half mile round trip between my house and the end of my street, and was pushing the distance further every day. I was on the mend, and although I was not quite out of the woods, the forest was getting much less challenging. Nancy had returned to her job, although she reduced her hours, and I was on my own for most of the day, under the watchful eye of my buddy Zeus.

Zeus, with whom I already had a very close bond, had become my inseparable companion. After four years, his puppy-like demeanor was beginning to subside, and he was finally following directions. Whether it be roaming from room to room or taking long rides in the car, Zeus very seldom left my side. The big yellow dog would sit in the passenger seat of my truck and remain perfectly still any time the truck was in motion. When I would come to a complete stop however, Zeus seized the opportunity to show his affection towards me by putting his paw on my hand, putting his head under my hand to make me pet him, or licking the right side of my face.

Our trips together also caused a number of humorous incidents as well. On one occasion Zeus and I drove to the bank on a hot spring day. When I went into the bank, I took my spare keys and left Zeus locked in the car with the air conditioner running. As I waited in line inside the bank, a woman walked in and in a loud voice asked, "Does someone in here own a green pickup truck outside?" I quickly spun around and said, "I do". The woman walked over to me and asked me to come outside. As I followed her all I could think of is that she hit my truck. Once outside she began to discipline me in an animated fashion about leaving my "poor dog" in a sweltering truck. "Did you pull me out of line for this?" I asked incredulously. "That poor dog is dying in there, it's 92 degrees out, how would you like it? Open your windows." I looked over to see Zeus sitting upright, his mouth slightly open and seemed to be in no discomfort whatsoever. "Lady, look at the damn dog, he's sitting in an air conditioned truck while you and I are out here sweating our asses off arguing about his wellbeing," It was now my turn to chastise the chastiser, and I took full advantage of it. "I know you are trying to help, but get all the facts before you start making accusations in public." I shook my head and walked back into the bank. As I made my way into the bank, I noticed that the line of people who were in front of me when I left had all been served and I was next. Being a person who hates standing in line, this event ended up being a pleasant diversion all thanks to Zeus.

Another time as I walked out of a supermarket, Zeus stuck his head out the window and began licking my face. An elderly couple saw his affection as they walked towards the market and called out. "He must really love you!" shouted the smiling older woman. "Oh, I love him too," I called back. Not to be undone, the husband shouted, "I wish my wife would treat me like that!" Well, being born without a filter, I could not keep my response to myself. "Why don't you try turning her over and rubbing her belly, you will be surprised what she will do for you!" I hated myself hearing each syllable exit my lips, but I could not stop. The response was mixed, he laughed, she smirked with a somewhat disdainful expression. That damn dog gets me in more trouble!

There was no question that Zeus was happy that I was home once again. The weather had finally warmed enough to sit outside and enjoy the sunshine. Each time I would sit on my patio, Zeus would run around the yard and somehow discover a ball that either he had discarded earlier or "borrowed" from a neighboring yard. He would drop the ball at my feet and look up into my eyes anticipating me to pick it up and throw it for him to retrieve. The first time I tried to throw his ball, I immediately realized that this was a mistake, for the throwing motion is not a natural movement for a healthy human body; never mind a human body with a newly sutured 14" wound in the center of its chest is even less natural.

I lifted my right arm with the yellow ball in my hand. As I began the throwing process, I could feel the pulling sensation in my chest, but once in the process of throwing, stopping is difficult; so, I didn't stop. I threw the ball while emitting a loud shrill caused by the pain in my chest. The ball traveled a disappointing 10 feet as I bent over at the waist, one hand on my knee, one hand on my chest. I felt a pain which I'm sure was similar to the pain the astronaut in the movie Alien felt when the creature jutted out from his abdomen. Zeus retrieved the ball, as retrievers will do, and followed me as I walked back into the house. Zeus dropped the ball just before entering the house with me, I walked over to the sofa and sat down and folded into the soft cushions. "Zeus, shut the door." I commanded. Performing the trick that I had taught him a few months earlier, Zeus ran to the door, stood up on his hind legs, and pushed the door shut with his front paws. Rather than rush to his bed and await the treat that usually follows his feat, Zeus seemed to understand the situation at hand, walked over to me, dropped to the floor and laid at my feet.

If I didn't already feel bad enough, Nancy's shortened work day had ended and I heard her car pulling into the driveway. I knew that I was in for a good ass chewing, and deservedly so, but knowing what I deserve and receiving it are two different things. I decided to suck it up, get in the most comfortable position on the couch and feign sleep. Nancy entered the house calling out her greetings and saw me lying on the couch. "Are you ok?" she asked. I looked up with my eyes, trying not to move any body part to prevent the pain associated with it. "Yeah, I'm just tired today."

Nancy walked over and kissed my forehead. I knew that I was going to be alright, I just needed a little time for the pain to dissipate. "Lay down, I'll get your lunch." No R.N., no P.A. and only few mothers could provide the love and level of care that Nancy devoted to me as well as my son, Mark. And as much as her love lifts me to the highest levels, her anger scares the living shit out of me. Even though I was not hungry, I welcomed her lunch because refusing it would be pointless. An hour later the pain was gone, but the lesson stayed with me for a while.

Wednesday morning began just like every one of the past mornings since I got home. It was hot already at eight in the morning. The paddle fan in the bedroom stirred the air somewhat, and when the occasional breeze flowed through the open windows, the cross ventilation made air conditioning unnecessary. Since I was still on the mend and had nowhere to go, my daily routine of waking to the sound of the 6 AM alarm had been replaced with a more comfortable schedule.

Nancy had started to leave the house earlier than usual since she shortened her days. Mark had also departed to get to his early classes. I climbed out of bed, performed my morning rituals, and made my way downstairs to the waiting panting of Zeus. Hearing me walk down the few stairs from the bedrooms, Zeus made it a habit of jumping out of his bed, picking up the first of his toys he could find, and then drop it at my feet once I entered the kitchen. This action, I later learned, was his way of paying tribute to me, like a pack wolf bringing a harvested prey to the alpha wolf.

I was still on the soft food diet because of my healing jaw, so this morning

I thought I would start the day without the traditional oatmeal, yogurt or scrambled eggs, and instead decided to go with a healthy serving of grits. Borrowing a line from the movie "My Cousin Vinny", I go by the adage that "No self-respecting southerner uses instant grits"; and even though my southern roots only go as far as Hanover, Massachusetts, my gastric preferences run to the more traditional of flavors.

As I was waiting for the water to boil, the home phone began to ring. The caller ID announced that the call originated from the Massachusetts General Hospital. I left the pan of water on the stove and answered the ringing phone. "Hello?" I said in a questioning voice. "Mr. Arienti, good morning, this is Sanjay, the cardiac fellow at the Mass General." By the time he had finished saying my name I already knew it was Sanjay. His voice and accent brought a smile to my face. "Hello Sanjay, how are you doing?" Sanjay's laughter could be heard coming from the other end of the line. "I am fine, but how I am is of no concern. Why I am calling is to see how you are." It was now my turn to laugh. "I'm well," I replied. "Feeling better and better every day." I looked over to the stove and saw the water in the pan was now boiling.

"I'm happy to hear that you are doing so well," commended Sanjay. "I just wanted to call you and let you know that we sent the tissue we took from your surgery to pathology, and they just informed us that they found light-chain amyloidosis. We sent it to the Mayo Clinic for them to take a closer look at it." In over 30 years in the medical field, I had never heard the term amyloidosis; but the way that Sanjay said it, with such a nonchalant voice, I thought it was something with which I should have been familiar.

I thought to myself that this cannot be anything serious because they would have called me into the Mass General to give me bad news, or at least explained what it was they were informing me of in detail within the confines of the conversation we were having. With Sanjay's tone, I decided that I would respond to the news with the same tone. "Oh, OK," I answered. Sanjay did not answer for a moment. In this moment of silence, I continued to assure myself that he was just making an obligatory phone call to tell me they are sending my tissue out. "Well, I will let your cardiologist know, and I will send you the results as soon as we get them." Sanjay's voice stayed constant, no added uplift nor additional concern. "Let us know if you have any problems or questions, ok?" "All right Sanjay, take care of yourself." I said in closing. "You too Mr. Arienti," and that ended the call.

As I hung up the phone I just stood there. I wracked my brain trying to remember any mention of the word amyloidosis or any derivative of the word, but nothing came to mind. With all the blood tests and tissue samples taken over the past few months, I was certain that this was just a minor chronic condition like anemia or arthritis. I wrote down what Sanjay had told me, folded the paper I wrote it on and stuck it in my pocket. By this time almost all the water in the pan had evaporated from the heat of the stove.

For a moment I thought of refilling the pan, but some reason I was no longer hungry. It wasn't that I was upset or even concerned, just the idea of food suddenly didn't interest me anymore. So, I decided instead of eating, it was a good time to take Zeus for our morning walk. I connected his blue leash to Zeus's collar and off we went.

It was only 9:30 and the temperature was already in the 90's. By the time we reached the end of Pine St. Zeus was panting; and truth be told, so was I. With my upper jawbone still wrapped with wires and healing, my ability to whistle had disappeared. Prior to this whole experience, a quick, short whistle would cause Zeus to stop immediately. Now my whistle sounded more like air escaping from a basketball. A snap of the leash alerted Zeus of a change in plans and together we made an about face and returned to our air-conditioned home.

As we entered the house, Zeus made a B-line for the kitchen and his water dish. I could hear him slurping up his nice cool drink, trying to get as much water inside him as quickly as possible. I removed my t-shirt, now saturated with perspiration and jumped in a warm shower, lowering the temperature every few moments until it began to cool my body down. As I looked down, I noticed that the scar from my surgery was beginning to develop a more pronounced appearance. This was nothing new, as every previous surgery I had produced a similar affect upon healing. Keloid is a type of tissue that appears on scars of people with southern European and northern African descent. People who have this condition have scars that protrude from the skin and usually have a pink or red hue the length of the scar. For those who are vain or overly particular about their appearance, keloid is a curse that takes years to disappear. As for me, it just makes a great intro to an interesting story.

After the shower I got dressed and went downstairs for a glass of juice. As I stood at the kitchen counter, I saw the note I had written earlier from my conversation with Sanjay. I picked up my laptop and against my better instincts, I went to WebMD.com to find out just exactly what this amyloidosis was. The reason that I have reservations with WebMD is because it seems for even the slightest ailment the final step is amputation or tissue removal; I never recommend looking at WebMD for anyone who has little medical knowledge or experience, especially when looking for a cure for jock itch.

When the information finally appeared on the screen, what I had expected to happen materialized, only this time the final step was heart transplant with a high death rate. Kicking myself in the ass for going against my better judgement, I immediately X'ed out of that screen and Googled amyloidosis; the results were not much better than the last one. According to the Mayo Clinic's web page, amyloidosis is a type of cancer similar to myeloma. It appears in the heart and the brain and usually occurs in people around seventy and over. There are three types, familial, which is genetic and can be controlled.

Senile amyloidosis usually occurs in geriatric patients towards the end of life and is an added complication with other more common ailments. Then I got to light chain amyloidosis, the type that Sanjay had said that I had. As I began to read, I had wished that I stopped at senile amyloidosis. The second sentence of the first paragraph caused me to pause, take a deep breath in through my nose and exhale through my mouth. This type of amyloidosis is much more serious than the others, with a mortality rate of close to 80%. I read on hoping to find salvation later in the article. Unfortunately, there was none.

The deeper I searched, a number of videos by a Doctor Falk began to appear. I clicked on one of them to find a man with an English accent not only explaining the situation in layman terms, his general prognosis was not as dire as the other articles, but more hopeful. He was one of only a handful of doctors in the world who were considered experts in the field of amyloidosis. The feeling of heaviness was somewhat relieved by this video and knowing that there are learned experts out there did offer me hope.

As I twisted in the wind for a few days waiting for my appointment with my cardiologist Dr. Berman to discuss this latest revelation. When the doctor finished examining me, I informed him of the phone call that I received from Sanjay. I asked if he knew anything about amyloidosis to which he replied "I have just a basic understanding about it, however I do know a doctor in the Brigham and Women's Hospital name Dr. Falk who is quite knowledgeable about the subject. I will put in a call to him to see if I can get you in."

It didn't dawn on me until I left the office, but the Doctor Falk mentioned by Dr. Berman had to have been the same man I saw on the video. I did not wait for Dr. Berman to make the call, for the moment I got home I called the Brigham and Women's hospital myself and reached Dr. Falk's office. When I explained my situation to the nurse, she reacted with a sound of surprise as well as concern. "Dr. Falk will not be back until July 24th, can you be in here on July 26th?" I answered with both excitement and relief, "Absolutely!" July 26th was three weeks away, but knowing that I was about to see one of the world's foremost experts in the field offered me more hope than I had since that infamous phone call.

CHAPTER 25

A number of years ago when it first opened, I went to the Holocaust museum in Washington D.C. Before that visit, I had read about the Holocaust, saw films and movies about it, but it never really affected me; possibly because I had no one who was personally involved in it. In addition, around that time the Holocaust was not made known as much as it is today.

As I stepped into the front door of the museum, I remember feeling uneasy just from the building construction alone. The bare brick walls, the exposed steel beams and girders, and the wired glass gave a visitor the sense of being in some type of a prison. I was then handed a little book that resembled a passport. I opened the cover to see a picture of a young man whose name I will never forget. Franz Spengler was a young Jewish man. His picture had the stamp of the Nazi eagle across it. There was German text on one page, and the other page told his story. He was 30, married with no children. He worked in his father's clothing store where he was a tailor. I began to follow the traffic trail of people meandering through the museum where I followed the events in both genuine and filmed exhibits. First, I saw how Franz was registered, and given papers and a yellow star to adorn his clothing. Next, the Spengler store was identified by Nazis had painted in yellow the word "Juden" on the glass window.

He was then removed from his apartment with his wife; allowed to take only one suitcase each. The home that they made together was now the property of the state, and the Spengler's were made to live in the ghetto. The hovel in which they were forced to live was tiny, cramped and shared with two other families. He now had to walk four miles each day to get to the store which was downstairs his former residence. They lived in the ghetto until one day they were taken from their apartment, put on two separate trucks and driven to train stations. They never saw each other again.

Once at the station they were made to board boxcars that were used prior for cattle and swine. The boxcars were barely washed out, if at all, and numerous truckloads of men, women and children were made to crowd into the cars. The number of people forced into the boxcar made it impossible for even the slightest movement. Sweat dripped into his eyes, and he was unable to lift his hand high enough to sooth the burning. The cries were deafening, children calling for their mothers, mothers screaming for the return of their children; men sobbing knowing that this was to be the last ride of their lives.

Once the train arrived at its destination everyone was made to exit the car, find their suitcase and register, where they were given a tattoo on their wrist, no matter their age. Their heads were then shaved with clippers and they were made to undress. They were then doused with delousing powder and made to don a blue and gray striped woolen suit that they were made to wear on the coldest night as well as the hottest summer day. The food they were given were scraps of stale bread and tainted meat. One day's rations was not enough to create one meal. Their sleeping quarters were nothing but wooden shelves with hardly 24" from one bunk to the one above.

As I continued through the museum, I saw the atrocities that innocent men, women and children were made to endure. The Germans said the acts were in the name of science, but were actually sado-masochistic rituals performed by people who called themselves doctors. I saw an authentic burlap bag of hair; I saw the genuine suitcases these people were made to carry. I saw the bunks that became these peoples only sanctuary, and I saw the striped woolen suits they were ordered to wear.

I then saw the boxcar. I walked up the ramp and entered the cavernous car. Although no one was in there when I entered, and no one followed behind me, I was overwhelmed by the feeling of claustrophobia. I could feel people pressing against me, prohibiting my movement. I felt the heat of the scorching sun one moment and the frigid cold the next. I could smell the stench of perspiration, urine and waste. I felt a trickle of sweat travel down my forehead, but whether or not it was intentional, I did not wipe it and allowed it to finish its trek and burn my eyes. I do not know if the boxcar was authentic or not, it did not matter; it had served its purpose.

I cannot remember the rest of the museum, as after the boxcar I was numb. The only thing I do remember was that I turned to the last page of the passport of Franz Spengler to be informed that he was killed at Auschwitz. There was no record available for his wife.

Maybe we should mandate that all students in the United States take a stroll through the museum to see firsthand the actions that although have been promised to never happen again, are still emulated by people in this country and in other countries around the world. Thugs in black uniforms adorned with swastikas, others with shaved heads and jack boots carrying torches in what they promote as peaceful demonstration can only evoke hatred and bring back horrid memories. On display in this museum was pure and unmitigated evil. It showed that man has the ability to commit unspeakable acts against mankind. Events of today make it evident that the evil of Nazi Germany was never truly eradicated from this world, it just changed faces. Like the people whom they mimic, there is no defense for the acts of today's Nazis, there is no apologizing for them. Once they have accepted hatred in their heart, they have abandoned any and all redeeming values that could have made them nice people; no acts of charity, no professional life, no loving family life. They are evil, nothing more. It is my belief that you cannot call yourself an American if you defend these people. You cannot say you love this country if their actions do not bother you. If you are offended by this and hate me, it is a hatred that I welcome with jubilation. I am by no means an example of goodness to be emulated; I just love and accept people for who they are; life is much easier to live that way.

CHAPTER 26

As I opened my front door to step outside, the heat hit me in the face like a blast furnace. It had been a very hot summer, even oppressive. Spending most of it in an air-conditioned house was not the worst situation in this type of weather. Immediately my glasses fogged up as I traveled from the comfortable atmosphere inside my air-conditioned home to the inferno awaiting me outside my door. A bead of sweat immediately formed on the top of my head and began its trek down my forehead and into my eye. It was not long before it was joined with many more droplets. It was August 11, 2016, and at 9:30 in the morning and it was already 88 degrees.

I hurried to my car to escape the searing heat. We have an attached garage, but like almost everybody's garage, ours was too full of clutter to contain a car as well. The morning sun had only been out for a few hours but had been beating directly on the hood of our Ford Escape. As the car door swung open, the heat of a blast furnace escaped, making the outside feel like a balmy day. I reached in without touching the leather seats and turned on the ignition. Once the engine began to run I heard the air conditioner kick on, and a feeling of anticipated relief washed over my body. I climbed into the car, closed the door and rejoiced as the temperature inside dropped to a comfortable level. After only five minutes outside, the brand-new shirt that I was wearing was already stained with perspiration, and the moist fabric stuck to both my skin and the leather interior.

As I waited in the driveway listening to local sports channel, I saw Nancy open the front door. The hot air hit her with the same intensity as it did me. She hurriedly locked the door, scampered down the front steps and joined me in the car. "Boy, is it hot out already!" Nancy commented as she wiped off the beads of perspiration from under her eyes. "Well, all we have to do is get out of the car in the underground garage," I explained. "It will be cooler down there, and the hospital is air conditioned. The rest of the day shouldn't be that bad." We backed out of the driveway and began our trip to the Brigham and Woman's Medical Center in Boston.

The Brigham and Women's Medical Center is a world-renowned hospital and a leader in the research, and treatment of all illnesses both internal as well as organic. It is rated the best hospitals in the United States, and probably, in the top 5 in the world. It is a bittersweet realization, but if you have to get sick in any way, Boston is the place to do it.

As always, the traffic crept slowly along the highway into Boston. The time of day or day of the week does not matter in Boston as it pertains to traffic, it is omnipresent. People from around the rest of the country seem to take sitting in traffic with a grain of salt. They sit back, listen to the radio, inch their car forward as the car in front of them moves, all without complaint. We Bostonians differ from our more rural counterparts just a bit. It is not uncommon to see a single person in a car screaming at the car or cars in front of him, or the second someone in front of you moves, the car behind you starts blaring their horn for you to travel the distance of one rotation of your tires. The one thing we do have in common with out of state drivers is that we both wave to people as we pass; only Boston people wave with just one finger.

When we finally arrived in Boston, we parked in the underground garage at the hospital. Although it was much cooler three stories below ground, the humidity made the air thick, and difficult to breath. We hastily made our way across the parking area and into the elevator enclosure; at last, cool air again.

Upon reaching the concierge desk, we asked the attendant where the cardiology department was. He directed us to a bank of elevators that would take us to that department. The hospital is huge, with buildings that reach longer than two city blocks. I honestly believe that it would take someone a week to visit every room in the series of buildings.

The sign on the wall opposite the elevator doors read "CARDIOLOGY" and was impossible to miss the moment the elevator doors opened. We followed the direction of the red arrow that led us down a long corridor until we reached a glass door. Imprinted into the glass in frosty letters were the words "Brigham and Women's Hospital Cardiology Department". We walked into the waiting room and approached the long wooden Formica counter next to the small obsolete sliding glass window situated in the middle of a wall. Fabric chairs with wooden arms and legs lined the walls of the office with a row of alternating seats resembling the configuration of a game of musical chairs.

An older Black woman sat behind the desk typing on a keyboard. There were two other chairs and work stations, but she was the only one there at the moment. "Can I help you?" she asked as she looked up from her monitor. "Hi, I am Bill Ari…" the phone rang right in middle of my sentence. "Excuse me," she said as she reached for the phone. "Brigham and Women's Hospital, Cardiology, please hold." Her attention immediately returned to me. "I'm sorry, what was your last name again?" I told her "Arienti". The woman looked up and down the computer screen with a puzzled look on her face. "Do you have an appointment?" she asked. "Yes, I have an 11 o'clock appointment with Dr. Falk." I responded. The phone began to ring again when a young man came from the back room and took a seat at the adjacent work station and answered the phone. "I'm sorry Mr. Rent, but I don't have you on the schedule." A smile appeared on my face, "No, my name is not Rent, it is R-E-N-T, spelled ARIENTI." The woman started laughing; "My goodness," she exclaimed…" I thought that I was going crazy. Here you are. Do you have an ID and your insurance card?" I handed her the two cards, in return she handed me a clipboard with a few papers on it. A pen was attached with a long-coiled cord was tied to the clip to discourage pilferage.

I sat down and began to fill out the questionnaire, laboring to remember my whole medical history and their respective years. As I filled it out, the woman behind the desk called to me as she held up my license and insurance card. Nancy stood up and stepped over to the counter to retrieve them. As I finished the paperwork, I stood up and before I could take a step, the door to the inner office opened and a young woman dressed in hospital scrubs emerged and called out "William A?" I took two steps to the counter, placed the clipboard on the counter, looked at the nurse and said, "That's me." She smiled at me, said hi and took Nancy and me to an examination room in the back office.

Holding a clipboard in her hand, she asked "Can you please tell me your name and date of birth?" "William," then I spelled my last name, and continued with "March 23, 1962." As I gave her the information, she read a white paper strip in her hand. Once I finished, she took the strip removed a piece of plastic from an adhesive strip and put the paper strip around my wrist. She then asked me to sit on the examination table where she took my vital signs. "Please remove your shirt and lay back," she requested. As I began to do that, she left the room. By this time, Nancy had found a chair in the room on which to sit. The nurse returned with an EKG machine on a rolling tray. She attached twelve electrodes to my chest, arms and ankles, allowed the machine to run for 20 seconds, then removed all of the electrodes. "The doctor will be right in," said the woman and took the EKG out of the room and closed the door as she left.

"What did the EKG say?" asked Nancy. "It looks like I have at least three blockages in my heart." Nancy's face turned pale, "Really?" I began to laugh, "How the hell do I know, I don't know how to read an EKG." Nancy shook her head as the color returned to her face. "Can you ever be serious?" I smiled for a response. Throughout my whole life, although years passed and my body matured, I took pride in the fact that I never really grew up. I make light of everything, no matter the severity; I still don't know if it is a coping mechanism or just a sick sense of humor. Either way, this attitude has served me well, allowing me to keep my wits about me while others lose theirs.

A few minutes passed when there was a knock on the door. A young man entered, black curly hair, glasses, tall, wearing a torn long lab coat. This was not the man I saw on the videos explaining amyloidosis. "Hi, I am Stephen Silverman, Dr. Falk's assistant. I'm just going to give you a quick examination, ask you some questions before Dr. Falk comes in and gives you the same examination and asks you the same questions." Being a stranger in a strange land, I just agreed without any protest or snide remark. He did exactly what he said he was going to do. Once his questions were complete, we engaged in a conversation, where my unfiltered personality began to present itself. The exchange was good, as his sense of humor was similar to mine. A knock came from the door, and the man whom I had seen on the video entered the room. Both his face and his voice were immediately recognizable as he greeted me. "Hello, Mr. Arienti? I am Dr. Falk." I reached out and shook his hand. "It's a pleasure to meet you, I have seen a number of videos in which you appear," I responded. Dr. Falk chuckled, "I hope I looked ok," replied the doctor injecting a little levity.

"So, I read your chart and I spoke to Dr. Berman; you have had quite the go of it, haven't you?" Nodding in agreement, I answered his question with, "You ain't kidding brother." The doctor asked me to return to the exam table where he listened to my lungs and heart. "Well, your heart and lungs certainly seem to be working quite well," explained the doctor, "how have you been feeling?" I told him that other than what was expected, I was feeling good. "I am going to send you to get some blood work. When you get that I will have the results right away," stated the doctor as he typed feverishly on his tablet. "You can go now," he requested as he held the door open. "The lab is right down the hall to the left. Please come back to this office when you're finished."

Nancy and I left the room and walked together down the hallway. "How are you feeling?" asked Nancy. "I'm doing fine," I responded as we walked down the long linoleum tiled floor. A sign saying "LAB" protruded from the wall above an open doorway. Nancy and I walked in and were pleasantly surprised to see that there were no waiting patients in the outer office, we were next.

There was no one sitting at the check-in desk, so I approached the back room and was immediately greeted by a rather curvy woman with whom I almost collided. "Can I help you?" said the woman in purple hospital scrubs. "Hi, Dr. Falk sent me down here for some bloodwork, my name is William

Arienti." The woman was not as congenial as the rest of the staff seemed to be. With what time of day it was, I surmised that I had interrupted her lunch. "You can take a seat in the waiting area; I will be right with you."

I returned to the waiting room and sat next to Nancy. Before my butt touched the cushion on the chair, Nancy asked, "What did she say?" I turned my head to face her and attempting to mimic the voice of the nurse, I said, "She told me...Go take a seat in the waiting room, I will be right with you." Nancy shushed me quickly. "Shhh, don't do that," she admonished. At that point I took Nancy's advice; I had forgotten that this woman would probably be the one who was going to be sticking a needle into my arm.

A few moments later the same woman entered into the waiting room. "William A?" she asked. Well, since the crowd in the waiting room consisted only of my wife and me, I didn't think that there would be any confusion, but protocol is protocol. I stood up and walked towards her when she requested to see my wrist band and asked for my date of birth. After comparing my information to her clipboard, she instructed me to follow her.

I was seated and an arm rest was positioned in front of me. The technician's demeanor had not changed since our initial meeting. When I worked as an EMT, I always felt compelled to engage with my patient, put them at ease and maybe even chuckle. As a patient I am the same way; I like to converse with my healthcare provider, no matter what level of care they may provide. I began to wonder how I could get this woman to lighten up a little, but my thought was interrupted when she wrapped a long blue rubber strip around my elbow and began slapping my inner forearm.

The technician quickly became frustrated, "Your veins are too deep." I nodded that I understood her challenge. "Try the back of my hand, they seem to be a lot more accessible," I recommended. The glare from her eyes told me that I should not offer my expertise to this highly trained individual. I now remembered an incident that had occurred to me years ago that would work perfect at that exact moment.

The tech found a vein in the back of my left hand, said "Little pinch," and inserted the needle. "One time I was at a firefighter convention in Chicago," I began to relate the story to the less than affable tech. "They were testing firefighters for Hepatitis B so that we could introduce it to our membership back home. The large area in which they were doing this was divided into little cubicles by metal rods and striped curtains. As we sat waiting for our turn, my friend Paul was called up and told to go into cubicle 12. My friend Al was then instructed to go into cubicle 10. I only had to sit alone for a few seconds when a very big woman stepped out of cubicle 11 and motioned me into her work area. She then performed the pre-extraction tasks, and then was about to insert the needle." I continued with little response from the tech. "Since it was a firefighter convention, and it was around 3:00, after lunch, I along with my buddies had a few beers in us already. The nurse, bending over my arm then said "Ok, little prick." To which my response to her was "OK fat ass." My buddies on both sides of me could be heard laughing as well as their nurses. My nurse began to laugh, and wiping her eyes of tears she said, "That's a new one for me, 20 years doing this, and no one ever hit me with that." Then she regained her composure and took my blood.

I closely watched the woman's face as I told the story. I saw her upper lip expand as she pushed her tongue between her lip and teeth. I watched her take in a deep breath and blow it out. I then saw the corners of her lips involuntarily begin to turn up, and that's when I knew that I got her. As she exchanged the full tubes in the intravenous that held my blood with empty tubes, she began to laugh, and then chuckled, "That's a good one." Unfortunately, the time it took to complete harvesting my blood lasted longer than her shift in personality, as she quickly returned to her more acidic tenor.

When she finished, I thanked her and returned to the waiting room to fetch Nancy, then together we walked back to Dr. Falk's examination room. Dr. Falk had seen our return from his office across the hall and soon rejoined us.

We began to have a conversation about my recent experience beginning April 6th up until the present. The Doctor occasionally interrupted the story with the same word, "Remarkable". When I had finished my explanation of my past few months, Dr. Falk responded, "You had best thank your lucky stars, somebody out there likes you". I nodded, smiled at Nancy and then replied, "I think I have a few guardian angels on my shoulders."

The computer on the small desk in the exam room suddenly pinged. Dr. Falk spun his chair around to face the monitor, keyed in a few characters, and a colored chart appeared on the screen. "Well, your test is positive that you do have amyloidosis, the light chain strain, but it is not uncommon for these tests to be off." I nodded; it was the answer that I had expected but with a hopeful chaser. "I will make an appointment with Dr. Jacob Laubach over at the Dana Farber Cancer Institute, he is quite experienced with this condition. He will be able to better determine your situation, and in what direction, if any, that we should proceed." I again nodded my head in compliance. "However, there is an upside," continued Dr. Falk. "Your surgery report and your ultra sound tell us that if you do have amyloidosis, it has not yet affected your heart, so you are completely non-symptomatic."

It was as if someone had pulled back a heavy curtain to expose a beautiful landscape on a sunshiny day. This was not a silver lining around a cloud, this was a parting of all clouds and the magnificent feeling of unfiltered sunshine on a cold winter's day. The change in my demeanor must have been quite noticeable as the Dr. looked at me with a twinge of disbelief. "So, if I am not symptomatic, that means that the amyloidosis has not yet reached or affected my heart, right?" The Doctor nodded his head, as I basically recited back to him his lecture that I had repeatedly watched on the internet. "You seem to know as much about this as I do," observed Dr. Falk. "Yeah, but I have you to thank for it" I shot back.

Having heard enough to digest for a while, I began to make my way off the examination table. The stiff paper beneath me that covered the table crinkled as I scooted off the table. As soon as my feet touched the floor, Doctor Falk rose from his chair and reached for my hand. "Thank you for all your help Doctor, if nothing else you have given me a foundation on which I can build hope." Doctor Falk smiled, "Well, you are a very fortunate man to have all this come to light so early in the process. Hopefully we can knock this right out of you with the proper treatment."

Nancy had approached while I was talking to the Doctor. She also reached out her hand and thanked the doctor with a warm, secure handshake. I looked at Nancy and asked, "All set?" Nancy said, "I am." Returning my attention to the doctor, I once again thanked him and wished him well as we left the office. As we walked down the hallway, Nancy asked, "How are you doing?" There was a pause for a minute as I repeated Nancy's question over and over in my head. How am I doing? I took in a deep breath, blew it out and smiled. I arrived with what could very well have been a death sentence and am leaving with the knowledge that I have a better than average chance of beating this thing. Nancy, unaware that I heard her question asked me again, "How are you doing?" To which I happily replied, "I'm doing alright." I took her hand in mine and we made our way to the elevators.

As the doors of the elevator slide open, in an instant the stench of trapped car exhaust and moist concrete permeated the vestibule. Although the air conditioner in the glass enclosure was continuously operating, the heat and humidity penetrated the walls, and made us aware of what awaited us outside of the glass door. When we pushed the glass door open, the feeling was similar to a walking into a tropical rain forest. The heat was stifling, the humidity was oppressive, and the odor was overwhelming. I thought to myself if it is so hot three stories underground, just imagine how hot it is outside.

We rushed to our car without running and hastily jumped inside. Nancy started the car and the air conditioner immediately began to blow cold air, causing our discomfort to last less than thirty seconds. Nancy backed out of the parking space, began to follow the maze of arrows towards the exit until we finally saw the rays of sunshine in its farthest reach down the ramp in the garage. It was now about four o'clock, not the ideal time to begin a car trip anywhere, but especially so in Boston.

There are many traffic rules that are recognized nationally as standard conventions; except in Boston. Green traffic lights mean go fast; yellow mean go faster, and red lights mean stop only if you are more than ten feet from the stop line. If you are within the ten-foot space, floor the gas pedal and drive staying close to the middle of the intersection to avoid the drivers who pull into the intersection because they think that they are in more of a hurry than you. Stop signs are suggestions and yield signs are ignored. Speed limit signs, especially on the expressway are completely disregarded, because you seldom reach the posted limit, and if by chance the gods shine down upon you and grant you an open lane, you are going as fast as your car can carry you to make up for the time that you lost in traffic. Blinkers, if they are to be deployed, are done so either when the car in front of you reaches the turn it is taking, or they stay on for nine to ten miles. Hand signs are allowed, but only one finger is visible. There are no road rage incidents in Boston because what other states consider road rage, Boston drivers consider driver etiquette. Welcome to Boston!

CHAPTER 27

The ride back home was a chance for me to sit back, reflect and concentrate on the day's events. It was as if a massive storm cloud had just floated overhead, obscuring a clear blue sky, but there were breaks in the cloud that allowed great beams of sunlight to shine through. I had prepared myself for the news, whatever it was prior to the appointment. Whatever the prognosis might have been seemed to be irrelevant to me; and it was at that moment I realized that I had an epiphany. I noticed that over the past few weeks I had been welcoming good news and celebrating its arrival. But any bad news was taken lightly, without the grief and pain that always accompanied it. Good news was eternal from the moment it was revealed, where bad news was fleeting, and would soon pass. It gave me pause, and then comfort. I looked at this new found outlook on life with exuberance, as it would grant me a better opportunity to see more of the goodness in life, no matter in what shape or circumstances it came.

My thoughts then turned to home and family. Although I had this new "gift", it was a gift that I could not fully share, or had not yet learned to share. Even though the news of the day was not devastatingly bad, it was not a clean bill of health, and I had to break this news to Mark. Mark is a big, strong, handsome young man. He is quite a friendly person and very compassionate whenever he encounters someone in pain or misfortune. Breaking this news to him without causing him any undue worry or despair would demand subtlety as well as discretion.

When we arrived home, Mark had not yet returned from school. Nancy unlocked the door and we entered the house. I was tired and proceeded directly to our big sectional couch and laid down. Zeus rushed to my side and began licking my face as I laid down on the soft pillows. I pushed him away and he laid down on the floor beside me. Nancy had to run out to the market for a few items which gave me the opportunity to sleep.

The ping sound on the home alarm system startled me out of my nap. "Nancy?" I called out. As Mark entered the front door he called back, "No, it's me." Zeus sprung to his feet and greeted Mark at the door, then returned to my side. "Marco!" I greeted him as he walked into the living room. "How are you feeling, Dad?" Asked Mark. "I'm doing OK, how was school?" As he opened the refrigerator door searching for a snack, Mark answered, "Not bad, I have a bunch of homework though."

When I heard the refrigerator door close, I asked Mark to come into the family room where I was now sitting up. "Can I see you for a minute?" Mark stepped into the family room eating a sandwich that he had just constructed. He sat down on the opposite side of the sectional sofa and inquired, "What's going on?"

Suddenly, my throat which was fine a moment ago got dry, and I felt my chest fall. I had a feeling like a golf ball had just dropped from my esophagus to the bottom of my stomach. I had not prepared the words I needed to inform Mark of my new dilemma, but I wanted to tell him before anyone else did, otherwise it would cause a distrust between the two of us. "Well," I began, "The good news is my heart is doing fine, and if there is anything that goes wrong, anything, they are confident that they can fix it." Mark nodded his head approvingly. "Well, that's good," he replied. "The bad news, is not really so bad because I have some great doctors." It was then I took in a deep breath in through my nose, held it and blew it out my mouth; my never fail coping mechanism. "Because I had the operation, the doctors found a problem in my tissue that if they didn't find would put me in a lot of trouble, luckily, they found it." Mark put his hand holding the sandwich on his lap. A sense of agitation was awash over his face. "So, what's going to a...hem, what's going to happen?" He stammered out his words with concern. I shook my head from side to side and said, "Nothing, they found it before it could do me any harm. They think it's a type of cancer, but they are sure that they can take care of it without too much trouble at all." Mark stood up and walked over to me, put his hands around my neck and said, I love you, Dad." I held back what would certainly be a flood of emotion, something Mark didn't need at that moment. It was funny, when I read about the cancer online, I was not emotional. When the doctor told me to my face that he believes it is a cancer, I was not emotional. But when Mark embraced me, it was as if the bar on a stable door was broken and out galloped a stampede of emotions. I cleared my throat and responded, "I love you Mark, more than you will ever know. Now get that goddamn sandwich off the back of my neck before I have crumbs down the back of my shirt."

Mark stepped back with his eyes full of tears. It seemed like he was holding them back so that I would not get upset. "Can I get you anything?" he asked. "I'm all set," I responded. Although we have had our ups and downs, like every parent, I knew at that moment that I could be proud of the way my son was raised by both of his parents. He was becoming a good man, a man with love, care and compassion for others. Intelligence, which Mark has, is of utmost importance for a man's future, but it is love, care and compassion that is paramount for mankind. Mark will be a good man.

The soft calypso music programed into my phone to wake me began to play. It was six in the morning, and I had a full day planned. Nancy and I would have to drive into Boston to the Dana Farber Cancer Institute to meet with my new physician, Doctor Laubach. I tried to let Nancy sleep a little longer, but she felt the movement in our bed and asked the time. I told her that she could sleep a little longer, but she refused, and got up with me.

Nancy began to make the bed, and I assisted her, first pulling the sheets taut and then lying the comforter flat. "Do you want to take a shower first, or do you want me to?" I asked. As Nancy put on her robe she replied, "Why don't you take one first; I'll go down and let Zeus outside." She opened the bedroom door and left the room; a moment later I heard her welcoming Zeus to a new day, almost like she would a child.

The bathroom floor tiles were cold, a refreshing feeling ran through my body as it was a nice change from the hot and humid night. I took a cool shower and let the streams of water flow over my head as I leaned with both hands on the front wall of the tub enclosure. Although a thousand thoughts were rushing through my head, I had a sense of calm about me. I was tranquil, not worrying what this day would bring, but rather how lucky I have been over these past few months to have some of the world's most notable doctors treating me. I took in a deep breath, held it, blew it out and smiled.

While I had been in the shower, Nancy had placed a towel, fresh out of the dryer, on the counter. The soft, plush and warm material absorbed the residual water that still clung to me. After I was dry, I brushed my teeth and lathered my face with shaving cream.

Nancy again entered the bathroom and asked if I was almost finished. I told her that I would be out in two minutes. "Are you nervous?" asked Nancy. A smile appeared on my face, "To be honest with you, Nan, not in the least. I feel fine." I continued to drag my razor across my face, removing the shaving cream and the hair stubble beneath it. "Oh, that's good. There is nothing to be nervous about anyway." Nancy's face betrayed her feelings, but it was alright, I had enough certainty for the both of us.

I rinsed the remnants of shaving cream off my face with cold water and dried it. As I slapped on some cologne, Nancy turned the shower on behind me. I walked out of the bathroom and into the bedroom to give her some privacy and closed the door. Walking by the bedroom mirror, I noticed the long scar on my chest. Just a couple of weeks ago there was no way I could have imagined just how much of a cataclysmic upheaval my life was to undergo.

The bedroom was really warm, and the humidity fully saturated the air. I found the lightest pair of shorts and shirt in my dresser. Suddenly the bedroom door burst open with a thump, and in burst Zeus, greeting me to the new day. "Go get my sneakers," I ordered Zeus even though my sneakers were only five feet away. Zeus scanned the room, then ran to my sneakers, picking up one with his mouth and began to run around the room before he placed it in my hands. "Good boy," I praised him as I pet his head and ears. I put the sneaker on and then instructed him to "Go get the other sneaker." Again, he scanned the room and reacted the same way with the remaining sneaker. He is a very smart dog, and I am sure that there are many more things that I could teach Zeus if I were as smart as he.

Now, fully dressed, I made my way down stairs with Zeus, fed him breakfast and let him outside to stretch his legs. I tossed him his Frisbee a few times, it was much less of a strain on my chest than throwing a ball. Zeus retrieved the Frisbee to me and ran again into the yard to catch the flying disc. After a few times, Zeus dropped the toy and ran into the woods. Moments later he emerged and returned to play. I guess he appreciates his privacy too.

Nancy appeared at the back door, dressed and ready for our trip into Boston. "Are you all set?" she asked. "Yup. C'mon Zeus, let's go." Zeus ignored my call, which is not unusual when he is in the back yard. "Zeus!" I shouted, "Come on, let's go inside," and then I said the magic word "…I have bacon." Zeus transformed from a golden lab to a greyhound as he raced back into the house, stopped as he entered the house, turned, jumped up and closed the back door; another trick that I had taught him. He then sat down awaiting his reward. Since we didn't have any bacon, I put some peanut butter on one of his biscuits and tossed it into the air for him to catch. It wasn't bacon, but I am sure he did not mind the substitution.

We locked the doors, entered the garage, and off we drove to the Dana Farber Cancer Institute in Boston. Traffic was light for a weekday, and after stopping for coffee at Dunkin Donuts, our journey was uneventful.

We made our way from the underground parking lot up to the seventh floor of the Dana Farber for my follow-up meeting with Dr. Jacob Laubach. Nancy and I sat and waited, admiring the expansive view of Boston through the oversized windows of the waiting room. "William A?" a voice was heard from the other side of the room. I arose from my chair and began to walk towards the woman who called my name. When I reached her, I turned around to see Nancy standing behind me. I smiled and told her that this was only to get my vital signs; I would return in five minutes. Nancy took a seat closer to where the nurse took me and began reading one of the outdated People magazines.

Once the vitals were taken, I rejoined Nancy in the waiting room. "Are you nervous?" she asked. The nonchalant attitude I had earlier was still there, but not as intense. I was somewhat nervous, but far from an extreme. Within the next few minutes, I was going to find out how sick I really was. I was already resigned to the fact that I had some type of cancer, but in my research, and my discussion with Dr. Falk, I had found that amyloidosis was a slow acting, more controllable infirmity when it is diagnosed in its most early stages, which mine was. But the cloud of myeloma hung over the sky, a more aggressive, dangerous and less controllable cancer than amyloidosis. My father, having died at 55, and my brother Charlie diagnosed with cancer at 54, I knew the odds were not in my favor. "No, I'm the luckiest guy in the world. For all these things to fall into perfect synchronization as they had how could things now go wrong?" I said with the most bravado that I could offer at the moment. "They got this early enough, so no matter what happens, they can take care of it without much effort."

I continued to look out the window until once again, the nurse emerged from the doorway and called out "William A." This time Nancy accompanied me to the office down the hallway. We entered the examination room and sat down on the matching chairs, leaving the desk chair for the doctor. The room was all white with white cabinets, a white counter, a white desktop and a long white tissue paper cover on the beige exam table. This was absolute clinical interior decorating; nothing relaxing, nothing peaceful or thought provoking; just sterile white.

The door opened and a tall, slender man with short hair, glasses and a lab coat entered the room. His boyish face made it easy to be comfortable in his presence. I stood up and reached out my hand. "Hi Doctor Laubach," I said as we shook hands. "I'm Bill Arienti, and this is my wife Nancy," I continued as Nancy reached out her hand from her seated position to greet the doctor. "Hi Bill, hi Nancy," said Doctor Laubach. "I am really impressed with your back story of these recent events. It is quite amazing." I smiled and shrugged my shoulders, Nancy laughed and joked, "Oh yeah, there is never a dull moment with Bill around."

The doctor took his seat at the white desk and signed onto the computer. "Well, your tests are back, the blood test and the urine test, and your numbers are not that bad, but do necessitate intervention." He said emotionless. "Let me tell you everything I know so far, then I will answer all your questions, ok?" "Sure, that's fine," I responded, anxious to hear all the facts he had discovered. "Well, your urine showed that your kidneys are functioning fully, and your blood tests were elevated, which is a concern. So, to better determine what we are facing, I am going to order a bone marrow biopsy. Amyloidosis is a lot like myeloma, but the cells in myeloma have lesions where the amyloid cells don't." My hopes of getting good news had to wait. This was not bad news; it was actually more like no news. Dr. Laubach read off the range of the blood cells that pertain to my disease. "The average person has a level between 12 and 25," the doctor informed us; "Yours is 140, high, but not outrageous, yet. I've seen people's level up to 350." Now I have been in the medical field for over 25 years, and I had absolutely no idea what he was talking about, but I let him continue; Nancy, on the other hand, didn't.

"Well, what does that mean?" interrupted Nancy. Dr. Laubach looked at Nancy and smiled. "Well, your bone marrow is making a protein that is cloning itself. Whereas when cells replicate, they are all somewhat different, but all of these proteins are exactly the same." The doctor attempted to get back to the subject at hand, when once again, Nancy spoke up. "Well, what does that mean, cloned cells? Are they in his other organs?" Again, the doctor stopped, smiled and explained "It means it's cancer and we have to treat it."

Now knowing all the while from my own research that I had either one of two types of cancer, I was a little anxious; not knowing precisely what I had, the anxiety within me turned to anger. I took a deep breath, blew it out of my nose, shrugged my shoulders and asked the doctor to continue trying not to let my reaction divulge my concern. "Well," continued the doctor, "We will do a bone marrow biopsy in a few minutes to tell us what type of cancer you have." I had no idea that I was going to have the biopsy right away. I had never had one but heard that they are quite painful. Oh well, another little challenge to overcome.

The doctor took a breath, this was long enough for Nancy to formulate another question. "Well, does h....". "Stop," I ordered. "Please let him finish before you ask any more questions." Nancy stopped; her look told me that she was not happy with my scolding. The doctor then continued, "Whatever the results of the biopsy are, we are going to have to start treating you right away." The words "immediately", "stat" or "right away" in medicine are never good, especially when it pertains to you. "We are going to have to start you on chemotherapy for four sessions," he began. "There is a three-drug combination. One of the drugs is administered intravenously, one is administered subcutaneously in your abdomen and one is taken orally." I nodded to let the doctor know that I understood his explanation. The question that I then asked was the one with the answer I most feared.

"Are there any side effects associated with any of the drugs?" Having had a father and brother waste away in front of me, suffering from nausea, starvation, blisters and mouths full of open canker sores, I had to judge myself to see if I had the courage to endure these plagues. I watched them as their pain grew to an unbearable level so that even morphine failed to soothe.

I was afraid to hear the answer but prolonging the inevitable would be senseless. "Well, there are a number of possible side effects, but the fact that you are younger and in otherwise good health and have a positive attitude, I don't expect that they will be that severe." The doctor sat back in his chair and began to recite a number of possibilities, "Nausea is most common, and you could experience constipation, diarrhea," "Not at the same time, right?" I interrupted in an attempt to break the tension. My attempt worked, the doctor did a double take and began to chuckle. "Well, I hope not," he said smiling. "I will give you an anti-nausea medication just to be sure, and you can take over the counter anti diarrhea or laxative to counteract those side effects if they occur."

Dr. Laubach began writing the prescriptions on a small pad of paper. As he wrote he once again began to talk; "Do you have any problem with numbness in your fingers?" His question caught me off guard. What would that have to do with amyloidosis? "Well, I had carpel tunnel surgery a couple years ago in my right hand, but that's about it." I informed him. The Dr. nodded, "If you feel numbness in your fingers or hands, call us immediately, we can counteract that if we handle it right away, but if there is any delay it may affect you permanently." There was that word again, "Immediately", and again it was pertaining to me. "It seldom happens, but I have to make you aware of it."

"Well, I guess they don't sound that bad, I should be able to handle them," I said with confidence. "Oh, I almost forgot," announced the Doctor. "God damn it," I thought to myself, "here it comes, I know it; pain, paralysis, mouth sores, hair loss, erectile dysfunction..." The Doctor continued, "Since one of the medications is a steroid, you might find it difficult to sleep or get easily agitated, so for that we will give you Ativan. Your immune system will be reduced, so I'm also giving you an antibiotic to keep you safe. "

To say that this was a stressful time for me would be an understatement, but it seems I do my best when tension is high. I took another deep breath, blew it out my mouth and smiled. "How long will I have to go through with this, I am going to Italy in October, and I am not going to miss it. I've been waiting a year for this trip." I informed the doctor. "You can go off the chemo for a little while, then get back on it when you return. I will give you a stronger antibiotic to take with you so that you will have a higher immune level."

There are times in life when someone can give you the best news in your life, but their somber demeanor makes you feel like they told you your dog died. Dr. Laubach, on the other hand, had such a calming, friendly approach that this life altering news had very little effect on me. He gave me a feeling of trust and confidence that was never needed more than at this moment in time.

"Now, one other thing," added the doctor. "I am also going to order a set of stem cells be taken from you. Once we have them, we can cryogenically freeze them and save them for up to ten years. This way, if anything were to happen within that time, we will have your stem cells available to inject back into your bone marrow to help you." That was a procedure I had never heard of before that day. "Does it require surgery?" I inquired. "No, but it is time consuming, two to four days for six hours a day." Explained the doctor. "You sit in a chair and they insert a large needle into your vein, then take your blood, extract the stem cells with a machine, then puts the blood back into your body." I had a procedure similar to this a number of times when I gave platelets in the past. The only real bad part was being harpooned by a huge needle. Then again, donating platelets only took 45 minutes.

The doctor again sat back and took a long look at me, "Are you alright? You understand everything I explained to you?" he asked. I looked around me to see if something was wrong, and after doing a quick survey, I shook my head and said "Yes, I'm fine, why?" "You have a very good attitude. That attitude will serve you better than you know during all of this," said the doctor with the sound of astonishment in his voice.

"Well, I look at it like this, everything that has happened to me throughout this whole series of events has led up to this moment," I reasoned. "If I didn't go to the class, I would have been dead. If I didn't forget my coat, I would have been dead. If I fell on a car, I would have been dead. If I didn't break my jaw, no one would have gone to the Mass General, and then I wouldn't have found out I have this disease. If I didn't seek out Dr. Falk, I would be walking around with a time bomb inside me. And if I didn't get to you, I most likely would have been dead in five years. So, all in all, if you look at it this way, I'm the luckiest guy in the world." The doctor looked at me somewhat quizzically and smiled, "You are amazing," he said shaking his head.

Nancy had not said a word in about thirty minutes, the doctor then asked if there were any other questions, so I looked at Nancy and said, "Go ahead." Both the doctor and Nancy chuckled. "Has he had this for a long time, he had been seeing an oncologist for a few years?" asked Nancy. "Well, Bill told me about the Gama globulin he had been diagnosed with years ago. If that's what you're talking about, the answer is no, but it may have developed into this," explained the doctor. "Remember, this was not found by symptoms, it was found by accident. If he had this five years ago, he would not be in such good condition. He would have shown up at his primary care physician with trouble breathing and chronic fatigue, the doctor would have probably treated him for congestive heart failure while the amyloidosis continued to grow undiagnosed within him." Nancy nodded, "How long will he have to be on chemo for?" The doctor took a deep breath, "At least four months, maybe more," estimated the doctor. "It depends on your protein count, if it is low, we can stop; but if it goes back up, then you will have to be on a maintenance program, but that won't be as bad as the treatment."

"Can I ask you a question," I said. "Go right ahead," allowed the doctor. "We live in Hanover, which is a good hour and a quarter a way without any traffic. We have the Dana Farber Cancer Institute in Weymouth, which is significantly closer. Would there be any way that I could get my treatments in Quincy and come back here every few weeks for you to examine and measure my progress?" Now, I know that this doctor is regarded as highly as a doctor can be and has an overabundance of patients to take up all of his time, but after asking him this question his expression changed from a humorous smile of a man to a sulking one of a disappointed child. "It's not that I don't trust you, or anything like that," I began, "but getting chemo in here would be an all-day ordeal. Weymouth would be much easier."

In the short time that we had known each other, it seems we had become friends. There was a mutual admiration for each other and the choice of the life paths we chose, and a genuine interest in each other's line of work. He was kind, informative and concerned, and in the world today, these qualities are difficult and sometimes impossible to find all in one human being. "You can do that," said the doctor. "I will set you up with my associate in Weymouth, Dr. Chi. She is a good doctor and quite capable. You then will come in here every three months for a progress examination." I, as well as Nancy, was relieved. Depending on the time of day, it could take up to 2 ½ hours to get into the Boston hospital and the same, if not more time to get home. With Chemo lasting about 3 hours from start to finish, I would be spending a full eight-hour day every time I went for treatments. Weymouth, being only a few miles from my home, would take less than a half an hour for the round trip.

With all the details seemingly arranged, the three of us rose from our seats, and wished each other well. As I shook Dr. Laubach's hand, I experienced a sense of inner peace and comfort. This was not an everyday, run of the mill doctor, but rather a true healer of both body and mind. I left the office without fear or apprehension, as his words of optimism continuously ran through my head. I truly wished he worked in the Weymouth facility because more than advice and guidance, he gave me hope.

"In a minute the nurse will be in to take you to the procedure room to get your marrow." Said Dr. Laubach as he walked out of the room. "Take care, and if you have any problems or questions please call me. "He seems really nice." remarked Nancy. "Yeah, he does." I agreed.

A moment later a knock came from the door, and the door slowly opened. In walked a young woman wearing hospital scrubs and a pair of bright white sneakers. "I'm going to take you for the bone marrow extraction, can I see your wristband please?" requested the nurse. I held out my hand allowing her to read the band. "What is your date of birth?" she asked. "March 23, 1962." The nurse released my arm and asked me to follow her. "You can wait in the waiting room please," she said to Nancy, pointing to the door that led out of the office. "I will see you in a few minutes." I assured her as we separated in the hallway.

The nurse led me down the corridor and into another white room, but this one had a hospital gurney in it. "The doctor will be right in." said the nurse, and left me alone in the room. About three minutes later a tall, slender, middle aged woman entered the room. "Mr. Arienti?" she inquired. "The one and only!" I said to create a laugh, it didn't work. "I'm here to take your bone marrow biopsy. Can you please tell me your date of birth?" By this time, I felt like I had told the world my date of birth, "March 23, 1962." "OK, please loosen your belt and lie face down on the bed," she instructed. I did what she asked when again the door opened and the nurse who brought me to the room returned. The two women gloved up, donned yellow paper gowns and masked their faces. I felt a cold liquid on my back, I assumed it was Betadine to stop infection. "OK, I am going to give you a couple of shots of Novocaine, and when you are numb, I will take your marrow" said the doctor.

I felt a sharp object penetrate my skin right about my pelvis in the center of my back. The area became warm, then I felt the pain in another location. I am not sure how many more shots I got as the anesthetic took effect quickly. After a few moments I felt a pressure on my lower back, but no pain. A moment later the pain arrived as a large needle found its way through the muscle and into the bone of my spine. It took only a minute, but I could not wait for it to be done.

As I buried my head in the pillow and took deep breaths, the doctor announced that she was done. "Please get up slowly" ordered the doctor as the nurse took both my hands in hers to help me up. I sat on the edge of the bed for a moment, then holding my pants up with my hand, I stood up without any difficulty or lightheadedness. I re-adjusted my pants and followed the doctor and nurse out of the room. As I opened the door to the outer office, I saw that the once crowded waiting room was now almost empty. Nancy stood up and approached me, "Are you alright?" she asked.

The feeling of relief and happiness that I earlier enjoyed with Dr. Laubach had for some reason disappeared, and in its stead was a feeling of irritability. I could not explain why I felt this way, but I could feel myself becoming an unpleasant person for no reason. "I told you that I'm fine," I barked, and we walked out of the office.

Usually I have a great memory for where I leave my car when I park it in a large area. Whatever the floor, the area, the lot may be, the location just sticks in my head. As we left the consult, I got into the elevator and pushed the button for the third parking level. We exited the kiosk and I began to walk to the area that I parked my car when I realized that I forgot where I parked it. Maybe it was all the information I just received, maybe it was psychological trauma from receiving certification of the news for which I thought I was already prepared. Whatever the reason, I could not find my car. I took out my keys and hit the alarm button to assist me in locating the vehicle, but no horn was audible.

"Are you sure we are on the right floor?" asked Nancy. My anger was interfering with my thought process and now was encroaching on my social graces as well. "Yeah, I'm on the right friggin' floor!" I snapped back at her. We continued to walk around the third floor, growing hotter with each step. The underground air was thick with humidity, which when combined with the remnants of lingering auto exhaust made breathing difficult. After walking in circles for fifteen minutes, we noticed we were once again at the elevator kiosk. "Let's try the fourth floor," I growled to Nancy as she followed me into the enclosure. I accidentally pushed the button for the third floor once again, and the elevator doors immediately separated, once again exposing the third-floor kiosk. "God damn it," I muttered as I realized my mistake, and then pushed the button for the fourth floor. "Are you alright?" asked Nancy. The way that I was behaving was totally uncalled for as my demeanor was directed towards the one person who was completely undeserving of receiving such a contemptable attitude.

The elevator stopped at the fourth level. Exiting the kiosk, I pressed the alarm button on my key to find my car right in the place I had parked it, twenty feet away. Nancy was silent as we walked to the car. After being together close to 35 years, she could sense my feelings better than I could myself. About 10 feet away from the car, I pressed the remote and unlocked the doors. We climbed into the car, started it and felt the comfort of the cool air blowing from the air conditioning vents. "Are you OK?" inquired Nancy.

She had not yet shifted the car in drive as I sat with both of my hands holding the seatbelt. I took a deep breath in through my nose and out of my mouth. On the exhalation, I looked straight ahead and said, "I'm pissed off." I don't know if that was a normal response to being told that you have a potentially fatal disease. Should I have been scared? Panicked? Depressed? Is there a correct emotion to have at this time? "This is unbelievable," I fumed. "I knew I had something, I knew what the news was going to be, but for some reason, I'm still pissed."

Nancy did not respond for a minute. Again, her insight into me was keen. She gave me the opportunity to sort things out in my head without any outside influence or pressure. We sat in silence for a moment while the noise of the air conditioner competed with the scratching static of the radio. I turned off the radio, replaced my hand onto the belt, inhaled another deep breath in through my nose and blew it out of my mouth in one loud whoosh. "It's over," I proclaimed. Nancy looked at me somewhat suspiciously.

"What?" she replied. "It's done, I am in the best hands and receiving the best care I possibly can. I have been the luckiest guy alive since this whole thing began, why should it run out now?"

Shaking her head slowly, Nancy's expression began to transform from deep concern to disbelief. "You're OK with this?" she questioned. "What choice do I have?" I replied with defiance. "Is sulking or feeling bad for myself going to make me better? Depression is only going to make this worse. So, I know the situation I am in, I know they found it early, I know that my chances are much greater than if I was symptomatic. I know that I'm going to beat this thing, I'm in a much better position than most people who are diagnosed with cancer, so I'm already ahead of the game."

It was Nancy's turn to take the deep breath in through her nose and out her mouth. "Well, I guess that's a good way of looking at it," she said, her look of disbelief now again transforming into the beginning of a smile.

"The only thing I don't want to do is tell my family right now," I told Nancy. With my brother Charlie quickly losing his battle with cancer, and my sister Marie and brother, Ernie absorbed with concern of Charlie's comfort, adding my situation to this already tenuous equation would be adding unneeded blades of straw to the back of an overburdened camel. Nancy agreed, and as the exit bar of the parking garage slowly lifted into a vertical position, we departed the automobile underworld and returned once again into the warmth, comfort and reassurance of sunlight.

CHAPTER 28

" Oh, it's cold and lonely in the deep dark night, I can see paradise by the dashboard's light." It was an omen, the one song from my days at Quincy High School that when I hear it, I remain in my car until it finishes, no matter if I am at my destination or not. Paradise by the Dash Board Lights by Meatloaf is not one song, but three separate songs that harmonize into each other, along with a momentary interruption of a baseball game by a Phil Rizzuto impersonator. There aren't many arrangements like this in modern music that are enjoyable to listen to; Queen's "Bohemian Rhapsody", and Billy Joel's "Scenes from an Italian Restaurant" are a couple of other quality ones that come to mind.

The song woke me from the previous night's sleep. I had forgotten to shut off my alarm; but if I had to wake up to anything, this song would have been one of my choices. As I lay in bed listening to how the music fit so perfectly together, I could hear the faint noise of Zeus's paws scratching on the hardwood floors. Faint was the sound at first, but with each second it became louder and louder. He ran up the stairs with a bound, and by this time he sounded like a Clydesdale on a cobblestone street. My bedroom door opened with a loud "Bang", as Zeus used his head as a battering ram to get into my bedroom. He ran over to my side of the bed, put his two feet up on my mattress and began licking my face, greeting me to a new day. He then dropped from the bed, ran around the room, picked up my socks from the day before, and returned to give them to me as some type of gift.

The next noise I heard was Nancy's clogs hurrying up the hardwood stairs. "Is Zeus in here? I told him to stay downstairs and let you rest," explained Nancy. At that moment I thought to myself, I had my favorite song, my wife, my dog all together in the same room, all I was missing was my so...... "Guess what I got on my biology test," asked Mark as he walked into the room. Now the world was right, I was with my family. "An 80?" I asked Mark. Earlier in the semester, Mark had a difficult time understanding certain areas of biology, but he had been working diligently, dedicating himself to clear this hurdle. "Close," answered Mark, "A 91." His answer produced smiles and congratulatory praise from both Nancy and me.

Mark kneeled down and began playing with Zeus. "What are you doing up here? Are you supposed to be in here?" Zeus was excited to be the recipient of Mark's attention. Trying to avert a catastrophe in my room, I warned Mark that Zeus had not yet been outside that morning, and if he gets too excited, we might have a problem. Mark stood up and smiled, "C'mon Zeus," called Mark as he walked out of the bedroom. Zeus obediently followed. "He's so good," I thought, but the thought manifested into a verbal blurt. Nancy replied, "I'm so happy that he's doing so much better in the class." Shaking my head, I joked back, "Well, I was talking about Zeus, but he's a good kid too." We both began to laugh.

I looked at the clock to see it was 8:48. The sun was forcing slivers of light through the small space between the shade and the window jamb. Although the breeze created by the paddle fan on our ceiling made the air in our bedroom comfortable at night; it was almost chilly first thing in the morning.

Since I am not a tea aficionado, I do not know the intricacies of one cup of tea from another; however, Nancy has an addiction to "Dunkin' Donuts" tea; medium, with milk and two sugar or Splenda, depending on whether or not she is dieting. I, on the other hand, am a huge fan of coconut coffee, extra coconut, cream and two sugars from just about any coffee shop with the strong exception of Starbucks. As I climbed out of bed, Nancy informed me that she was taking a quick ride to Dunkin's for coffee and tea, and she would be right back. As Nancy approached the front door, Zeus galloped away from Mark and headed to the front door. "Are you going to Dunkies with me?" The sound was unmistakable, Zeus was turning in circles around the front door in excitement. I was hoping that Mark had taken him outside already.

It was well past my morning constitutional, and now that I was wide awake, it was reminding me that time and tide wait for no man. I jumped out of bed and headed for the bathroom. After answering natures call, I showered in the well-lit cool water shower. Nancy had just taken towels out of the dryer, so I took one from the middle of the pile, still warm, and dried off. When I looked in the mirror in front of me, I noticed that the incision from my surgery was beginning to manifest itself into a larger scar. My past medical history includes a tendency for my surgery scars to protrude and slightly discolor, making them unsightly; but I began to laugh thinking that if this was the only reason women on the beach would avoid me, I was pretty damn lucky.

After shaving and brushing my teeth, I dressed and was happy to see a cup of coconut coffee sitting for me on the kitchen countertop. Nancy sat on the couch, sipping her tea and watching the previous night's episode of "Outlander". She had become enthralled with the show, and asked me, as well every other member of our immediate and extended family and circle of friends to watch it. The biggest drawback of the show for me is that the characters speak with a Scottish brogue, and I only understand that language after having a few beers.

Suddenly, the phone began to ring, and the words Dana Farber Cancer appeared on the top right-hand corner of the television screen. Nancy instinctively pushed the pause button on the remote control to save her place as I picked up the phone and placed the receiver to my ear. "Hello," I greeted the caller. "Good morning, may I please speak to a mister Bill Arienti?" responded the voice on the other end of the line. "Speaking," I returned. "Hi Mr. Arienti, this is Karen from the Dana Farber Cancer Institute in Weymouth. We were wondering if you could come in this afternoon for a consult with Dr. Chi." I had no plans for the rest of the day, and asked Nancy if she was busy. Nancy thought for a moment, then not being able to recall any prior engagement, said that she was available.

"Great," said Karen cheerfully. "Could you come in at 3, we will do some blood work, a quick physical exam and a consult with Dr. Chi. All in all, it will be about 2 hours." I jotted down all the information on the back of a junk mail envelope and let her know that I would be there. I ended the call, but before I could press the end call button, Nancy was already asking questions.

"OK, before you start," I began, holding up my right hand as I hung up the phone with my left. "The Dana Farber in Weymouth asked if I could come in tomorrow at 3 for an exam, some blood work and a consult with Dr. Chi. It will take about 2 hours." My information was followed by a barrage of questions from my very concerned wife. As she asked the questions and I kept answering "I don't know," I gave her the envelope with the information and said, "This is all I've got." Nancy then informed me, quite adamantly, that she was going to go to the appointment with me. I had every intention of bringing her with me, but I decided to give her the satisfaction of domination.

The Dana-Farber building in Weymouth is very familiar to me from my job as an EMT. I often transported South Shore Hospital patients across the street to the Dana-Farber for chemotherapy and radiation treatments. Little did I know that I would be receiving treatment there myself.

The medical oncology unit was located on the third floor, one floor higher than the bridge from the parking garage enters the building. We parked the car, crossed the bridge and took the elevator to the third floor. As the doors opened up, we were greeted with a bright, cheerful office. I made my way to the reception desk, told them my name, and was given a clipboard with a stack of papers. "Could you please fill out these forms before we draw your blood?" asked the middle-aged woman behind the desk. I took the clipboard and joined Nancy in the waiting area.

I took out my wallet and removed my health insurance card, my medication insurance card and my license. I began to fill out the forms that seemed to be exactly the same with the exception of the bold lettered label at the top. After filling out half of the forms, I was pleased to see that the remaining paperwork were pamphlets for policy, procedures and privacy. I turned in the completed paperwork along with my insurance cards and license to the woman at the desk. She inserted the three cards into a tiny copy machine and returned them to me. "They will be right with you." Commented the woman. "Can I please see your left hand?" I gave her my hand and she expertly wrapped a white paper bracelet with black printing around my wrist. I sat down with the new adornment and waited barely a minute when a blonde nurse with what sounded like a Slavic accent called out "Bill, Bill?"

I stood up and began to walk towards the voice. Nancy also rose from her chair, but I stopped her and instructed her to stay, as this was only a blood test. Nancy sat back down and I followed the blonde nurse with the Eastern European accent to the lab.

The lab was a collection of small stalls, each complete with a blood drawing chair, a stool, a blood pressure machine, computer keyboard and monitor and a rolling cabinet stocked with needles, test tubes and bandages. In a common area of the lab was a large scale, a vile machine if there ever was one. "Please take off your shoes and stand on the scale," instructed the nurse. "We need to get a baseline weight on you."

Not having known that I was going to be weighed, coupled with the ninety degree weather outside, my foot attire that day was a pair of sneakers sans socks. Now I am in no way a germaphobe, nor do I have any hang-ups about my feet. However, I am uncomfortable placing my bare skin onto any medical device found in a hospital or other medical office building. I am sure that I come in contact with more germs walking barefoot on the beach, or even around my house, but I have a phobia about coming in contact with any medical equipment that may have been used by another, including scales. Rather than complain at my very first visit, I did what I was told.

Now, never in my life could my body have been described as slender. Chubby, husky, rotund, those were some of the more charitable adjectives that had been used in reference towards me. As a child and adolescent, I blamed this on my Italian mother. Every night at dinner my mother, a phenomenal cook, would create these epicurean masterpieces. Since there were six of us eating, she would make extra large amounts to ensure everyone's appetite was satisfied. Since my mother grew up during the depression, the idea of throwing any food away was taboo at my house, and leftovers, well, unless we had Chinese food, leftovers were not looked upon kindly. This meant that we would all have heaping dishes of food, and after finishing more than our share, my mother would always say here, have some more; and I don't think I ever said no. As time went on, I realized that as other kids in school were tall and thin, I was tall and fatter. I was not really over the top fat, like my mother never bought men's Bermuda shorts for me to wear as pants, but we would always have to go to the last bin when looking for pants in the boys section.

However, being a fat kid did offer me one lesson in life, you have to have thick skin to get along in this world. When you are a fatter kid, one of three things happen, you crawl into a shell and be depressed your whole life, or you lose weight and fight to stay thin forever, or you embrace your size, accept you for who you are, and let the comments and insults roll off your back. I chose door number three. Over the years my skin became pretty callous against not only fat comments, but pretty much any insult hurled at me for virtually any reason. I never took things to heart which is probably why I have the attitude I do.

As I stepped onto the scale, I said in a joking voice, "vile machine", which solicited a chuckle from the nurse. "I hate these things too," she shot back. Before the readout on the screen, I reached out and pressed the kilograms button and smiled at the nurse, "I'm lighter on this scale," I joked and we both laughed. She was a very friendly woman, and I would soon find out that every nurse in this unit was just as friendly, helpful and kind as the next. Having worked around terminally ill patients for a number of years, I recognized the full measure of devotion each of these women and few men had to giving hope to those with very little left. It made me look back on my career and hope that I gave every patient I transported over the years the same level of grace and dignity these people offered me.

I stepped off the scale when the numbers appeared, slipped back into my sneakers and proceeded to follow the nurse to her station. I sat down in the chair provided and allowed her to take my vital signs as well as three vials of blood. "Are you getting a port?" she asked me.

Suddenly, with this one question, reality set in. For a few years I had worked for a private ambulance firm that transported patients back and forth to kidney dialysis treatments. These patients would have large prominent protuberances under their skin and running down their arms or across their chest and protruding out of their skin. The dialysis machine is plugged into these ports to prevent veins and arteries from collapsing during the treatments. This was unacceptable to me; I had been stoic, strong and determined throughout this whole process, but the thought of having a port anywhere on my body made me uneasy, to say the least.

"Do I need a port?" I asked the nurse. She must have heard the nervous apprehension in my voice, because her eyes shot over to me with concern. She began an attempt to reduce my recognizable anxiety by explaining that not everyone requires a port, and being an otherwise healthy younger man, my veins should be strong enough to accommodate the medications.

Unfortunately, her more positive assessment fell onto deaf ears. The thought was now firmly secured in my mind, and nothing short of a physician's direct assurance would cause it to waiver. The nurse completed her duties of drawing blood and taking vital signs and instructed me to return to the waiting area.

Nancy had been sitting in the waiting room, alone in a room full of people. I returned to the seat next to hers when without hesitation Nancy asked, "What did they say?" I was quite sure that Nancy did not know exactly what a port was, nor what they looked like. The thought of having one, even after I left the lab continued to press on my mind. "They just took my vitals," I answered Nancy, not wanting to have to define a port and then describe what it looks like. Nancy sipped her tea and I sipped my coffee and we waited for the doctor to see us.

"Bill?" A voice floated through the waiting room. "Bill?" I stood up to see another nurse, tall, thin and blonde. She was middle aged and had a very welcoming smile. Nancy stood up beside me and together we walked towards the nurse. "I'm taking you down to see Dr. Chi," explained the nurse as we followed close behind her down a long hallway and into a small examination room. "Right in here please," said the nurse. We followed her directions and took seats near the window. "Dr. Chi will be right in," said the nurse and closed the door as she walked out of the room.

The wait was not more than a few seconds when we heard a knock on the door immediately before it swung open. An Asian woman in what looked like her late 30's, wearing a longer white lab coat entered the room. She greeted both Nancy and me with, "Hello, I am Dr. Chi." As she began to extend her hand, I raised up from my chair and accepted her hand into mine, firmly shaking it while looking into her eyes. Nancy did not rise but reached out and shook her hand as well.

"Well Mr. Arienti, It looks like you have had quite an interesting year," said the doctor, her Chinese accent was very slight as her speech pattern was precise, avoiding contractions and fully pronouncing every syllable of every word she said. "Well, that is one way of looking at it I guess," I chuckled as Dr. Chi sat down next to me. She began our conversation by saying, "Well, how are you feeling today?" I smiled, opened my hands to an upward position and with certainty I said, "I feel great."

The Doctor began to chuckle, "Well, I guess we are ahead of the game," she replied. She asked me to remove my shirt and sit on the examination table. I unbuttoned my shirt and pulled off my t shirt, handing them to Nancy. I sat on the paper covered table and awaited the icy touch of Dr. Chi's stethoscope; she did not disappoint. After a quick examination she began to inspect the inner part of my forearms. Reaching into her pocket, the Doctor retrieved a long, thick blue rubber band and wrapped it around my left arm just below my elbow. She slapped my arm a few times below the band and then removed it. Dr. Chi then reapplied the band to my right arm and again slapped my arm before removing the band. "Well, your veins look pretty good, I don't think you need a port."

Her words were a refreshing cool breeze on a hot August day. "Wow, those are the words I was hoping to hear you say," I said in one long exhale. Nancy looked confused, "What is a port?" she asked. I explained to Nancy what a port is, what it does and what it looks like. My words did little to quell her curiosity, as her demeanor never changed. "You have good veins," said Dr. Chi. "They are deep, but they will handle the I.V."

The Doctor again sat in her chair and reviewed my chart on her computer display. Well, your numbers are a little high, so we are going to start giving you chemo next Thursday, if that's ok with you." Since I knew that this was a lifeline that I could not pass up, I immediately agreed to the proposed day. "OK then, so we will do Fridays for four cycles. Each cycle consists of four weeks, then a week off," explained the Doctor, "Are Thursdays going to be OK?" I responded with an affirmative, then looked at Nancy. I guess I should have done that in reverse and asked Nancy first, but what's done was done.

"Thursday you just need to come up to this floor and register at the desk, they will handle everything from there. It will take about 4 hours for the whole procedure." For a number of years, I had transported cancer patients to and from both chemotherapy and radiation treatments. I had seen firsthand the affects these treatments produced in even the strongest patients. Although I knew that this would ultimately lengthen my life, regardless of how good the ends would be, I was not looking forward to the means.

"What's a port?" I had hoped Nancy had forgotten about this part of the examination conversation. "A port is a shunt that goes directly into a vein or artery so that a patient can receive intravenous medications without further damaging any already damaged blood vessels." I gave Nancy the most clinical definition of the equipment and procedure that I could come up with, hoping that it would end the inquiries. "Why are you so happy that you don't have to have one?" Well, so much for hope. "Sometimes when they put in a port, they have a large shunt subcutaneously that resembles a snake crawling under your skin. Other times it's just a big tube sticking out of your body, both of them look pretty bad." Nancy's demeanor became less curious and more agitated.

"When did they tell you that you would need that?" I took a deep breath in through my nose and blew it out my mouth, my old pressure relief valve.

To be honest, I did not want to even talk about this, but Nancy had been so responsive to my every need, every call that I felt my discomfort was irrelevant. "They didn't say that I needed one, they said that I might need one. They told me when I was in the lab." Being open and honest is always the way to go, but this time it was just causing more and more friction. "Why didn't you tell me when they told you?" Playing conversation chess in my head, trying to figure out my contenders next three moves was always one of my strongpoints. I thought Nancy's last question was my opportunity to get out of the conversation. "Well, to be honest with you, I have seen hundreds of these ports, and I get sick every time I see them. I was afraid to even think about having to get one, and from the second they mentioned it, all I did was pray that it didn't need it." I was not lying; I was praying my hardest to whoever would listen not to have a port.

Nancy's agitation suddenly turned back to compassion. "I didn't know that it bothered you that much. I'm so sorry; you should have told me so that I could have helped you through this." Finally, this conversation was coming to an end. "I know how much you want to help me Nan, but there is nothing that you could have done or said that would have consoled me if I needed a port, but thank you for caring."

No matter how many times people have told me that I was unlucky, or how sorry they were for me, I laughed. I am a smiling man who in all honesty should have been dead. From here on in I am playing with the house's money, and I intend to invest of it what I must, and splurge all I can.

With the chemotherapy regime scheduled, and its side effects on me not yet known, I decided that I wanted to take a break and get away for a few days. Both Nancy and I always enjoyed the Southern Maine seacoast, so we decided to go up to Kennebunkport for an extended weekend. We had just bought a new, used car and decided that taking if for a long ride while it was still under warranty made sense.

I started to call hotels and found that many of them were already booked before the upcoming weekend. I finally found one that was strategically named to attract travelers. The Kennebunk Port Inn was located in Kennebunk, the town next to Kennebunkport which is right on the water. This inn was not what one thinks of when they imagine an inn; no Victorian or New England farm house by the ocean in a quaint Maine village, it was a motel, on a major highway that ended up being quite a distance from the water. The place was not all bad, as it was the impetus that finally caused me to download the Trip Advisor website. Although we were disappointed in the facility, the location, the distance to the beach and the town, it was clean, and they were hospitable, so we stayed and chalked it up to a learning experience. We had dinner and went back to the room for an uneventful night.

The next day was quite hot; so hot in fact that at eight in the morning the concrete walkway had already reached a temperature well above the point of toleration for bare feet. We decided to go to the beach, but first we needed the equipment to adequately enjoy ourselves. After breakfast we drove about five miles south looking for a beach shop to procure some necessities. After driving five miles on a main road in a beach community and not finding any kind of surf shop, we turned around and tried the other direction. Finally, our quest was over; we found a beach shop.

Being the only beach shop in the area, we were at the mercy of jackals. For the price of two beach chairs, two beach towels and a small umbrella for Nancy, we could have eaten in one of Maine's best restaurants. We then stopped to pick up something for lunch on the beach, and off we went.

It seems that our idea was not so novel, as everyone in southern Maine had seemed to flock to the beach that morning. Parking at the beach was at a premium, and the parking police were out in force. Sometimes the universe gives and sometimes it takes; today was a giving day. As I drove down to the best section of the beach, a ball bounced across the street in front of me. I slammed on the brakes as two children ran out to retrieve it. The car in front of me continued driving and as luck would have it, a couple returned to their car on the street giving me the ideal position of which to take advantage. Six feet from the beach, ten feet from the stairs and a spot on the beach in an ideal location.

After setting up our spot, I paused for a moment. This would be the first time that I would be removing my shirt, standing out in public bare chested with a huge scar down the center of my chest. Of all the things I can use to describe myself, the one thing that would never enter my mind was self - conscious of my appearance. I had a scary sensation that the moment I removed my t-shirt, a child would scream in fright at the scar, and instantly thirty thousand eyes would in unison turn towards me and just gasp. I know how stupid that sounds, but I never said that I was intelligent.

I took a deep breath, grasped the bottom of my shirt and stretched it over my head to hear seagulls squawking, waves breaking on the shore, children playing, and a variety of music coming from speakers across the beach. No one noticed. No one even batted an eye. I was not a monster; I was no more disgusting than I was before the surgery. The only alarm came from Nancy, a fair skinned beauty who is ever vigilant in skin protection. "Hurry up and put some sun screen on your chest!" she called out, rifling through her beach bag to find her bottle of sun screen. I laugh when she protects her skin with such enthusiasm. She is much less protective than she was a few years ago, as I would joke that Nancy's beachwear consists of a sun hat, a long sleeve t-shirt, long pants and 200 sun screen on her hands and feet. Whatever she does, it works because her skin is still as supple as it was when I first met her over 35 years ago.

The Maine ocean water, usually frigid even in summer, was not only bearable, it was actually refreshing. Not as warm as the Caribbean, but far from the glacial bearing water we expected. The day was enjoyable, soaking up the summer sun, cooling off in the soothingly pleasant water. As I relaxed, I was able to disassociate myself from the situations at home. My brother's sickness, as well as the sickness of my best friend had continued to deteriorate their bodies, and time was not their ally. It was a strange feeling that I was experiencing at this time. I was more concerned with their welfare than I was the impending chemotherapy regiment that I was about to experience. As an EMT, I had seen the effects of chemotherapy, the weight loss, the nausea and vomiting, the lethargy and loss of strength. I should be quaking knowing what I know, but my mind went back to a previous position; I am living on the house time now. Every day is a gift, some days will be better gifts than others, but the fact that I am still able to enjoy the world around me, hold close my family, experience the pleasure of good food; then a few days of discomfort is a pretty good trade. At this time, I was much more concerned about them, their suffering, and the fates of their families when their final certainty has arrived.

The weekend trip to Maine was a rejuvenating and delightful time.

CHAPTER 29

When one walks on a beach, their feet sink in the sand. The depth of their imprints is dependent on their weight and the water content of the sand. Unless the footprints are immediately washed away by the surf, there is no way to take a step into sand without leaving some sort of sign that they were there. In our world, sand is often considered insignificant. A tiny grain, almost microscopic in size, has virtually no value, but has the potential to be so much more.

One grain of sand will not make any impact whatsoever if dropped into a hole of any size. A grain of sand will not cause a car to gain traction on a slippery road. A grain of sand cannot strengthen concrete in the slightest. It has no monetary value even in a country with a monetary system that has a currency denomination less than one-one hundredth of a penny. A grain of sand is worthless, one would come to believe.

However, take that one grain of sand and put it on a french-fry before eating it, you will certainly know of that grain of sand's existence. Place it between your eye and your eye lid and you will surely recognize it. Rub it against your glass or place it between pieces of glass; a single grain of sand can cause more damage than one could imagine.

Now take that same grain of sand and place it within an oyster. Leave the oyster to live and flourish for up to six years, and that grain of sand will miraculously turn into a pearl. The pearl is not worthless, the pearl is not useless. A pearl has a number of uses including esthetic value, and depending on the quality of that pearl, it could be quite valuable.

As many grains of sand as there are on a small beach, there are as many people in the world. If one person decides for himself to be useless, worthless, then their existence on this earth will be little more than an irritant. That person would be the proverbial grain of sand in society's collective eye. Although this type of person does exist, they are truly a microcosm in the world. No one wants to be useless; no one wants to be worthless. All people, unless they are suffering from a severe psychological ailment, desire to be of worth and make a difference in this world.

The levels of ambition and drive may differ greatly among all the people of the world, but with the same caveat as mentioned above, no one is void of all ambition and self-worth. Everyone has it within themselves to make a difference, no matter how small, no matter how noticeable. From holding a door open to writing a check for ten million dollars to a charity, each person makes a contribution to this world based on their personal situation and their ambition to make a difference.

In the scope of the vastness of the universe, none of us are any more significant than that grain of sand is to us. We may decide that we are comfortable being that unchanged grain of sand and exist just for the sake of existing. We may join other grains of sand and become the medium that makes concrete impenetrable, allows tires to gain traction on ice, fills bags that save cities from floods.

Or you can decide to be that one grain of sand that sacrifices itself to make a better world, to offer himself, his work and his being to improve the world. To understand that his ambition will not only improve him but will improve the world around him. Each of us has the ability and the choice, we can be content being a grain of sand, or we can excel, and be the pearl. The choice is yours.

CHAPTER 30

Having worked at South Shore Hospital for a number of years, I was very well acquainted with the Dana Farber Cancer Institute building immediately across the street. The Dana Farber had brokered a partnership with South Shore Hospital to treat people on the South Shore of Massachusetts who are suffering from cancer without having to go into Boston. The building contained an office for radiation therapy, MRI, diagnostics, and chemotherapy. Each specialty was equipped with state-of-the-art equipment and technology. As a satellite facility, this was most definitely one of the best.

We pulled into the parking garage connected to the Dana Farber at 8:40 for a nine o'clock appointment. After I had passed a number of open parking spaces on the lower levels, Nancy asked me where I was going. I told her that if we drove up to the third level, there is a bridge that connects to the second floor of the facility. Reaching the third level, we observed that there were a number of open parking spots. I pulled the car in, turned off the engine, and with my hands still gripping the steering wheel, I took in and released a long, deep breath. This was my way of saying "Geronimo", as I opened the door, exited the car, and walked with purpose to the door that led to the bridge. Nancy followed close behind, having to jog to keep up with my pace.

Walking across the glass bridge, it was obvious that the engineer worked with well-informed interior designers and psychologists to make the bridge a comfortable, and not in the least threatening. A soft carpet covered the floor, which made walking relaxing. Upholstered benches lined the way where one could sit and just look out through the glass wall into eternity. There were small tables that offered pamphlets on a number of different topics that someone living with cancer might find informative. At the end of the bridge was a small glass cabinet displaying stylish hats and other headwear for women whose hair had been taken by radiation therapy.

Entering the building, we took that elevator to the third floor. As the doors opened, the check-in desk was directly ahead of me. The younger woman behind the counter smiled at me and asked my name. "Hi," I said. "I am William Arienti." The woman touched a few keys on her computer keyboard and informed me that she had found my name in the database. "May I please see your license?" she asked. I pulled my wallet from my front pocket, opened it and produced my driver's license. She glanced at it, gave it back and then tore a paper wrist band from the printer. "Can you please tell me your date of birth?" she requested. "Three twenty-three sixty two," I responded. "OK, that's you," she declared. "Can I see your right hand please?" I extended my hand towards her as she wrapped the paper band around my wrist and secured it with self-adhesive tape. "They will call you in a few minutes for bloodwork," she stated. "Until then, you can take a seat."

Nancy had already found two seats together and was sitting in one with her purse occupying the other. The waiting room was almost full of people of assorted ages and differing levels of their cancer's progression. Some people sat alone; others sat with a companion to help them through their procedure. Sitting in this room awaiting my turn to be called into the treatment room caused me to reflect on all the patients I had taken to their chemotherapy treatment and radiation. I used the memory to put things into perspective, for as bad as my situation seemed, there was no possibility of me receiving radiation for my cancer. Even now, I chuckled to myself, I'm still the luckiest guy in the world.

My name was called out and I told Nancy to remain in her seat, this was only bloodwork. An older woman, still very attractive with a blonde ponytail, asked me to follow her. As we walked towards the lab the woman asked me if I was related to Charlie Arienti. "He is my brother," I replied. The woman smiled, "He is such a nice guy, he did so much work to put this facility together." Her words brought a smile to my face. As I am sure that you have already discovered, I am very proud of my family, and when I hear a member of my family being praised, it brings me great joy. "Thank you," I responded. "He really is a dedicated guy. He is in a tough battle right now, but he is living life on his own terms." The nurse's smile faded into a look of concern. "I had heard something about him being sick, is it bad?" she questioned. I nodded my head, "He is a fighter, but even the greatest fighter can fight for only so long."

We approached the scale where I removed my sneakers and stepped onto the black matt covering the stainless-steel tray. A few seconds later a number appeared in red light emitting diodes. "Fucking liar," I grumbled, which solicited full laughter from the nurse. She instructed me to sit down in her cubicle where she took my vital signs as well as three vials of blood. When she finished placing labels on the vial the nurse instructed me to return to the waiting room where I would be called soon.

Other than a radio playing soft music and local advertisements, the waiting room was almost silent. No one seemed to talk or communicate in any way, they just waited silently to be called for their treatment. As I sat down, Nancy gave me a look of bewilderment, but she also said nothing. We sat for a few minutes looking up at the ceiling or counting squares in the rug below our feet until we again heard my name; "William," once again was called out by a nurse. We stood up together and followed the nurse to a small office, much like the one in which I had been examined by Dr. Chi a few days earlier. "The Doctor will be right in," announced the nurse, who turned, left the room and closed the door behind her.

"How are you doing?" asked Nancy. To be honest, I think that she again was more nervous than I. "I'm fine," I assured her. I was not just saying that to placate her, I really was fine. I did not know what side effects, if any, would be affecting me, and worrying about something that may never happen makes no sense to me.

A few seconds later there was a knock on the door followed by the sound of the door latch turning and the soft squeak of an opening hinge. "Hello Mr. Arienti," said Dr. Chi as she extended her hand for me to shake. As I took her hand in mine, Dr. Chi turned towards Nancy and nodded, "Hello," she said warmly as she greeted Nancy. Nancy responded with "Hello Doctor."

"How are you feeling today? Are you ready for your first treatment?" Dr. Chi sounded much more excited than I felt. I did not yet know her well enough to read her. "Well, if I'm not ready now I guess I never will be," I responded. Dr. Chi requested that I sit on the exam table where she placed the bell of her stethoscope on my upper back to listen to my lungs. "Please breathe deep," she asked as she moved the bell from side to side, then up and down. When she finished with my back, she moved to my chest and told me to breathe regularly. After a few moments Dr. Chi took the stethoscope away, stepped back and asked, "All ready?" I took one more deep breath, blew it out, stood up from the exam table and with confidence proclaimed, "Let's do this."

Dr. Chi opened the door and allowed Nancy and me to pass before her. She led us into the treatment room and looked for a small private cubicle for me. Near the far corner of the room was an unoccupied cubicle with a window that overlooked the street outside. The doctor instructed me to sit in the large beige reclining chair, and instructed Nancy to sit in one of the other two seats in the cubicle. I carried a bag with some belongings, including my laptop computer, and now placed it on top of the small hospital table. I again took a deep breath and readied myself for the procedure.

It was not long before a woman who appeared to be in her mid to late 40's wearing hospital scrubs greeted me and welcomed me to the treatment center. "Hi, I'm Kelly, I'll be your nurse for today." Kelly placed a warmed blanket over my legs and asked me if I would like something to drink. Knowing that I would have to take some pills, I requested some cranberry juice. "Would you like something to eat as well, we have cookies, and the sandwiches will be up shortly," she inquired. Since I had eaten a big breakfast, I was not at all hungry, "Thanks, but I am all set." "Well, if either one of you want something, everything is right over there in the kitchen area, help yourself," she said, smiled and turned to walk away. I have to say that I was very impressed with the level of care they had already provided.

The reclining chair was exceptionally comfortable. I reached down to grab my bag, but Nancy saw what I was doing and took the bag by its black strapped handle. She then lifted the bag and placed it on my lap. I unzipped the bag and removed my laptop and cord. I asked Nancy to plug the cord into the red electrical receptacle, to which she responded, "I don't think you are supposed to use them, why don't you wait and ask the nurse if you can when she comes back." Again, Nancy shows her absolutely propensity for following directions, even if she does not know what the directions are. I was not going to fight with her today, it just wasn't worth the effort; plus, I had a full battery on of which to draw. I opened the top, turned on the computer, opened a word file and began typing. Nancy sat by watching me, I did not want to be rude, but I just wanted to occupy my mind while I waited for the procedure to begin.

It was not long before Kelly returned with a full I.V. bag and the tubes necessary to empty it into my awaiting veins. "Do you have a port?" asked Kelly. "Thankfully, no," I answered. "You get the pleasure of digging for my veins." Kelly smiled, "Good, I always love a challenge. Are your veins that deep?" I looked down onto my arm, returned my look to her and said, "Well, I personally have never tried, but most of the people that have said I do."

Kelly took my hand in hers, looked at the backside of my hand, slapped it a couple of times. She then reached over to the surgical table and took a long blue band of rubber. She wrapped the band tightly around my upper arm and tied it securely. Again, she took my hand and slapped the back of it. "There's a nice fat one," she said as she took the needle from the table, removed it from the package and then squeezed my hand. "OK, pinch," she warned and slid the needle quickly through my skin and into my vein. A little flash of blood appeared in the base of the needle alerting her that her aim was true, and she was into my vein.

Once the needle was in, she slid the plastic tube that tightly covered the needle into my vein and removed the needle. She secured the tubing first with transparent tape, then a number of adhesive tape strips. Once she was satisfied with her work, she attached the long plastic tube to me, the other end already attached to the IV bag hanging from the tall pole. As she adjusted the control, I could see the saline slowly form drops inside a bulb. Once the drop was too big to hang onto the tube, it detached itself and fell into the small reservoir at the bottom of the tube. The more she adjusted the control, the faster the drop grew in size and dropped into the waiting fluid below.

Kelly then turned, took all the wrappings from the items she had just used, and threw them into the trash barrel. "I will be right back with some of your medications," she said. "Do you want water or juice to swallow your pills with?" "I'll have some cranberry juice please." I responded. Upon hearing my request, she again left us alone in the cubicle. "How you doing Bill?" asked Nancy. I know that I tease the hell out of her, but she is really an amazing woman to have put up with all that I have put her through during our 30 plus years of marriage. "I'm fine, this is just saline they are putting in me now," I responded.

I continued to type even with the IV in my hand. Other than the tape, it did not constrict my movement in any way. At the end of the thought that I was writing, I paused and looked up. It was at this moment that I began to survey my surroundings. Although I had been in this ward a number of times before, it was always as the caregiver, never the patient. As a caregiver you do not notice the people around you, all attention is fixated on your own patient. Now that I was on the other side of the coin, I began to observe the unit. Each cubicle had a curtain for privacy, but none were drawn, allowing the patient to see out, and everyone else to see in. I did not want to be intrusive or seem nosy, so I just quickly perused the other cubicles.

For the first time since I received the news, I began to feel the uncertainty that comes with cancer. The people in all the other cubicles that I could see were suffering from more advanced cases of cancer. A gray pallor, lack of energy, missing hair and emaciation had already grasped many of the people receiving the same procedure that I was. I looked quickly, never letting my eyes settle on any one person so as not to intrude on their privacy.

I took a deep breath and sighed. Was this my future? Did they find this fucking cancer in time, or am I in the fight of my life, for my life? Will the chemicals that they are pumping into me cause me to feel nauseous? Will they cause unbearable joint pain? Will they cause blisters inside my mouth making eating impossible? "STOP IT!" I shouted to myself inside my own mind. "This is not my lot in life, this will not happen to me, I will not allow this to happen to me." I took in a deep breath, expanded my lungs to their capacity. As I inhaled, I again looked into each cubicle to grasp with my eyes each person's anguish. In that breath I took in the pain of every person in that room. I took in their fear, their sorrow, their hunger and their nausea. I held it all in my lungs for twenty seconds, trying to use their advanced illnesses as an inoculation, a vaccine of a live virus to give my body the ability to form a greater resistance against the cancer circulating through my body.

When the pressure on my diaphragm became too intense for me to contain it any longer, I allowed my breath to exit my body through my mouth, assisting it by flexing my chest muscles to put a greater level of pressure on my lungs. The air of pestilence, along with the reservoir of stale air I had reserved in the far reaches of my lungs was now out of my body, completely. When it had finally finished, I began to cough from my hypopnea and began to experience the feeling of syncope. I then turned to the window that overlooked the street, aimed my glaze up into the sky and as I coughed, I took in a new breath, a breath of clouds, a breath of sunshine, a breath of blue sky.

The exercise worked; the apprehension left my body with the contaminated air. A sense of calm, tranquility and confidence replaced any lesser feeling of anxiety. I felt a smile in my soul that transferred into my body and finally emerged onto my face. I thought that it was just a feeling of serenity, but as Kelly approached me, she noticed something. "Now that's a smile." she chuckled. She placed a white Styrofoam cup with a straw and a small clear plastic cup on the surgical table. Nancy looked at me and noticed the smile as well. "What's so funny?" she asked. "Nothing," I responded, "nothing at all."

Kelly stood in front of her computer terminal and began entering data from the keyboard. After a few moments she turned towards me, in her right hand was a scanning device like the ones seen in grocery stores. She asked me to hold up my wrist so that she could scan the white paper bracelet around my wrist. I obliged her request, then she asked me my name and birthdate, to which I replied "Herbert Schwartz, October 31, 1948."

A smirk appeared on Kelly's face, "Smart ass," she grumbled. "I have to do this, now no kidding, what is your name and date of birth?" I answered, "William Arienti, March 23, 1962." Again, Kelly smirked and chuckled "smart ass" under her breath. She then removed a package of pills individually wrapped in a plastic cover with an aluminum foil backing. Kelly squeezed five pills out of the package into the small cup and then handed it to me along with the cup of cranberry juice.

"These are the steroids, the first part of your treatment," offered Kelly. "The pharmacy is making up your chemo now, it should be here any minute. They have to mix it specific to your weight and your blood levels." I never knew just how precise chemotherapy was. I always thought that they had all these different chemicals mixed up and stored, waiting for the next victim to arrive. "OK, that's fine," I emptied the small cup of pills into my mouth and washed them down with the cranberry juice. I then I sat back into the reclining chair and returned my attention to my laptop.

Ten minutes later, Kelly again returned carrying a small plastic bag with a yellow marking on the front of it. Before reaching my cubicle, Kelly stopped and placed the bag on a surgical table near her desk. She then took a blue paper surgical gown from a stack of neatly folded ones. She donned the gown and then stretched latex gloves over her hands. Once again, she lifted the plastic bag and asked another nurse to help her. Then the two nurses walked to my cubicle with what I could only surmise was my chemo. The second nurse, a younger, blonde and tall woman greeted me with a smile. "Hi, can you please tell me your name and date of birth?" This time I answered correctly. As I spoke, the nurse stared at the bag Kelly had been carrying, comparing my words to the printing on the bag's label. Once finished, the other nurse thanked me and returned the bag back to Kelly.

Kelly proceeded to remove a smaller bag from inside the plastic bag and laid it on the surgical table. She then began to type into the computer again, scanned my bracelet and asked my name and date of birth. She then took the small bag, hung it next to the IV bag on the pole, pulled a long rubber tube from the bottom of it and inserted the tip into a port on my IV line. This was the real thing that I was about to experience.

Once connected, Kelly began to adjust the flow of the drip by installing the tube into a machine located midway down the pole. After a few beeps and boops, numbers appeared on the front of the machine and I saw the first drip from my little bag of death drip from the hanging bag, into the reservoir, down the long tube, through the machine and into my cancer infected body. I sat back not knowing what to expect. I looked at Nancy whose gaze had not left me. I shrugged my shoulders, gave her a wink, then closed my eyes and let my mind wander to anywhere it desired.

The loud piercing beep from the machine startled me out of a semi catatonic state and brought me back to the matter at hand. The bag had emptied its contents into my awaiting body. The noise alerted the nursing staff that their assistance was required to remove the empty container. Again, Kelly donned the gown and gloves. She entered my cubicle, pressed the buttons on the machine to stop the beeping, disconnected the tube from my IV connection, then reached up and took the bag from the pole. She then carefully placed the small bag along with the tubes and any other device associated with it into the original bag from where she had removed it. She then wrapped the bag tightly, sealed it, turned and stepped on the pedal of the metal red and black hazardous waste container. The top of the container slid open as she applied more pressure to the pedal until it was open sufficiently enough to accept the bag without any force. She removed her foot and the top of the can slid shut.

Kelly removed her gown, then her gloves and disposed of them in the trash. She then put on clean pair of latex gloves, turned back towards me and quickly tore the adhesive tape from my hand. "I like to get the tape off like that," explained Kelly. "The shock distracts you from the pain this way." Her logic was true, well partially true. The shock did stun me, but what little discomfort I felt was irrelevant. A thick piece of gauze was then placed over the spot where the intravenous tube entered my body, and Kelly quickly pulled the tube, extricating the equipment from the back of my hand. A strip of blue fabric tape was wrapped around my hand to hold the gauze in place, and my first session of chemo therapy was complete; or so I thought.

I began to attempt an escape from the comfort of the reclining chair when Kelly held up her hand in a manner that would imply that she wanted me to halt. I sat back in the chair, "Not yet sweetie, you still need your shot of Velcade," revealed the nurse. I returned to the reclining position and waited for Kelly to return. Nancy then asked me how I was feeling. "I'm fine," I responded. Having transported many people to and from chemotherapy and radiation treatments, it was more likely than not patients would experience side effects, from lethargy to vomiting. It seemed that almost everybody experiences some kind of effect once the treatment was complete, so not feeling any changes was a very welcomed non-event.

Again, Kelly shuffled back to my cubicle with another plastic bag in her hand. She repeated the medicinal administering process once again, then asked me to pull up my shirt. I started to raise the short sleeve shirt on my arm when Kelly stopped me. "No, this shot goes into your belly," she explained.

I lifted my shirt from my waist and exposed my ample belly. "This is going to look like the Marines on Iwo Jima." My joke caused Kelly to erupt in laughter. "That's a first for me," laughed Kelly. Even Nancy chuckled at the comment. The nurse pinched a small area of my abdomen, then inserted a very small gauge needle into the skin. Slowly, she pushed down on the plunger of the syringe, pushing the medication into my subcutaneous layer. After about 15 seconds, Kelly removed the needle from my body, dropped it into the sharps container, and placed a Band aid onto the tiny wound. "Now you're done!" she exclaimed.

Nancy and I got up and began to walk towards the elevator. I walked at my regular gait, but by the time I got to the elevator bank I noticed that I had slowed down. By the time we reached our car, I was exhausted. Nancy took over the driving duties, and home we drove.

When we reached our house, we made our way in. I sat down wanting to do nothing more than sleep; but sleep never came. As a matter of fact, sleep eluded me for almost 24 hours, until the effect of the steroid wore off. I wanted to sleep, I needed to sleep, I was dying to sleep; but my mind was running like a hamster on speed running on a wheel. This, I determined, would be my side effect; which in all honesty would not be that bad if this was the total effect.

━━╲╱━━CHAPTER 31━━╲╱━━

A s I sat in my living room on March 2, 2018, the lights in my house, just like almost every other person's lights in Massachusetts, went out. Since we are renting a house in Duxbury, Massachusetts while we build our future home, I did not have my generator connected to my electrical box, so we remained in the dark all night, illuminated only by candlelight. In the darkness, my wife watched the progress of the winter storm on her phone while I began to reminisce about my younger days in Quincy, Massachusetts; more specifically, my summers in Quincy.

Summers were planned way in advance by all the kids in the gang (when the word gang did not have a nefarious meaning). Baseball, hiking, frog catching, mountain climbing all in the confines of Faxon Park. Fishing at Echo Lake, where the Adams Heights Men's Club is now located. We would plan on an occasional visit to the quarries for a swim and to watch the high school kids jump and dive from heights that made us cringe to think about. Maybe we would take a ride on the MBTA and a trip to Jack Horner's Joke Shop at what is now Downtown Crossing in Boston, if we could all scrape up some money. We would head down to Wollaston Beach whenever we could; if we went with our parents, we would stay around Tony's Clam Shack; if we went on our own, we would challenge the rapids at the opposite end of the beach. We would beg our parents to take us to Fenway for a Red Sox game, Nantasket Beach for a day of fun at Paragon Amusement Park, and deep-sea fishing in Plymouth on the Capt. John's boat fleet. Any day that we did not have an adventure of some sort planned, we would head down the "Square" (Quincy's shopping area), starting at Coleman's Sporting Goods and work our way down to PVC Head Shop. If it happened to rain on a day, we knew that we always had the Strand Movie Theater the Lincoln Movie Theater, and the Wollaston Theater, all with a $1.25 admission to keep us busy. Each headline movie followed a Three Stooges short that we could very well see on TV that night.

But as a young boy growing up in Quincy in the summer, one event more than any other was anticipated from the day the last bell rang at school; the Quincy Center Sidewalk Sale, culminating with the Miss Quincy Bay Beauty Pageant. The stores in the Square would set up tables and bins in front of their businesses and pile on them all the surplus items that they could not get rid of throughout the previous year in the hopes that someone would take a second look for a reduced price. Novelty T- shirts were always a big hit with us, especially if they had a questionable decal on them. We would always stop by the Armed Services Recruiting Center where they would give away free posters of servicemen and women in uniform posing in positions that sent a feeling of courage and patriotism running through our veins.

A little further down the street we would stop at Jason's Music and Luggage store where invariably Mike da Winger would be hanging out. Mike da Winger was the pseudonym of lifetime Quincy resident Michael Zadrozny. Mike was older, but no one really knew how old. He was somewhat mentally challenged but was what I believe is called handicapable. He was known by all as Mike da Winger for a reason that you will soon read.

Mike would stand against a signpost, his bike, his only means of transportation, not far away, and greet us all with a big hi when we would call out his name. His hair was always styled in a crew cut, and there was always a devilish smile of a young boy across his face. Mike would talk to us for a while, telling us that music performers like Wayne Newton, Guy Lombardo, Johnny Cash, Perry Como were all a lot of "haws", they "gotta go", and he "had to huk'em". Once we left him and began to sample the wears of Jason's, the attention of the manager was trained directly on us, which was a bad idea, because we had no intention to steal anything. However, while the manager's back was turned, Mike was stuffing 45 rpm records up his shirt for his nightly "winging" session on top of Capitol Supermarket. Whenever Mike was able to get his hands on records, he would take a position on the roof of the Capitol Super Market that happened to overlook a large parking area below. Mike would then read the artist's name on the record, say his distinctive "Gotta Go", and in a sidearm manner fling the record off the roof and into the parking area. For all the hundreds of records that Mike had "winged" over the years, it is truly amazing that at least to my knowledge, no one ever caught an LP or a 45 in the head, (Again, another phrase that unfortunately has a different meaning in society today). As dangerous an action this was, hearing someone call out "Mike is winging" brought a crowd to the roof of Capitol Supermarket.

On the last night of the sidewalk sale, we would all gather together and make our way up to the Miss Quincy Bay Beauty Pageant, where one of us always had an older sister, cousin or neighbor participating. We would all cheer for the young ladies who were known to us and boo the ones who were not. We would always laugh as the contestants, dressed in bathing suits, were escorted down the stage and runway by what we called dirty old sea men (yes, I know). The officers of Quincy's yacht clubs were usually white-haired men, and would dress in white pants, a blue blazer and a white commodore's hat. If you ever saw Ted Knight in "Caddy Shack", you get the picture. More often than not, it was the young ladies who had to help them down the stage rather than the other way around. At the end of the pageant, we would cheer for the winner, and whoever in my group that knew how would wolf whistle at the highest decibels.

Then every year, as sure as the days got shorter and the leaves began to turn, that dreaded Thursday morning in August would arrive. That Thursday morning arrived after the Wednesday Patriot Ledger Newspaper would announce the annual Quincy Bargain Center Back to School Sale. Without any prior notice, my mother, as well as almost every mother in Quincy, would wake us up at 7:30 on that morning, hurry their children into their clothes and push breakfast down their throats. My mother would then pile us in the car without saying a word, and we would oblige clueless. As I look back, she was like a pet owner taking her loving dog to the vet to get neutered.

As we drove through the square, the picture became clearer and clearer, then when we turned the corner at Clifford's Flowers, there was no going back. Our mothers had slyly brought us to the Bargain Center, known to all as "The Bargie", to join in the procession known as "The line of tears". Mothers from all around the South Shore raced to be the first in line, herding their children like cats against the tall brick wall on the crooked sidewalk that lined the potholed street across from the rotten smelling fruit stand. This was a Quincy child's version of the gates of hell. And once those frosted glass gates finally opened, the stampede of palomino mothers dragging a child in each hand would gallop into the store, spinning to locate the children's department, and kicking up the dust just like in the ring of a rodeo. Troughs of shoes piled high without any designation of size, color, style were tied in pairs with a white string. Mothers would dig through those piles like prospectors searching for gold in a pile of dirt until, EUREKA!

Loads of polyester pants labeled double knit, boy's turtle neck body shirts with zippers, unfolded and wrinkled button-down shirts were mounded on gray wooden troughs. It was not uncommon to see two mothers, each holding a sleeve of the same shirt, attempting to rip the shirt from the grasp of the other mother. The boisterous manager, Elliot Levine would shout out over the din, "Ladies, you rip it you bought it". There were piles of underwear without packages, socks stapled together, and racks and racks of yellow raincoats. What made things worse for me is that my mother had to buy clothes for me in the husky section. For those of you who don't know what husky is, it is the section where pants were sold for old, short, fat men who would not object to wear anything, except for these pants. So, rather than do the humane thing and destroy these clothes or send them to Miami where taste in clothing is suspect, the manager of the Bargie pawned them off on mothers for their unsuspecting and soon to be psychologically damaged sons.

Once an overloaded pile of clothes and shoes had been amassed, mothers would carry their pile to the long check-out line. Since the Bargie had no shopping carriages, all goods had to be carried around from trough to trough by the mothers, and it was up to their children to follow behind closely and gather the refugee articles of clothes that escaped from an unsuspecting mother's grasp. After paying, all the items would be stuffed beyond capacity into the thinnest of thin paper bags; so thin it seemed that compared to them, tissue paper was like corrugated cardboard. Shopping complete and bags fully packed, we trudged out through the dust, like mules beginning a long journey into the Sierra Madres. We would haul the bags out of the store, down the broken sidewalk, across the pothole street and into the wretched parking lot where, like clockwork, all the sides and bottoms of the bags would simultaneously tear through, dropping our new clothes, shoes, coats and underwear into a combination of dirt, loose asphalt and children's tears.

After our mothers would stop screaming at us for dirtying the clothes already filthy from the store, we would make our way to the car, unload our armfuls of new, soiled garments and climb in to the back seat. Once in the car, our mothers would say I'll be right back, I'm going to get some fruit. Scientists have said that when exposed to excessive temperatures for prolonged periods of time, children can experience brain damage. Well, picture three or four kids in a dark blue 1966 Pontiac Catalina sitting in full sun with vinyl dark blue seats in August with the windows up because otherwise someone might kidnap us. After 10 minutes of screaming, sweating and crying in the car, the idea of being kidnapped was actually a most welcome thought.

CHAPTER 32

The brightest of days can never be fully appreciated until one experiences the darkest of nights. This is the analogy that I often use when I lose someone whom I love in my life. No one knows better than me that death is a part of life; sometimes a welcomed part, more often, not so much. Although I believe that the physical body is just a vessel to contain the real being of a person, it seems that we, as humans mourn the expiration of the vessel with greater emotion than we celebrate the true essence of the person that will stay within each of us forever.

After a day of relaxation and enjoyment, Nancy, our dog Zeus and I returned home. It was a very warm day, about 80 degrees at around 4:30. Once home, we sat down for a few minutes to catch our breath and read the mail. Nancy then picked up the cordless phone and dialed the phone number of our friends Ruth and Paul. You may remember Paul from the very beginning of the book; this was the family that I would cook for while Paul fought his battle with cancer.

Nancy's face lost its expression and her pallor faded from the rosy brown hue that spending a day in the sun produces to a very pale beige. Although the phone was pressed tightly to her ear, I could hear the panic in Ruthie's voice. Nancy said "OK" and hung up the phone. "Ruthie asked if you could bring your medical equipment up, Paul is failing fast". The urgency in her voice alerted me that this was not an ordinary situation.

Without a word, I ran to my bedroom, got my stethoscope and pulse/ox device and ran up to Paul's and Ruthie's house. There were cars in the driveway as well as on the street outside their home. The front door was open, but the screen door was closed. I ran up their stairs while hearing a labored breath through the screen. Without notifying anyone inside, I opened the door and entered into the room to the left. Paul's hospital bed had been moved downstairs into the living room where we all would often sit and laugh. Surrounded by his family softly murmuring words of love to the unconscious man, the devotion this man instilled into his friends and family was evident. Above the prayers I could hear Paul's labored breath. The family separated just enough to offer me access to my friend.

I placed the earpiece of my stethoscope into my ears, then placed the pulse oximeter device upon his finger. I then placed the bell of the stethoscope onto the center of his chest to hear his heart, beating slowly, beating weakly. This heart that he gave to each us and every person he met was now coming to a rest. I listen to his lungs for a moment and his breaths were very shallow and barely discernable.

I removed the stethoscope from my ears and watched the LED numbers on the pulse oximeter quickly decline. His oxygen level went from 90, to 85, 70, numbers too low to sustain life in a human. His pulse followed suit, dropping from 40 rapidly to zero. I held his hand in mine, put my free arm around Ruthie, and whispered in her ear, "He's at rest now Ruthie." Although small in stature, Ruthie is one of the toughest people I have ever known. We met long before we moved to Hanover, as we met in junior high school in Quincy, MA. We knew each other for years and Friends in school and afterwards as well. It was an amazing coincidence (there is that funny word again) that after all these years, we lived less than one hundred yards from each other. She is sweet, funny, a great friend and even a greater parent. Nancy and I had become very close to Ruth and Paul, as close as family.

Ruthie sat down on the bed next to Paul's body, trying to be stoic for the sake of her children, but her emotions broke through her tough façade in bits and pieces. Their children and family closed in to bid farewell to this kind, and wonderful Lebanese man. I backed away so as not to interfere, removing the pulse oximeter from his finger. Taking deep breaths, I held back my tears and put my arm around Nancy who also had moved to allow access for the immediate family. As I said in the first pages of this book; Paul did not have friends, everyone who had the pleasure of knowing him considered him family.

Just the night before I had invited Paul and Ruth's three children, Emily, Sophia and Elijah to come down to my house for a chat. When they came, I explained to them the feelings that they were about to encounter. The loss they would feel, and that nothing anyone can say will ease the pain they will feel. Having lost my father at eighteen, I knew the realm that they were about to enter, and knowing the reluctance Paul would have preparing his children this experience, as a close friend, I felt that the mantle of responsibility had fallen onto my shoulders.

Although I knew that the time was quickly approaching, I had no idea it would be the next day. Now that the time had come, I was quite surprised how well they accepted the passing. The three of them were sad and upset, but they weathered the moment with great maturity and understanding, a type of composure that would not be expected from people that so young.

The wake for Paul were befitting a nobleman, a man of great renown or fame. We arrived early to lend support to the family, the same idea many more people had as well. We were arrived to find a full parking lot and a line of people outside the door standing under a canopy, being shaded from the glaring sun on a hot August afternoon. The line was stalled. For ten minutes we had not moved a step. When we finally reached the entrance of the viewing room, we saw people relating the many stories of care, friendship and laughter they shared with Paul. It dawned on me at that moment that Paul was more than a man who came to a new land to make a new life; he was a man who brought happiness to everyone he met. In his previous life as an officer in the Lebanese Army, the atrocities he was made to witness were inhuman; in his later life, everyone he touched was enriched.

Life never takes a break. While fighting the effects of chemotherapy, progressing through the process of my retirement from the fire department and mourning the passing of my close friend, my brother Charlie took a turn for the worse. Earlier he had made the decision that quality of life outweighs the quantity. Being able to join in fewer celebrations with friends and family dwarfs knowing that outside his bedroom, many more celebration were being held. Without life, there is no living, and so Charlie decided to fulfill his days with pride and honor. Although he had the ability to end his suffering by his own hand, he stayed the pain and suffering, and lived out the last of his days taking measures only to relieve the pain.

Charlie was taken from his home on Friday night, September 9, and taken to hospice in a nearby town. He never again regained full consciousness; his extent of awareness was a slight blink when his agonal breathing was quieted. Saturday brought members of our immediate family together so Charlie would leave this world knowing that he was loved. On Sunday morning, September 11, 2016, Timmy, Charlie's younger son arrived from a trip he had taken. He said his goodbyes to his father whose few moments of slight awareness had ended.

Ginny, Charlie's wife, sitting at his left hand began to speak to her husband; thanking him for the years of enjoyment the two had shared, letting him know that her love for him would endure whether or not their bodies did. When she had finished, Charlie continued to breath with great difficulty. Each breath was accompanied with a snore to fill his lungs as much as possible.

My sister Marie, then in a tearful voice, told Charlie that he had done a wonderful job in life, that he was a great brother, husband and father. That his legacy would live on through the goodness which he instilled into his children.

Kenny, Charlie's elder son then thanked his father for all the love and care he had given him throughout his life; he could never have had a greater father. Because of his dad's teachings, travels through his own life would be on a much kinder road.

My brother Ernie, then, with great emotion spoke of the bond he and Charlie had forged throughout their life. How he respected Charlie and enjoyed the many moments the two had shared throughout his life. Charlie continued to struggle to breath. His blinks had long since ceased.

I then spoke. I told my brother that so many people, once notified that their time on earth was coming to an end, would cower into themselves, wallow in self-pity, and succumb to their mortality. I commended Charlie for not only putting the ailments of his body behind him, but for living a life that was richer, replete with travels, experiences, events and occasions. Since he was notified of his illness, he had done more than the vast majority of those who had lived a full life. I told him that throughout our lives we all make mistakes and do things that we later regret; it is human nature, nothing more. He should not be bound by those mistakes, they are all forgiven, they're nothing more than shadows of a time long past. His journey through life has been one of great success, and he should be proud of the accomplishments he made through his career, the great life he created for his family, and the exceptional job he did raising his two sons. It was now time to rest; to let go of the ties that kept him here. It was now time to sleep and go on and be at peace. His challenges were overcome, his duties, complete. Go now, be at peace.

Again, Charlie snored taking in a breath of air; it was his last.

Much like Paul's services, Charlie's too brought many friends, family members, neighbors and coworkers together. Although I stood inside, flanking the casket with the rest of my immediate family, I could not comprehend the line of people parading through the funeral home. From 4 PM until 8 PM the line never slowed from a stream, there was never a break.

Because few people knew that I had cancer, when I made my way around town people would offer me condolences, and then follow up with, "Well, you know what they say, they always come in threes." After years of saying that phrase myself, I realize just how foreboding it truly is. I knew that I would not be the third, at least not soon. But there is nothing like a cold splash of water in the face to cause you to wake up. From that moment on, I have never said, and will never again say that phrase.

Chemo continued without any major occurrences. Having seen how chemo ravages bodies, my greatest complaint (and I do not want to even say it was a complaint) was that it made me lethargic. The effects were cumulative, as with each session of chemotherapy, the longer the lethargic feeling would last. What was once a day and a half quickly became two, then three. Fortunately, that was the extent of the effects. After three days I could once again feel a rise in energy; until the next time.

During these times, Nancy was a godsend. She would sit with me during the process, drive me home afterwards, make me lunch, keep me comfortable, and ensured that my every need was met. Just walking from the chair to the bathroom felt like climbing three flights of stairs to me. What made matters worse was Nancy did not want me to sit outside in the sun. It was mid-September, the temperature was still high, and sitting in a lounge chair on the deck would have been a welcomed event. However, Nancy, who is not the most ardent of sun worshipers, felt the heavy doses of medication I was receiving would make me susceptible to sun burns. So instead, I sat inside and became a big fan of shows like "Hot Bench."

Days quickly became months, and before I realized it my appointment with Dr. Laubach was at hand. Nancy and I traveled into the Dana Farber in Boston one morning in early January. I had received chemo the previous week, so this would be an ideal time to check my blood levels. I was looking forward to the visit. I not only respected Dr. Laubach, I actually liked him for his demeanor, his nature and his genuine concern for both my physical as well as psychological wellbeing. He is someone who I would cherish as a friend.

I had now received five months of chemotherapy treatments. Five out of what was to be eighteen months of treatments. Like every other trip into the Dana Farber, we parked in the garage, registered at the desk, and proceeded to the lab for my blood work. We then went upstairs for breakfast and wasted time until my appointment with Dr. Laubach.

Nancy and I sat in the waiting room for a period until my name was called for the staff to take my vitals. Nancy now knew that this was only the preliminary call in, so she didn't move when my name was called. I went through the regular procedure with the nurse and returned to my seat next to Nancy. Unlike our other times in this office, there was no fear or apprehension. I knew what to expect, and my past experiences put me at ease. Nancy turned the pages of a Better Homes and Gardens magazine when "William A" was called out by a nurse.

We both rose to our feet and walked to the nurse. She checked my armband to see that I was who I said, and then led me down the long corridor to Dr. Laubach's examination room. We entered the room, took our seats and I turned to Nancy and said, "Now please hold your questions until the end, OK?" Nancy's less than pleased look appeared on her face, but she knew what I had meant. She nodded when a knock came from the door and Dr. Laubach entered the room.

We both stood to welcome the Doctor, shaking his hand in a warm greeting. The Doctor sat in his chair in front of his computer screen and pulled up my file. He made small talk as the computer's memory searched for my information. The conversation came to an abrupt end as Dr. Laubach leaned in closer to the screen. "Well, how have you been feeling, any complaints?" asked the doctor. I answered while shaking my head side to side, "No, I feel pretty good."

Dr. Laubach continued to look at the screen and nodded. "Well, let me tell you, looking at your numbers, you are doing great." His response was not the traditional way a doctor gives you news, but much more incredulous. "I figured it would take a year to 18 months of chemotherapy for someone with the numbers you had when you came in, but your numbers are now within the normal range." Dr. Laubach continued, "I am honestly amazed by your reaction to the drugs, this is incredible."

My response was as subdued as it was when he informed me that I had cancer. I did not dance around in a euphoric celebration but smiled a smile of relief. "So, does that mean I am done with chemo?" I asked. I felt Nancy's hand in mine but was afraid to look at her because I did not know what her response would be. I knew if she was crying, I probably would have started to cry myself.

"Well, here is what I want to do," began the doctor. "Because your numbers are so good, I want to harvest some of your stem cells, once we have them, we will freeze them for ten years. If you happen to have a relapse of this or any other type of cancer, we will hit you with a heavy dose of chemotherapy and wipe out the cancer along with your immune system. We will then give you back your stem cells and regenerate your immune system but without the cancer. Consider it another lease on life."

This was absolutely amazing to me. What did I do in life to deserve this? I was fortunate enough to have been in the exact place I needed to be when my valve got stuck to return me to the living. They found a deadly cancer in me that goes unnoticed on almost everyone else. Now they not only drove the cancer out, but told me that if I get cancer again, they can cure it. Although I did charity work, I did nothing compared to so many others to deserve these three new leases on life.

When I dealt with terminally ill patients who told me that they were going to die, I often told them that they cannot leave this earth until they fulfill the specific duty they were sent here to perform. We don't know what it is and might not even know if or when we did it, but once it is done, we can then leave the earth. I don't know what my job is, or was, but if the universe is giving out extra leases on life like it has granted me, well, I must certainly have a big job yet to perform.

Peace

ABOUT THE AUTHOR

Bill Arienti is an author and career firefighter (now retired), who despite a near death experience, heart surgery, and subsequent cancer diagnosis, has resumed living his life with gusto even in the face of ongoing chemotherapy. He recently designed and subcontracted the building of his new dream house in Manomet, Massachusetts, where he lives with his wife Nancy, their son Mark and golden Labrador retriever Zeus. His first book, "The Gift is in the Giving" is available through all major bookstores and Amazon.com.

ABOUT KHARIS PUBLISHING

Kharis Publishing is an independent, traditional publishing house with a core mission to publish impactful books, and channel proceeds into establishing mini-libraries or resource centers for orphanages in developing countries, so these kids will learn to read, dream, and grow. Every time you purchase a book from Kharis Publishing or partner as an author, you are helping give these kids an amazing opportunity to read, dream, and grow. Kharis Publishing is an imprint of Kharis Media LLC. Learn more at https://www.kharispublishing.com

CONTEMPORÁNEA

[!]

Federico García Lorca nació en Fuente Vaqueros (Granada) el 5 de junio de 1898, y murió fusilado en agosto de 1936. Se licenció en Derecho (1923) en la Universidad de Granada, donde también cursó estudios de Filosofía y Letras. En 1919 estuvo en Madrid, en la Residencia de Estudiantes, donde convivió con parte de los que después formarían la Generación del 27. Viajó por Europa y América y, en 1932, dirigió la compañía de teatro «La Barraca». Sus obras más emblemáticas, en poesía, son el *Romancero Gitano* (1927), donde el lirismo andaluz llega a su cumbre y universalidad, y *Poeta en Nueva York* (1940), conjunto de poemas, adscritos a las vanguardias de principios del siglo xx, escritos durante su estancia en la Universidad de Columbia. Entre sus obras dramáticas destacan *Bodas de sangre*, *La casa de Bernarda Alba* y *Yerma*. Con esta colección, DeBols!llo presenta toda la obra publicada o representada en vida del autor andaluz.